Representations
of Women

LADY BLESSINGTON, ELIZA COOK, AND CAROLINE NORTON

Three eminent female writers of the nineteenth century, as portrayed by artist Arthur Miles in the February 13, 1847, number of *Reynolds's Miscellany*. What the accompanying article said of them applies to all the women writers represented in this book: "Long, long after their fair hands shall have mouldered in the dust, will their works continue to be appreciated and admired."

Representations of Women

NINETEENTH– CENTURY BRITISH WOMEN'S POETRY

Kathleen Hickok

CONTRIBUTIONS IN WOMEN'S STUDIES, NUMBER 49

GREENWOOD PRESS
WESTPORT, CONNECTICUT • LONDON, ENGLAND

Library of Congress Cataloging in Publication Data

Hickok, Kathleen.
  Representations of women.

  (Contributions in women's studies, ISSN 0147-104X ;
no. 49)
  Bibliography: p.
  Includes index.
  1. English poetry—19th century—History and
criticism.   2. Women in literature.   3. English
poetry—Women authors—History and criticism.   4. Women
—Great Britain—History—19th century.   5. Feminism
and literature.   I. Title.   II. Series.
PR585.W58H52   1984   821'.7'09352042   83-13029
ISBN 0-313-23837-5 (lib. bdg.)

Library of Congress Catalog Card Number: 83-13029
ISBN: 0-313-23837-5
ISSN: 0147-104X

First published in 1984

Greenwood Press
A division of Congressional Information Service, Inc.
88 Post Road West
Westport, Connecticut 06881

Printed in the United States of America

10 9 8 7 6 5 4 3 2 1

Copyright Acknowledgments

Grateful acknowledgment is made of the permission to reprint in two chapters of this book material that
appeared, in a slightly different form, in two earlier articles.

"The Spinster" uses material from "The Spinster in Victoria's England: Changing Attitudes in Popular
Poetry by Women," published in the *Journal of Popular Culture*. Reprinted by permission from the *Journal
of Popular Culture*, Volume 15 No. 3 Winter 1981, pp. 119–31.

"Elizabeth Barrett Browning" uses material from " 'New Yet Orthodox'—The Female Characters in
Aurora Leigh," published in the *International Journal of Women's Studies*. Reprinted by permission from the
International Journal of Women's Studies, Volume 3 No. 5 September–October 1980, pp. 479–489.

For my parents

Contents

viii   Contents

Acknowledgments

Looking back over the years I have spent in writing this book, I find many people and institutions to thank. My mentors and colleagues at Iowa State University, the University of Maryland, and elsewhere have included Kathryn Seidel, Barbara Bowman, Joyce Rothschild, Margaret Cruikshank, Rosanne Potter, Frank Haggard, Susan Galenbeck, Gretchen Bataille, Bill McCarthy, G. Allan Cate, William S. Peterson, and the late John W. Kinnaird. All of these people generously gave time and attention to my intellectual, practical, and sometimes emotional needs. Iowa State University gave me several monetary grants and releases from coursework at times when I particularly needed those essentials for scholarship: money and time. In addition, the librarians and staffs at the Library of Congress and the University of Maryland were unfailingly gracious and helpful.

My family—George, Mary, Michael, and Lisa Hickok—encouraged me at every stage of my work. Brenda Laughlin gave me a place to live and much moral support. I particularly appreciated her patience and good humor in the last crucial days before my deadline. Nancy Tepper and Eann Rains provided friendship and much needed periods of respite from intense concentration. And finally, my typists, Karen Smith and Sheryl Kamps, were a constant pleasure to work with. Their intelligence and perceptivity in the preparation of my manuscript were invaluable. To all of these people, and to my many women's studies students who have taught me so much over the years, I am forever grateful. I hope the book justifies the energy and confidence they have given me. Any errors, of course, are strictly my own.

Representations
of Women

Introduction

"From their own constitution, and from the station they occupy in the world, [women are], strictly speaking, relative creatures."[1] Thus did Mrs. Sarah Stickney Ellis describe English women in 1839. Her popular series of books—*The Women of England* (1839), *The Daughters of England* (1843), *The Wives of England* (1843), and *The Mothers of England* (1844)—is representative of the so-called courtesy books which undertook in the nineteenth century to describe for English women, especially middle-class women, their proper character, duties, and "sphere." The issue of woman's role and status in society had become controversial in England with Mary Wollstonecraft's *A Vindication of the Rights of Woman* in 1792, followed in 1798 by Mary Hays' *Appeal to the Men of Great Britain in Behalf of Women*, and was to remain so throughout Queen Victoria's reign. Radical new ideas about human equality—stimulated by the French Revolution—and the changing socio-economic picture in England—associated with the transition from a rural to an industrial state—educed numerous formulations of and challenges to current ideology about women.

In addition to the courtesy books, a flood of political tracts, social essays, and periodical literature appeared, offering facts and opinions on various aspects of woman's life: her education, her proper work, and her legal, economic, and social condition. Novelists and poets participated in the ongoing debate as well, through their depiction of female characters, and sometimes, as in Tennyson's *The Princess*, Coventry Patmore's *The Angel in the House*, and George Eliot's *Middlemarch*, through directly dealing with some aspect of the issue. Admittedly, these diverse kinds of sources—whether literary or nonliterary—do not necessarily describe the actual experiences of individual nineteenth-century women. But they do reflect widely held contemporary beliefs and ideals concerning feminine behavior, and they therefore indicate a relevant context and provide norms for comparison.

I believe we can best evaluate the representations of women by nineteenth-century women poets if we examine their work in the context of contemporary thought and in comparison with other writers' depictions of female characters. Several studies have applied this contextual approach to the images of women in the nineteenth-century novel; most of these studies have included the work of male as well as female novelists.[2] But women poets of nineteenth-century England have, with only a few exceptions, received such scant attention that a great deal of poetry written by women who were significant literary figures in their day and who considered themselves to be serious artists is today virtually unknown. To retrieve their contributions from oblivion and to view them in a clarifying focus is a challenging but satisfying task; in order to succeed, we must immerse ourselves in nineteenth-century British culture. My intention, then, is to connect the representations of women in nineteenth-century women's poetry with their contemporary social (and to a lesser extent, literary) contexts. To this end, I have consulted a wide range and variety of published materials and assembled a sort of cultural backdrop against which the various female figures emanating from the pens of women poets can move. The first of these is woman herself.

In referring to woman's "constitution," her "station" in life, and her status as a "relative" rather than an independent being, Mrs. Ellis expressed the conventional wisdom on the subject. Women were generally thought to be differently constituted from men, not only physically, but emotionally and intellectually as well. Furthermore, they were seen as existing—legally, economically, and socially—chiefly in relationship to others, specifically their families. All the different patterns of female life in the century were regarded as preparation for, fulfillment of, or deviation from the "normal" role of wife and mother.

Even such figures as the young unmarried woman, the spinster, the prostitute, the professional woman, and the female laborer were regarded by society throughout most of the nineteenth century in terms of the role they were *not* filling, the "relative" role of wife and mother. Young, unmarried women were doubly relative. They were presently daughters of fathers, and they were, from their childhoods, "women awaiting marriage,"[3] future wives of future husbands. They were in preparation for the dual career of matrimony and motherhood. The woman who failed to fulfill this vocation—the spinster— was seen as a sad, lonely, frustrated old maid, whose chief hope was to attach herself to a family as a sort of surrogate mother figure.

Alternately, she might become a working woman at any of various points on the status scale: a career professional (for example, a writer, or, later in the century, a nurse); a poor but genteel working woman (a governess or seam-stress); a domestic servant; an industrial laborer; or, worst of all, a prostitute. Or she might devote herself to an "aged parent" and remain in the role of daughter all her life. Toward the end of the century, these alternative roles or life-patterns all expanded and acquired more dignity. Even the prostitute received a great deal of attention and a modicum of aid and support. But for most of the nineteenth century, the woman who did not achieve marriage and motherhood was, in the majority view, the woman who had failed. It remained for the "New Woman" of the seventies, eighties, and nineties to insist on the right not to be defined by society solely as a "relative" creature.

Because I have organized this book around the most significant social/liter-ary images of women generated by nineteenth-century British culture, certain important genres congenial to women writers of the era have been omitted: amatory verse, self-referencing lyrics, devotional poems, children's rhymes. But although some significant aspects of women's poetry are thereby exclud-ed, the subject areas of these genres are *not* overlooked; love, self-revelation, religion, and motherhood all figure prominently in the more public formula-tions I have chosen to investigate. My approach also precludes, on occasion, other valid possible readings of individual poems—archetypal, psychological, biographical, Marxist, etc. But one cannot do everything at once, and a femi-nist socio-cultural heuristic yields numerous insights into the complexities of a large and long-neglected canon of poetry. There is more than enough to con-sider: after an initial chapter on womanhood in general, I address, in turn, daughters, wives, mothers, fallen women, spinsters, working women, and "New Women."

Of the women poets who treated these important figures in nineteenth-century England, the best known today are Emily Brontë, Elizabeth Barrett Browning, and Christina Rossetti, all of whom have been accepted, albeit somewhat grudgingly, into the canon of Victorian literature. However, there were throughout the century many other women writing poetry, much of it extremely popular and highly praised in its day. John Stuart Mill wrote in 1869, "We may safely assert that the knowledge which men can acquire of women, even as they have been and are, without reference to what they might be, is wretchedly imperfect and superficial, and always will be so, until women themselves have told all that they have to tell."[4] It is indeed enlighten-ing to study the depiction of women by women and to study it in the context of popular thought about women. For viewed from this new angle English women's poetry of the nineteenth century reveals its own particular strengths and weaknesses, as well as its own illuminations and blind spots, especially in the critical area of woman's changing role and status as a social being. Further-more, the work of minor but popular poets—Felicia Hemans, Letitia Landon,

Caroline Norton, Eliza Cook, Adelaide Anne Procter, Dora Greenwell, Jean Ingelow, Emily Pfeiffer, Mary Elizabeth Coleridge, "Michael Field," and twenty-five others—provides an even more particular context for assessing the representations of women by major figures such as Emily Brontë and, more exhaustively, Elizabeth Barrett Browning and Christina Rossetti.

In choosing the minor poets to consider, I was guided by both the popularity and the merit of the writer—two characteristics which were often mutually exclusive rather than complementary. Thus, the overall quality of works under consideration is unavoidably uneven. There were many volumes of mediocre poems by representative, popular women poets as well as fewer books by women who were not well known by the general public but whose poetry was of excellent quality or was decidedly unconventional in its depiction of women. I included poetry written for adult readers by women who were, for the most part, English—not Scottish, Irish, or colonial. At both ends of the period, I excluded poems which were not published during the nineteenth century, but I did not disqualify writers like Alice Meynell whose work spilled into two centuries. Of course, I was limited to the poetry which was available to me; fortunately, the Library of Congress collection of women's verse is quite extensive.[5] An appendix lists alphabetically the many lesser-known poets whose works appear in the book, with their birth and death dates, salient facts about their lives, and references to significant critical or biographical studies.[6]

The inclusive approach I have adopted has several advantages. It brings these lesser-known poets to light, allowing us, for the first time in more than a hundred years in some cases, to describe and evaluate their achievements, to discover common themes and genres in their work, and to examine trends and changes in the literary history of women. Furthermore, it enables us to analyze more confidently the ways in which the better-known writers were linked with their culture and their literary peers; so that, turning in the final chapters to Elizabeth Barrett Browning and Christina Rossetti, we are better poised to evaluate their own outstanding contributions to the literary representation of women.

Although some characteristics of women's poetry in the nineteenth century can be identified as Romantic or Victorian by theme or by aesthetics, the literary history of women ultimately cannot and should not be defined solely by the literary history of men. Important differences in both education and experience make the trajectory of women's literature distinct from men's. In the first place, women writers seldom received the classical education that serious poetry seemed to call for.[7] What's more, as Elaine Showalter reports, "Victorian critics agreed that if women were going to write at all they should write novels," not poems.[8] Romantic critics were no more open-minded. Margaret Homans describes how, in those crucial early years of the century, the vocation of poet was conceived of by all relevant traditions as unequivocably male, causing women writers serious psychological hardships in their struggle for poetic identity.[9] Joanne Feit Diehl finds that even the poems of major, well-educated writers like Elizabeth Barrett Browning and Christina Rossetti reveal "a sense of struggle, an awareness of the expense . . . of attaining one's own poetic voice."[10]

Popular women poets, particularly, were not writing for the intellectual, elite male reader of William Wordsworth or Matthew Arnold, but for a less educated, middle-class female reader of giftbooks and periodical verse. Consequently, much of their poetry was narrative and descriptive; despite the frequent appearance of tropes, it was essentially literal and representational—just the kind of poetry that lends itself well to socio-cultural analysis. Even the major writers all wrote a quantity of this kind of verse: Barrett Browning's innovative verse novel *Aurora Leigh*, for example, arose partly from the nineteenth-century female genre of narrative poetry with a contemporary setting.

In any culture, the interplay between literary and nonliterary texts is mutually reinforcing; this was especially true in the Victorian period, with its proliferation of novels and periodical literature of all kinds. As Steven Marcus points out, writers of both literary and nonliterary texts are "powerfully informed and influenced by preconceptions of what it is they are writing about."[11] Furthermore, as Edwin Ardener has shown, the expression of uniquely female experience is frequently muted by the dominant male culture.[12] These facts help to explain why female "characters" in women's poetry often seem to owe more to the images and conventions of the dominant culture than to the lived experiences of the poets themselves. Marcus notes also that writers' "representations or imaginations of society often differ from their conscious and explicit awareness of what it is that they are doing or describing."[13]

Applying this idea to women's literature, Dale Spender suggests that "women writers have at times told the male/public what they wanted to hear and have reinforced the dominant group's definition of reality in the process. They have supported the tunnel vision of males and have been accomplices in the reproduction of patriarchal order by portraying females in the distorted forms in which males have cast them, even while they, as women writers, were aware of the falseness of this image."[14] Sandra Gilbert and Susan Gubar hypothesize also that a woman writer "herself secretly realizes that her employment of (and participation in) patriarchal plots and genres inevitably involves her in duplicity or bad faith."[15] For all these reasons and more, the interaction between literature and culture is, in the case of women artists, quite complex. Literary and social conventions are at once enabling and inhibiting: they provide an acceptable structure within which to write, but at the same time they restrict what can be written. To observe women poets of various capabilities struggling with this dilemma is painful, but it is also encouraging; for nineteenth-century women writers, working within the imposed limitations, managed covertly to convey a great deal more than is visible at first glance. In order to fully understand, however, one must be a sympathetic reader attuned to the idiom and conventions of the day.

Indeed, wide and concentrated reading of nineteenth-century women's verse reveals a curious state of tension between conventional ideas about women and reaction against those ideas. True, the bulk of women's poems did tend to reinforce prevailing ideals of womanhood; poems which expressed protest or even doubt about their tenability were relatively few and far between. And shifts in emphasis from the old ideal to the various new ones seem to have been consistently deferred until the changed climate of social opinion had minimized the risk. Still, the frequency and directness of unconventional poems about women did increase steadily between 1800 and 1900. We will see how women poets chose variously to reject or endorse woman's essential relativity to man and to accept, defend, subvert, or even defy conventional stereotyping. Among the lesser poets it was generally true that the more conventional their poetry, the greater their popularity—and the lesser their enduring value. Meanwhile, though, a cautious tradition of subtle protest appeared. We will see, for instance, how woman's love was often linked with sadness, even bitterness, over man's faithlessness or woman's unhappy lot in life. We will also observe that women poets resisted presenting the conventional feminine ideal as if it were actually possible to achieve. Poems written in a spirit of protest but in a sort of code were also prevalent during the nineteenth century—more so than poems that straightforwardly defied convention.

Numerous recent studies of women writers have pointed to both their need and their strategies for "simultaneously conforming to and subverting" patriarchal literary and cultural standards.[16] Katharine Rogers found "some evidence of feminist feeling" in "even the most timid and conventional" women writers of the eighteenth century—if one (sensibly) defines feminism not as "single-minded, systematic campaigning for women's rights," but as "particular sensitivity to their needs, awareness of their problems, and concern for their situation."[17] Annis Pratt agrees that a "note of protest, accompanied by the countertone of accommodation or acceptance" frequently appears in the female novel of development from the 1790s to the present:

"Even the most conformist of women authors admit elements of intellectual, erotic, economic, and spiritual rebellion into their narrative structures."[18]

Virtually everyone now studying the subject agrees that women's literature has a covert or clandestine quality. Showalter notes, "The feminist content of feminine art [1840–1880] is typically oblique, displaced, ironic and subversive; one has to read it between the lines. . . . "[19] Cheryl Walker, speaking of women's literature in nineteenth-century America, says, "Something inheres in women's poetry that has the force of a secret kept by a clandestine group."[20] Judith Newton points out that "subversion, indirection, and disguise are natural tactics of the resisting weak, are social strategies for managing the most intense and the most compelling rebellions."[21] It will come as no surprise, then, to find among women poets in the nineteenth century (as among women novelists) "a kind of covert solidarity that sometimes amounts to a genteel conspiracy."[22] Certainly—for better or worse—the women writers of any era reinforce one another's literary themes and methods and support one another's innovativeness or conformity.

For as Showalter says, "It can be argued that women have constituted a subculture within the framework of a larger society, and have been unified by values, conventions, experiences, and behaviors impinging on each individual."[23] United by a common awareness of the force of social expectation that they would perform chiefly as daughters, wives, and mothers, even those writers who were living differently in the nineteenth century were cautious in contradicting the received wisdom. Consequently, they produced a great deal of poetry depicting women in the most socially acceptable roles—ideal English girl; dutiful, submissive wife; devoted, angelic mother. Yet even here, we will find not merely isolated instances, but a real tradition of subversion and covert protest. While reluctant to offer outright endorsement of alternative roles, women poets nonetheless reversed their attitude toward "unprotected" women from hostility to sympathy. Thus, it became no longer necessary to depict fallen women as irrevocably damned or to portray spinsters as ridiculously unattractive. Furthermore, the working woman's cause was not only recognized, but sometimes loudly propounded. Only the "New Woman" failed to enlist women poets' sympathies to any appreciable extent; she was, perhaps, too outrageous to be tolerated by their audience.

It is certainly true that "when we look at women writers collectively we can see an imaginative continuum, the recurrence of certain patterns, themes, problems, and images from generation to generation."[24] Even Elizabeth Barrett Browning and Christina Rossetti, the twin stars of nineteenth-century English women's poetry, participated in the general tendencies of their literary peers. Elizabeth Barrett Browning was the more directly feminist of the two;

her contribution to women's literature with *Aurora Leigh* represents both a sociological and an artistic triumph. But Christina Rossetti also, in her own quiet way, contributed significantly to the understanding and portrayal of women by representing them within an essentially independent female context.

Furthermore, while it remains undeniable that on the whole women's poetry was convention-ridden and tradition-bound, it is also true that not all the conventions and traditions of feminine verse were limiting or inauthentic in their representations of women. We will see that women poets as a group, as a literary subculture, devised during the nineteenth century a cluster of distinct female traditions, many of which are still appropriate vehicles for women's self-expression and cultural solidarity today. For example, literature addressing the death of the mother, which as Showalter says "has become one of the most profound occasions of female literature,"[25] is a legacy, in part, from nineteenth-century women poets as diverse as Eliza Cook and Elizabeth Barrett Browning.

Although no woman poet can be named whose depiction of women in the nineteenth century was always original or authentic, none can be named whose work was never so, either. Among the most consistently honest in their representations of women were Augusta Webster, Amy Levy, and George Eliot. Poets like Jane Taylor, Caroline Norton, and Adelaide Anne Procter were foremothers of many women writing poetry today. Even the most mediocre and conventional of the popular women poets occasionally give us flashes of insight into the true experience of nineteenth-century womanhood. The pertinent question is not, really, why women poets in the nineteenth century so often adhered to conventionality in their representations of women (although that is surely a significant issue and will be addressed presently), but how and why so many of them managed to transcend convention, bequeathing to modern writers and readers a fascinating record of their partial success.

Implicit in much that I have already said is my decision not only to describe and analyze, but also to evaluate the poems I am presenting. The criteria I employ differ significantly from nineteenth-century expectations for "female poetry." I have not totally rejected contemporary standards, however, but recast them from a feminist critical perspective. For just as male literary history does not adequately describe the characteristics and development of women's literature, male literary criticism often does not meet women's poetry on its own terms. Dale Spender puts it very well in her discussion of the double standard of literary criticism, noting "that males have determined the criteria of what constitutes good writing, that they have then also controlled the means of making decisions about what good writing gets published and what does not, [and] that they have also had the power to rank published writing, making or breaking the reputations of women writers."[26]

Nineteenth-century commentators, editors, and critics rewarded the "feminine" qualities of sentimentality, domesticity, delicacy, and moralism in poetry by women; however, they actually preferred a type of poetry which they saw as inappropriate and perhaps even impossible for women to write—poetry with the "masculine" virtues of intellectuality, breadth, strength, and preoccupation with ethics.[27] While I have continued to appreciate women poets' orientation to the female world and their moral standards within it, I have chiefly valorized poems in which the emotional force of the writing conveys a slightly different and, I would argue, more genuine or honest relationship to that subject matter. I am not judging women's poetry by the presence or absence of feminist tendencies *per se*, but rather by the imaginative and/or authentic quality of its representation of experience. It is possible to do this without ignoring the aesthetic achievements of the various authors, because, it seems to me, genuine engagement with subject matter and beauty of artistic expression are, in a talented writer, intimately related.

Returning, then, to the question of why so much popular nineteenth-century women's poetry remained basically conservative in its representation of women—the answer is complex. For one thing, many women poets undoubtedly accepted the validity, if not the attainability, of contemporary ideals of womanhood. As Lynne Agress has suggested, many of the lesser women writers, especially, were probably victims of their own naiveté. They had grown up in a sexist society and they accepted their role. As women of their times, they perpetuated what they had themselves been taught to believe.[28] Walker cautions also that "we should not underestimate the attraction of an identity model that seemed to provide both security and status." For the cult of domesticity offered women "a sense of importance, satisfaction, and solidarity with other women."[29] The irony is that many truly extraordinary women had therefore to regard their own lives and achievements as second-rate because they were not centered exclusively on husband and family.

In 1837, Robert Southey wrote a letter to Charlotte Brontë advising her to remember her place. "Literature cannot be the business of a woman's life and it ought not to be," he admonished her. "The more she is engaged in her proper duties, the less leisure will she have for it, even as an accomplishment and a recreation."[30] He apparently meant that the author of *Jane Eyre* ought to peel potatoes and embroider handkerchiefs instead of writing novels. Unfortunately, many women writers responded to dicta such as this "not by protest but by vigorous demonstration of their domestic felicity. They worked hard to present their writings as an extension of their feminine role, an activity that did not detract from their womanhood, but in some sense augmented it." Ultimately, this tactic was, as Showalter says, "a trap," for the result of the "domestication of the profession" was insipidity and renewed artistic commitment to conventional women's roles.[31]

However, we should also acknowledge the alternative possibility that some women poets were not thoroughly committed to the ideals their poetry came to exemplify, but were nudged into an uncongenial conservatism by the demands and expectations of their audience. After all, most women who wrote for the popular press did so in order to earn money; thus, it was important that they not offend the tastes of their reading public. The essentially middle-class constituency for their poetry wanted its comforting conventions about women to be reinforced, not challenged. These readers desired to be instructed and amused, to be presented with the accepted vision of exemplary womanhood, preferably in a sentimental and entertaining form. Publishing in annuals, giftbooks, and literary and ladies' magazines, women poets were able to meet those needs exactly; consequently, their works flooded the new middle-class market. As Vita Sackville-West has observed, the contents of these periodicals, especially of the annuals, were "exceedingly ladylike." Their popularity continued undiminished until the middle of the century because they so accurately reflected the public taste.[32] Women who wanted to publish their verses were almost compelled to write to the standards of this medium which (especially early in the century) was the most accessible one, and thus they could not often risk alienating their audience by openly challenging its most cherished notions about womanhood, even if they were moved to do so.

As for expressing sexuality, or describing female physical experiences such as menstruation or parturition, Victorian ideas of propriety effectively prevented that. Organizations like the Society for the Suppression of Vice and the Proclamation Society attacked "obscenity" in the press along with "blasphemy" and "sedition." Between this kind of outright censorship and the more insidious self-censorship which writers exercised in deference to public morality, not only women poets but nineteenth-century writers in general had to "tone down" their work.[33] However, as Showalter has pointed out, "While Victorian prudery prevented men as well as women from expressing themselves, it operated much more oppressively on women, because virtually all experience that was uniquely feminine was considered unprintable."[34] Furthermore, as Patricia Stubbs explains, "Finding new ways of writing about sexuality and new images of women was a political as well as an aesthetic struggle. It meant attacking a whole ideology and the network of state and social controls which had evolved to re-enforce it."[35] We must not fault women poets, therefore, for not writing more openly about female sexuality and other intimate feminine subjects in the nineteenth century, but rather acknowledge the boldness of their occasional attempts to broach these subjects at all.

Besides the public's expectations for their verse, women poets had also to contend with the current notions about women's proper "sphere," duties, role, etc., which tended to confine them to the appropriate feminine subjects, themes, and attitudes. As early as 1792, Mary Wollstonecraft complained that "the fear of departing from a supposed sexual character has made even women of superior sense" adopt sentiments which "rob the whole sex of its dignity."[36] In striving to fulfill their feminine "mission"—to guide, uplift, and influence society towards righteousness—women poets tended to concentrate upon representing ideals to be pursued—whether familiar, conventional ones or radical, new ones—rather than upon representing social realities to be deplored. Even among writers who most consistently propounded the old ideas, the awareness of discrepancies between the female figures in their poems and the women actually existing in society may well have been greater than has generally been recognized.

Clearly, it was necessary to please in order to publish. As Spender says, "The crux of these difficulties for many women writers is that they must write for men. They are doubly dependent on men in that they depend upon the dominant group's definition of them as women and they depend upon the dominant group's evaluation of their writing."[37] Harriet Taylor Mill called the resulting behavior of literary women "the servilities of toadyism," including "disclaiming the desire for equality or citizenship, and proclaiming their complete satisfaction with the place which society assigns to them."[38] Certainly the critical rewards for innovativeness in women's writing were virtually nonexistent. In her "Survey of Critical Attitudes Toward Women Writers, 1790–1870," Nellie Jones reports, "Women who conformed to accepted *mores* suffered less in critical comment than those who grappled with political, economic, social, or moral evils of the day. Women who were sweetly feminine, mawkishly sentimental, or moralizing escaped lightly in comparison with their more aggressive sisters."[39] It is no wonder, then, that women poets were reluctant to enter the fray of social controversy by challenging powerful prevailing codes of expression.

George Eliot was appalled at the contemporary caliber of women's writing, mostly because of its obvious inauthenticity. In an 1836 article in the *Westminster Review* on "Silly Novels by Lady Novelists," she ridiculed the absurdly false representations of reality by incompetent women writers of "mediocre faculties," who she felt might better serve society by abstaining from authorship entirely. To serious women writers, she urged a more professional attitude and the cultivation of those qualities which contributed to true literary excellence: "genuine observation, humour, and passion" and "patient diligence, a sense of the responsibility involved in publication, and an appreciation of the sacredness of the writer's art."[40] Eliot's irritation is certainly understandable; because she herself was capable—in verse as well as fiction—of conveying experience with depth and breadth, she expected that all serious writers could do so if they chose.

However, many women writers were living in such sheltered circumstances that they lacked significant, fundamental human experiences from which to create their art. In 1896 Georgiana Hill noted the failure of women's poetry to keep pace with the times and wondered whether it was "from lack of imaginative and creative power, or because they have not seen enough of life."[41] Fully three-quarters of a century later, Germaine Greer summed it all up:

> The difference in the conditions of women's work, their exclusion from the frank and free intercourse with kindred spirits, the inaccessibility of the mainsprings of a literary tradition nourished by classical sources, and the general phenomenon of *otherness* and cultural isolation provide adequate explanation of the inability of women poets to keep a footing with men at the highest level.[42]

Thus, although it is somewhat misleading to generalize about "the women poets" of any era, it *is* possible to advance various plausible explanations for the fact that, overall, women's poetry in the nineteenth century tended to adhere to conventionality in its representations of women.

Fortunately, the spirit of human creativity is not easily stifled. Despite all the forces ranged against them, the popular women poets of nineteenth-century England succeeded in creating a lively and challenging body of poetry. The rewards of investigating it after all these years are both informative and aesthetic. As for the outstanding literary achievements of Elizabeth Barrett Browning and Christina Rossetti—two women who led very different lives and held very different opinions about women and society—they cannot be fully explained in socio-cultural terms. The union of human authenticity and literary excellence in their poetry is, as always, attributable to the transcendent nature of artistic genius. But placing them once again in the social and literary context of their era is like setting the last and most luminous jewels into a crown studded with small gems: both the jewels and the crown suddenly shine forth in full glory.

1
Representations of Woman, 1792–1901

In the closing decades of the eighteenth century, rationalists and revolutionaries infused the intellectual and emotional discourse of England with exciting new ideas about human rights and personal dignity. Writers like Mary Wollstonecraft daringly extrapolated from "The Rights of Man" a notion of "The Rights of Woman," touching off a reactionary explosion of conservative, didactic publications lasting for most of the next century. These publications took many forms—social essays, courtesy books, fiction, poetry, etc.—all primarily aimed at justifying woman's inferior position in English society by reference to her "nature" or her "constitution" and articulating for her emulation a womanly ideal responsive to the felt needs of industrial (male) English society. The ideology thus formulated, the "cult of true womanhood" as it has been aptly labeled, was widely disseminated, particularly among the middle classes.[1]

Based on the apparent physical inferiority of woman to man, as attested to by scientific authorities like Herbert Spencer and Alexander Walker,[2] woman was assigned "the attributes natural to her weakness: resignation, patience, timidity, tact, gentleness, tenderness, consideration, unselfishness."[3] To give one representative example, in *Woman in Her Social and Domestic Character* (1831), Elizabeth Poole Sandford urged women to cultivate the "female virtues" of dependence, gentleness, elegance, softness, grace, agreeableness, delicacy, domesticity, and piety. The faults they must counteract were, like their innate virtues, "almost always attributable to their weakness": women must guard against vanity, insubordination, fanaticism, fickleness, gossip, romantic folly, want of judgment, and want of decorum.[4] From out of such requirements arose the composite figure regarded by her Victorian contemporaries as the ideal woman.

Of course, no individual human could really achieve this perfection of womanhood. Furthermore, the security, power, and wealth of the aristocracy and, conversely, the poverty, toil, and illiteracy of the working class made the passive and delicate feminine ideal much less relevant for both upper- and lower-class women. It was middle-class women and girls, the chief and most susceptible audience for social instruction, who were constantly urged, at least in print, to exemplify the womanly ideal.

The dispiriting effect (upon women) of the prevailing doctrine of male superiority was only partially countered by the belief that man and woman were, again by "nature" and/or "constitution," complementary beings, with different but significant contributions to make to each other and to society.[5] John Ruskin, in his famous lecture *Of Queens' Gardens* (1864), explained, "Each has what the other has not: each completes the other, and is completed by the other: they are in nothing alike, and the happiness and perfection of both depends on each asking and receiving from the other what the other can give." However, it is obvious also that Ruskin considered woman's role to be secondary: Man "is active, progressive, defensive. He is the doer, the discoverer, the defender. . . . His intellect is for speculation and invention . . . her intellect is not for invention or creation, but for sweet ordering, arrangement, and decision. . . . Her great function is Praise."[6]

The twin doctrines of male superiority and the complementarity of the sexes together provided the chief justification in the nineteenth century for an extreme separation of "spheres," with men commanding the public sphere of business, politics, and power, and women ensconced in the private sphere of emotion, spirituality, and moral influence. When the rationalist/feminist philosopher John Stuart Mill objected to this social structure in *The Subjection of Women* (1869), the *Edinburgh Review* countered by saying, "We cannot flatter Mr. Mill or his disciples, with any hope that the fundamental question between man and woman can be greatly altered; and we altogether reject his hypothesis that woman is man in petticoats. It is not so; it never was so; and devoutly we trust never will be."[7]

Of course there was constant dissent from the conservative position; otherwise it would not have required such continual reiteration. Since the late eighteenth century, a few writers and thinkers had been opposing the inferences drawn from woman's "constitutional" weakness. Most of these dissenters had not rejected, necessarily, the argument that men and women were different, or even that women were, in some respects, inferior. Rather, they challenged the morality and social utility of the dominance/submission structure that had been built around the "complementary" differences between the sexes. In *A Vindication of the Rights of Woman* (1792), Mary Wollstonecraft articulated the following goal:

I wish to persuade women to endeavour to acquire strength, both of mind and body, and to convince them that the soft phrases, "susceptibility of heart," "delicacy of sentiment," and "refinement of taste," are almost synonymous with epithets of weakness, and that those beings who are only the objects of pity . . . will soon become objects of contempt.[8]

In 1798, Mary Hays frankly found both the argument of male superiority and the conclusions drawn from it to be suspect in motive:

If, then, the intellectual superiority of men, is anything but well proven, let us not draw a certain and constant conclusion from an uncertain and fluctuating cause; let us not say, that the weakness and dependence of women, make them the more amiable, the fitter, and the better companions for men. No, let us not say so—But I will tell you what we may safely say; that these would if true, make women much more convenient companions—much fitter tools,—much more submissive and hypocritical slaves. . . . [9]

And in 1844, Anne Richelieu Lamb [Dryden] asserted in *Can Woman Regenerate Society?* "that the male and female of the human family are of equal importance in creation," and "that the incapacity of woman can be proved only after she shall have had equal privileges with man for development, for it is precisely according to her real value in herself, that she can ever be of any value to others."[10] Although feminist thinkers and writers such as these were clearly a minority in nineteenth-century England, their numbers steadily grew; by the turn of the century their ideas were slowly finding some acceptance.

Probably the most significant change they effected was the modification of woman's status as "relative." In 1792, Wollstonecraft insisted that although "connected with man as daughters, wives, and mothers, [so that] their [women's] moral character may be estimated by their manner of fulfilling those simple duties," nevertheless "the end, the grand end, of their exertions should be to unfold their own faculties, and acquire the dignity of conscious virtue."[11] Such thorough reform as this took a long time to secure and met great resistance. Halfway into the nineteenth century, Harriet Taylor Mill echoed the cynical tone of Mary Hays more than the conciliatory tone of Mary Wollstonecraft. In "The Emancipation of Women" she bluntly exposed the power imbalance inherent in the conventional ideology of relations between the sexes:

> In practice self-will and self-assertion form the type of what are desig-
> nated as manly virtues, while abnegation of self, patience, resignation,
> and submission to power . . . have been stamped by general consent
> as pre-eminently the duties and graces required of women. The mean-
> ing being merely, that power makes itself the centre of moral obliga-
> tion, and that a man likes to have his own will, but does not like that
> his domestic companion should have a will different from his.[12]

The public debate over women's appropriate role and status was extremely heated in the 1850s and 1860s as proposed changes in law and custom began to receive serious consideration. In the same year that "The Emancipation of Women" appeared (1851), Coventry Patmore published a lengthy, conservative assessment of "The Social Position of Women" in the *North British Review,* in which he persisted in defining woman as a being always relative to men:

> Lawmakers have perceived and acted upon the plain and unalterable
> fact, that those interests can never be sufficiently distinguished from
> the interests of men to warrant any extensive serious considera-
> tion. . . . A married woman entirely identifies her interests with those
> of her husband; or if not, she is in imminent danger of identifying
> them with those of some other man, which the law very properly
> provides that she shall not do where she can be hindered.[13]

Historical analyses of the position of the early nineteenth-century English woman agree that although law and custom were nominally structured for her protection, their effect was to put her at a severe disadvantage, "for women were but relative to men, and had no real standing of their own."[14] According to Sir William Blackstone's authoritative *Commentary on the Laws of England* (1765), "By marriage, the very being or legal existence of a woman is suspended, or at least it is incorporated or consolidated into that of the husband, under whose wing, protection, and cover she performs everything; and she is therefore called in our law a *femme covert.*"[15] Any money a woman might inherit or earn by her labors became, unless secured to her by settlement or allowance, part of a matrimonial or family estate in the control of a man. Thus, married women were without any direct economic or political power in society and without any responsibility under law. The *femme covert* was civilly dead. Her property, earnings, liberty, conscience, even her children all belonged to her husband: "My wife and I are one and I am he." The *femme sole,* or independent woman, had only a few civil rights: she could, under certain circumstances, control property, sign a contract, write a will. No woman, of course, could vote.

The obvious assumption was that most women could not cope with financial, economic, or political responsibility and if they could avoid it would
prefer not to try. This theory approached absurdity when applied to independent single women, working women, educated women. But these women
were not perceived as the norm; the homebound wife and mother was the
norm.

Yet, despite the vehemence with which courtesy book writers and conservative journalists and politicians clung to the old ideal throughout the century, it
was rapidly losing ground to the new. Indeed, "after 1830, the old ideal and
the new [feminist] ones existed side by side. They cannot be disengaged without some distortion; opposition to dominating ideals naturally exists at all
times, and a change is not a break but a shift of emphasis."[16] By 1869, with
the publication of John Stuart Mill's essay *The Subjection of Women* and Josephine Butler's collection of essays by various writers on *Woman's Work and
Woman's Culture*, the new ideal of female integrity and self-dependence had
been clearly delineated and forcefully presented, and society as a whole began
to adopt it. As a consequence, by 1900 Ray Strachey could proclaim that
"women were, in the main, free both in their persons and their properties,
their money and their souls."[17]

Although, as Vera Brittain has pointed out, women's position in 1900
"would not suggest freedom to the young woman of today,"[18] nevertheless
many crucial alterations had been made in women's legal, social, and economic status. After about 1870, women had made continual gains in civil
"life," including the right to hold a number of public posts, the right to vote
in most municipal (though no Parliamentary) elections, and the recognition of
their responsibility under the law. The Married Women's Property Acts of
1870, 1882, and 1893 gave married women rights to their own earnings and
property and allowed them to sue and make contracts.[19] A woman's right to
her children, granted in part in 1839, was extended in 1876 to make her their
guardian on their father's death.[20] The obvious tendency of these changes was
toward the recognition of women's ability, right, and responsibility to function as independent civil entities, rather than as extensions of men. Other
important advances for women were achieved during the nineteenth century
also—especially in the areas of education, career opportunities, and protection
of working women from exploitation—gains not obviously related to
women's roles as wives and mothers.

In 1896, Georgiana Hill, in her history of *Women in English Life*, could
state with easy assurance, "The conception of woman's place in society has
undergone a process of re-making in this century." Hill observed that
woman's "sphere" had greatly enlarged, that marriage and motherhood had
become less important as a career, and that girls were no longer content to live

only through their fathers, brothers, or husbands. Furthermore, the ideal of what was excellent and desirable in a woman had been created anew:

> Qualities which used to be thought admirable, such as physical weakness and mental indolence, are pitied or condemned. Neither the role of pleasure nor of domesticity suffices. A woman is expected to share in all the social and intellectual activities around her, to follow and understand, if she does not play any definite part.[21]

Within society, the shift in emphasis from the old ideal to the new had apparently been completed. Women were no longer "strictly speaking, relative creatures," but independent human beings, at least in potential.

The nineteenth century is for this reason a fascinating era in both the social and literary history of women. A survey of English women poets' depiction of women during the century reveals three distinct stages (though with some overlapping, of course). In the years preceding Victoria's accession in 1837, the literary image of woman as domestic angel began to take shape and achieve precedence in poetry by women, despite some few earnest objections by feminist writers and occasional humorous poetic jibes from female aristocrats. Then during the years from 1837 through the mid-sixties—the years of Queen Victoria's most active wife-and-motherhood—the apotheosis of the womanly woman coexisted with subdued criticisms of that ideal. Finally, from the late sixties through the turn of the century, direct modifications and outright rejections of the *status quo* grew more numerous and frequent; not coincidentally, the artistic quality of women's poetry took a dramatic turn for the better also. An overview of popular women poets' representations of woman *per se* will demonstrate how contemporary social ideologies, which gave structure to the imaginative expectations and responses of nineteenth-century readers, inevitably shaped the products of those poets' artistic expression.

The first, most obvious thing one notices about women's poetry of the age is that the most popular subject of women's poems was love. Indeed, *most* narrative poetry by women in the nineteenth century was concerned with episodes of love: filial, romantic, marital, maternal, or religious. Between 1827 and 1844, five short pieces, all titled "Woman's Love," appeared from various hands: Letitia Landon, Mary Ann Browne, Caroline Lamb, Caroline Norton, and Fanny Kemble. All of these poems focus on woman's constancy in romantic or marital love and connect it with some kind of sorrow—either death or betrayal. A typical (and very trite) example is this stanza by Landon:

> Timid as the tale of woe,
>   Tender as the wood dove's sigh,

Lovely as the flowers below,
  Changeless as the stars on high,
Made all chance and change to prove,
  And this is a woman's love.[22]

From Caroline Norton:

To keep unchanged thy calm, pure, quiet love,
If he, inconstant, doth a new one prove. . . .
Oh! this is woman's love—its joy—its pain.[23]

From Fanny Kemble:

A maiden meek, with solemn, steadfast eyes,
  Full of eternal constancy and faith . . .
Looking with little hope unto the morrow;
  And still she walketh hand in hand with sorrow.[24]

In each of these three poems (and also in Mary Ann Browne's), woman's love is presented as innate and is characterized by the conventional feminine virtues. Yet the most revealing aspect of these very conventional poems is surely the consistent association of this kind of love with abandonment and sadness.

Women were frequently reminded that the burden of sacrifice and self-effacement in love was theirs. Dinah Craik in "Leonora" (1859) refers to this as "Womanhood's meek cross," which replaces "girlhood's flowery crown."[25] Letitia Landon puts it this way:

There is a feeling in the heart
Of woman which can have no part
In man; a self-devotedness,
As victims round their idols press,
And asking nothing, but to show
How far their zeal and faith can go.[26]

It is impossible to overlook the Christ identification of the nineteenth-century woman's martyrdom. Of course, the "idol," the object of all this worship and the beneficiary of all this sacrifice, is man. Even Eliza Cook, who was something of a feminist, wrote approvingly, and in religious diction, of feminine selflessness:

The Heart—the Heart that's truly blest
  Is never all its own;
No ray of glory lights the breast
  That beats for self alone.[27]

Certainly, however, one must keep in mind the difference between the received ideal and women's actual behavior. Nor did all women poets express agreement with these views.

For example, Caroline Lamb's version of "Woman's Love" contradicts the idea of woman's devotion as naturally constant; in fact, in the first three stanzas she sounds an almost misogynistic note, reminiscent of eighteenth-century satiric attacks on woman's love.

> Did ever a man a woman love,
> And listen to her flattery,
> Who did not soon his folly prove,
> And mourning rue her treachery?
>
> . . . .
>
> [For] were she pure as falling dews,
> That deck the blossoms of the spring,
> Still, man, thy love she would misuse,
> And from thy breast contentment wring.

In the final stanza, however, Lady Caroline expresses a resentment which may have informed the other writers' poems as well.

> Then trust her not though fair and young,
> Man has so many true hearts grieved,
> That woman thinks she does no wrong,
> When she is false and he deceived.[28]

That woman's love is accompanied by grief is often, in women's verse, the fault of man, whose love is not unfailing. Like Caroline Lamb, Caroline Norton and Fanny Kemble, at any rate, had personal reasons for holding this view.[29]

As a companion piece to her own "Woman's Love," Mary Ann Browne wrote "Man's Love," in which she pointedly accused men of innate inconstancy:

> When woman's eye grows dull,
>   And her cheek paleth,
> When fades the beautiful,
>   Then man's love faileth. . . .
>
> He goes from her chamber straight
>   Into life's jostle,
> He meets at the very gate

Business and bustle;
He thinks not of her within,
    Slightly sighing,
He forgets, in that noisy din,
    That she is dying.[30]

Of course, when the woman is identified as dull, pale, faded, and slight, is it particularly surprising that the man should prefer jostle, bustle, and din? Apparently, the woman in this poem is literally dying, rather than suffering from malaise or frustration. But Browne's juxtaposition of woman's decline and man's busy, full life suggests that one possible consequence of separating female and male "spheres" is a debilitating constriction of women's activities, which carries even worse implications for women than does men's inattentiveness or infidelity.[31]

Even in the poetry of Queen Victoria's favorite poet, Adelaide Anne Procter,[32] there appeared at times a strong note of cynicism about male/female relationships. In "A Warning," for example, Procter offers this advice about love:

Treasure love; though ready
    Still to live without.
In your fondest trust, keep
    Just one thread of doubt.

Trust no prayer or promise;
    Words are grains of sand:
To keep your heart unbroken,
    Hold it in your hand.[33]

In "A Parting," also by Procter, the tone is ambiguous. Ostensibly, the female speaker is comforting the man who has deceived and is about to abandon her, by expressing her sincere appreciation to him—first, that his love made her happy for so many years, and second, that his betrayal turned her heart toward God. However, it is impossible to ignore the irony in lines like these:

I thank you that you taught me the stern truth. . . .
    That vain had been my life, and I deceived,
And wasted all the purpose of my youth.

I thank you that the heart I cast away
    On such as you, though broken, bruised and crushed, . . .
Upon a worthier altar I can lay.

I thank you for a terrible awaking. . . .

In eleven stanzas delineating the man's mistreatment of the woman are fourteen "I thank you's." The concluding stanza, which appears to deny the irony of those preceding, can also be taken two ways.

> Farewell forever now: in peace we part;
>   And should an idle vision of my tears
>   Arise before your soul in after years
> Remember that I thank you from my heart![34]

Is this a benediction or a curse?

One lengthy feminist work, composed in verse, vainly attempted to promote recognition and amelioration of woman's universally miserable condition. Lucy Aikin's four "Epistles on Women," which appeared in 1810, neither assert the need for perfect equality between men and women nor refute the doctrines of male authority and separate spheres. However, surveying the oppressed condition of women throughout history and in all parts of the globe, Lucy Aikin calls upon her readers to "grasp the sisterhood of womankind," and to recognize "that it is impossible for man to degrade his companion without degrading himself, or to elevate her without receiving a proportional accession of dignity and happiness." She insists that all virtues and vices are neither masculine nor feminine, but simply human, and she warns against the substitution of mere chivalry for real respect. Otherwise, it must be woman's fate

> To bow inglorious to a master's rule,
> And good and bad obey, and wise and fool;
> Here a meek drudge, a listless captive there,
> For gold now bartered, now as cheap as air;
> Prize of the coward rich or lawless brave,
> Scorned and caressed, a plaything and slave,
> Yet taught with spaniel soul to kiss the rod,
> And worship man as delegate of God.[35]

The final line refers to John Milton's "He for God only, she for God in him," implying a relativity of woman to man which Lucy Aikin declined to acknowledge.

However, a poem by Lucy Aikin's aunt, the popular writer Anna Barbauld, more closely typifies the emergent image of the womanly woman. Anna Barbauld's "The Rights of Women" begins by echoing her niece's poem:

> Yes, injured Woman! rise, assert thy right!
> Woman! too long degraded, scorned, opprest. . . .

> Go, bid proud Man his boasted rule resign,
> And kiss the golden sceptre of thy reign.

It soon develops, however, that this glorious feminine revolution is to be accomplished not by warfare or by debate, but by "angel pureness," "grace," "soft melting tones," "blushes and fears," "wit and art." Even then, the victory will prove an empty one, because woman (whose very nature it is to love) will soon find "That separate rights are lost in mutual love."[36] Thus Anna Barbauld answers her niece's appeal to masculine justice with a counter appeal to feminine virtue and womanly love.

When women addressed the issue of womanly perfection, the titles of their poems (e.g., "Beatrice" or "The Visionary Portrait") often revealed the author's awareness that her subject belonged to the realm of ideality, not reality. Faced with the problem of representing the ideal in a more or less realistic situation of some kind, the woman poet frequently resorted to the device of a male speaker. By presenting the woman through the eyes of a male admirer, the author could make elaborate idealization seem more credible. Thus in Mary Howitt's "Beatrice: A Lover's Lay" (1835), the young woman is addressed by a young man who finds her gentle, social, cheerful, pious, duteous, meek, beautiful, loving, and faithful. He compares her with various supernatural beings: a saint, an angel, a sylph, a fairy, and a (benevolent) "syren." He even refers to the "witchery" of her smiles. In the last stanza he states his intention to ask her father for her hand.[37] The modern reader's overall impression is that this feminine paragon can exist only in the young man's worshipful imagination.

In "The Visionary Portrait," Caroline Norton's male speaker entertains a "sweet vision" of the ideal woman as he sits musing beside his lonely hearth. Not surprisingly, his first requirement is that her life be exclusively devoted to his: he dreams "of one who might / For ever in his presence stay; / Whose dream should be of him by night, / Whose smile should be for him by day." Then he describes her ideal physical and personal qualities:

> Let youth's fresh rose still gently bloom
>   Upon her smooth and downy cheek,
> Yet let a shadow, not of gloom,
>   But soft and meek,
> Tell that *some* sorrow she hath known,
> Though not a sorrow of her own.
>
> . . . .
>
> Let her be full of quiet grace
>   No sparkling wit with sudden glow

Bright'ning her purely chiselled face
And placid brow. . . .

The poem emphasizes the passivity and stasis of this visionary portrait of
womanhood. Recurring references to insubstantialities (dreams, a rainbow, a
fading mist, a shadow) reinforce the unreality of it all. Yet in the poem's
valentine-like conclusion, the speaker yearns, "Oh! dream of something half
divine, / Be real—be mortal—and be mine!"[38] Woman is entreated to literally
personify the contemporary ideal of femininity.

That this was an impossible task is the theme of Jean Ingelow's "Family Pictures" (1850). The female narrator of this poem describes a family portrait she
has cherished since childhood. It depicts a lovely woman in an attitude of
repose. She is surrounded by flowers; her adoring little daughter is at her side.
This woman, with her meek eyes and placid forehead, has been the narrator's
ideal of womanhood. Now an adult, she confronts the pictured ideal:

What?—did nothing come to ruffle
Or disturb thy quiet mood?—
Was thy kindness always valued,
And thy meaning understood?—
Hadst thou never days of trouble,—
Fretful moments such as these?
Were thy children ne'er unruly,
Nor thy husband hard to please?

I have stood and look'd upon thee
Often when I was a child—
Thinking that when I grew older
I would be as calm and mild . . .
Oh! delusion deep and vain![39]

The ideal Victorian woman was a delusion, a vision, a portrait—not a human
being.

In a much later poem (1883) Fanny Kemble describes an ideal woman who
is more colorful, vital, complex, and physically present than many of her fore-
bears. In "What Is My Lady Like?" the difficulty of embodying the ideal in
the real is resolved by representing the woman exclusively through simile.

WHAT IS MY LADY LIKE?

What is my lady like? thou fain wouldst know—
A rosy chaplet of fresh apple bloom,
Bound with blue ribbon, lying on the snow;
What is my lady like? the violet gloom

Of evening, with deep orange light below.
She's like the noonday smell of a pine wood,
She's like the sounding of a stormy flood,
She's like a mountain-top high in the skies,
To which the day its earliest light doth lend;
She's like a pleasant path without an end;
Like a strange secret, and a sweet surprise;
Like a sharp axe of doom, wreathed with blush roses,
A casket full of gems whose key one loses;
Like a hard saying, wonderful and wise.[40]

This woman is not static and passive, domestic and delicate. Note that several images convey threat, which, however, is immediately tempered. We have the sound of the flood, not the rushing waters; and the axe of doom is wreathed with roses. Kemble's "lady," though still essentially benign, reflects the tendency later in the century to allow the ideal woman more individuality and strength—so long as she still elicits (masculine) approval and maintains her prescribed position with regard to men generally.

Poem after poem in the nineteenth century makes this necessary deference to men seem unavoidable. For in literature as in life—and especially in women's poetry—woman's manifest destiny was marriage and motherhood. Numerous poems appeared throughout the century with the purpose of reflecting upon "woman's lot" and/or outlining the "natural" stages of woman's life. Most of these poems convey a tone of melancholy and a philosophy of patient and passive resignation.

One of Felicia Hemans' most popular and frequently anthologized pieces, "Evening Prayer at a Girl's School," predicts that the adolescent girls in the poem will soon inherit woman's burden of mingled joy and woe.

Her look is on you—silent tears to weep,
    And patient smiles to wear through suffering's hour,
And sumless riches, from affection's deep
    To pour on broken reeds—a wasted shower!

. . . .

Meekly to bear with wrong, to cheer decay,
    And, oh! to love through all things—therefore pray.[41]

To the uninitiated, it may be necessary to explain that "suffering's hour" probably alludes to pregnancy and childbirth, and "broken reeds" to children who die in infancy. Notice that the only advice that Hemans offers these young women, in light of their inevitable future, is "therefore pray."

In a poem appearing in three installments in the *Ladies' Companion* for

1850, Mary Howitt delineates "The Three Ages of Woman." In the first stage of their lives, women are "Life's Young Angels," "daughters, sisters,—angels! / With bright un-tear-dimmed eyes." But maturity brings "many a bitter woe" to adult wives and mothers ("Life's Guardian Angels"). Once the children are grown, her function in life is over, and it only remains for woman to be "Approaching the Unseen."[42] Similarly, Jean Ingelow's "Songs of Seven" (1863) traces seven predictable stages of woman's life: "Exultation," "Romance," "Love" (marriage), "Maternity," "Widowhood," "Giving in Marriage," and "Longing for Home" (preparing for death). The last stanza of "Longing for Home" is worthy of quotation for the simplicity and directness of statement with which it carries its burden of sorrow and loss.[43]

> I pray you, what is the nest to me,
>   My empty nest?
> And what is the shore where I stood to see
>   My boat sail down to the west?
> Can I call that home where I anchor yet,
>   Though my good man has sailed?
> Can I call that home where my nest was set,
>   Now all its hope hath failed?
> Nay, but the port where my sailor went,
>   And the land where my nestlings be:
> There is the home where my thoughts are sent,
>   The only home for me—
>   Ah me![44]

Ingelow's poem illustrates the lifelong dependency of the "typical" woman upon a husband and family. When husband and children both are departed, life becomes meaningless and it is time to die.

In one final and slightly unusual poem of this genre, "Baby's Turn" (1860), the religious poet Frances Ridley Havergal predicts that in the infant girl's future, it will be

> Baby's turn to care for others, and to kiss away the tear,
> For the joy of ministration to the suffering or the dear,
> For the happiness of giving help and comfort, love and life,
> Whether walking all alone, or as a blessed and blessing wife.[45]

Frances Havergal was not married. The special difficulties of women in patterns of life other than marriage and motherhood will be considered later. The most important point in recounting the "Stages of Life" poems is the force of the conventional belief that all women were cut out to be wives and mothers and were thus fated to be dependent on men. Before law and custom could be changed—and major changes *were* effected before the turn of the twentieth century—societal attitudes such as this had first to be challenged and revised.

One hopeful poem, Dora Greenwell's "Bring Me Word How Tall She Is: Woman in 1872," anticipated positive revisions in the relationship of men and women to be produced by the current changes in social ideas. The title is from *As You Like It:* " 'How tall is your Rosalind?' / 'Just as high as my heart.' "

> At length, in stature grown,
> He stands erect and free;
> Yet stands he not alone,
> For his beloved would be
> Like him she loveth wise, like him she loveth free.
>
> So wins she her desire,
> Yet stand they not apart;
> For as she doth aspire
> He grows, nor stands she higher
> Than her Beloved's heart.[46]

It is still too soon, in 1872, for woman's stature to equal her mate's. Though "wise" now and "free," she still stands no higher than his "heart." However, even this kind of guarded optimism was scarcely the norm in women poets' assessments of the relations between the sexes or in their meditations upon the probable destinies of women.

Often, women poets expressed their dissatisfaction with woman's lot in life obliquely, through image, symbol, or metaphor. The poem of captivity, for example, was very popular. In Emily Brontë's Gondal poetry is "The Prisoner" (published in 1846) about a young woman locked in a dungeon. A visitor to the vault mocks her with "Confined in triple walls, art thou so much to fear, / That we must bind thee down and clench thy fetters here?"[47] Consider the situation of the mid-Victorian woman—confined by convention to home and hearth, hindered in her attempts to improve herself, and twitted by masculine critics for her inferiority of body and mind. The captive in "The Prisoner" yearns for the freedom she will find in death.

The imprisonment imagery which is so prevalent in Emily Brontë's poetry has only recently been attributed to any sense she might have had that her life was restricted because she was a woman.[48] More often, critics have referred this imagery to her mysticism; presumably, it expressed her soul's wish to break free of the confinements of the flesh.[49] Overall, Brontë's work has generally been read as philosophically Romantic (or, sometimes, anti-Romantic);

seldom has it been placed in historical context.[50] One reader insists that neither her novel nor her poetry represents "a criticism of this life, but an evocation of another, and, like its author, it is not to be compared."[51] Another declares that the "sociological approach" to Brontë has been "a notorious failure."[52] Yet, without denying her high level of intellectual sophistication and her metaphysical understanding of life, we must still acknowledge that Emily Brontë was not *sui generis,* but a woman artist writing and publishing in nineteenth-century England. And according to Sandra Gilbert and Susan Gubar, "dramatizations of imprisonment and escape are so all-pervasive in nineteenth-century literature by women that . . . they represent a uniquely female tradition in this period."[53]

Two final stanzas of "The Prisoner," which were first published in 1915, incorporate the captivity images of the caged bird and the broken chain. The caged bird, as an emblem for the soul, for poetic aspiration, or for woman's general plight, was a recurrent image in Victorian women's poetry.[54] Other examples include Brontë's own "The Caged Bird," Dinah Craik's "The Canary in His Cage," and Emily Pfeiffer's "The Winged Soul." Dora Greenwell's "The Broken Chain" (1861) conveys the emotional difficulty of breaking a chain that is strengthened by both love and custom.

> Captives, bound in iron bands,
>   Half have learned to love their chain;
> Slaves have held up ransomed hands,
>   Praying to be slaves again;
> So doth custom reconcile,
>   Soothing even pain to smile;
> So a sadness will remain
>   In the breaking of the chain.
>
> But if chain were woven shining,
>   Firm as gold and fine as hair,
> Twisting round the heart and twining,
>   Binding all that centres there
> In a knot, that like the olden
>   May be cut, yet ne'er unfolden;—
> Would not something sharp remain
>   In the breaking of the chain?[55]

Dora Greenwell was a conservative, devout single woman, and an invalid for most of her life.[56] Yet surely in "The Broken Chain" she has explained the reluctance of the average (and therefore married) Victorian woman to rebel against her situation.

Another poem by Greenwell, titled "The Sunflower," has recently been revived in anthologies of women's poetry because of its metaphorical representation of nineteenth-century woman's relationship with man.[57] Woman, of course, is the flower, man the sun. The opening stanza begins, "Till the slow daylight pale, / A willing slave, fast bound to one above, / I wait." The lines that most clearly validate a feminist reading of the poem are, "I must droop / Upon my stalk, I cannot reach his *sphere*; / To mine he cannot stoop" (emphasis added).[58] Cora Kaplan declares "The Sunflower" to be "an extremely sexualized, submissive poem" with "troubling masochistic nuances." Yet, as she quite rightly notes, it simultaneously contradicts the conventional association of women and flowers. "The sunflower is a coarse, common flower; Victorian women were supposed to keep themselves shaded from the sun, folded, like the rose."[59] In an enlightening essay, Kaplan goes on to show how the flowers lavishly strewn about in women's poetry in the nineteenth century often carry symbolic messages about women's perceptions of their lives and of their very nature.

Granting the validity of this kind of interpretation, let us just examine two additional poems of this type. Emily Pfeiffer's sonnet "Learn of the Dog" (1881) is another and rather less flattering treatment of the theme of "The Broken Chain."

LEARN OF THE DOG

Poor friend and sport of man, like him unwise,
  Away! Thou standest to his heart too near.
  Too close for careless rest or healthy cheer;
Almost in thee the glad brute nature dies.
Go, scour the open fields in wild emprise,
  Lead the free chase, leap, plunge into the mere,
  Herd with thy fellows, stay no longer here,
Seeking thy law and gospel in man's eyes.

He cannot go; love holds him fast to thee
  More than the voices of his kind thy word
    Lives in his heart; for him, thy very rod
Has flowered; he only in thy will is free;
  Cast him not out, the unclaimed savage herd
    Would turn and rend him, pining for his God.[60]

Woman is the over-domesticated dog, the "friend and sport of man," who stands too close to his heart to be cheerful or carefree. Though a life of activity and freedom in the company of her own kind may look natural and appealing, woman's love for her master prevents it. To make this reading of the poem seem obvious, simply substitute "she" for "he" throughout the poem wherever the antecedent is the dog, and bear in mind that the poem's title asks the reader to "Learn of the Dog."

A final example of a woman poet who adopted a symbolic mode in order to comment upon woman's role vis-à-vis man is Mary Elizabeth Coleridge (Samuel Taylor Coleridge's great-grandniece). "In Dispraise of the Moon," for example, contrasts the aridity and pallor of the (traditionally feminine) moon with the brightness and nobility of the (traditionally masculine) sun. Declaring, "I would not be the Moon, the sickly thing," she rejects the principle of woman's life as reflected light. For "Light in itself doth feed the living brain; / That light, reflected, but makes darkness plain."[61] "Beware!" (1894) suggests that beneath the conventional exterior of the most pliant of Victorian women, hostility might be lurking.

BEWARE!

Her yellow hair is soft, and her soft eyes
  Are as the dove's for meekness. Only feel
The softness of the hand in mine that lies!
  The sheath is velvet, but the sword is steel.

Soft are her footsteps; and her low replies
  The lover's woe like softest music heal.
Ah, let him still remember and be wise,
  The sheath is velvet, but the sword is steel![62]

An ambiguous sexuality is conveyed in the metaphor for the woman's contradictory nature: a steel sword (masculine) and a velvet sheath (feminine). As a woman both strong and soft, masculine and feminine, her love capable of wounding as well as healing, the heroine of "Beware!" represents the ideal Victorian woman merging with the *femme fatale*. Precisely because of her benign appearance, the poem suggests, the woman of concealed strength (perhaps *all* women?) could actually be dangerous to men.[63]

Writing in the 1890s, Mary Coleridge thus moves beyond criticism of woman's traditional role, to intimation of its potentially ominous consequences—not for women, but for men. Furthermore, the symbolism in "Beware!" is less covert, and requires less elaborate decoding, than that in "Learn of the Dog" or "The Sunflower." Yet even here, the conceptualization remains attached to the conventional imagery of womanhood.

The continuing power of that imagery, and women poets' various strategies for confronting it, are addressed in the next three chapters, which examine women poets' representations of women in their conventional roles as daughters, wives, and mothers.

2
Daughters

Having explored some of the ways in which women poets responded to basic nineteenth-century attitudes about women, let us examine their representations of women in different possible social roles. Taking a more or less chronological approach, we begin with daughters. The English girl was the subject of a great deal of sentimental verse in the nineteenth century. But while a few perceptive women poets addressed such significant issues as education, sexual awakening, and female friendships, most were content to emphasize maidenhood as a time of personal preparation for the ambiguous but inevitable destiny of marriage and motherhood.

In 1774, one Dr. John Gregory, on the point of death, published *A Father's Legacy to His Daughters*, a small courtesy book which saw numerous successive editions and enjoyed great popularity for over half a century. Dr. Gregory recommended that the desired feminine characteristics of daintiness and passivity be feigned where not naturally existing. A robust healthiness should be enjoyed in grateful silence because "when a woman speaks of her great strength, her extraordinary appetite, her ability to bear excessive fatigue, we [men] recoil at the description in a way she is little aware of." Dr. Gregory further admonished, "if you happen to have any learning, keep it a profound secret, especially from the men, who generally look with a jealous and malignant eye on a woman of great parts and a cultivated understanding. . . . Be even cautious in displaying your good sense."[1] In recommending that his daughters conform to the stereotype of the endearingly shy, weak, ignorant, and helpless young thing, Dr. Gregory seems to have been totally unperturbed by the duplicity of life to which he committed them. The point was to fulfill the character expectations of society, so as to be asked in marriage.

In his first volume of *Poems* (1817), John Keats captured the sentimental appeal of the sweet, helpless young girl:

> Ah! who can e'er forget so fair a being?
>   Who can forget her half retiring sweets?
>   God! she is like a milk-white lamb that bleats
> For man's protection.[2]

Only in a leisured society could such an ideal of femininity seem appropriate. And indeed, by the beginning of the nineteenth century, many middle-class women began to find they had less real work to do than ever before. Thus it became their goal in life "to realize the type of female perfection which the breadwinner of the family expected to find in his wife and daughters."[3] It became the hallmark of such a "lady" first to be idle and admired (during the Regency period) and then, additionally, to be sheltered and protected (during the early Victorian era). It was not until the second half of Victoria's reign that the idea of female usefulness and participation in society began to regain acceptance. Even then, the popular courtesy books continued to preach reticence, duty, delicacy, and accomplishment and to justify the constriction and monotony of middle-class women's lives by insisting that the preservation of home and family life depended upon them.

Probably the most crucial factor affecting a girl's life was, in reality, the quality and extent of her education. Unlike boys, who usually went away to school, most middle-class girls received what little education they got from their mothers and in their own homes, especially at the beginning of the century. If a girl had brothers at home, she could sometimes share their tutor; or if her father had an extensive library and would allow her to use it, she could try to educate herself. A fortunate girl might even get a solid liberal education if she were upper class; or if she were part of a new radical family, perhaps Quaker or Unitarian, which valued intellectualism in women; or if she were simply extremely lucky.[4] She could not, of course, acquire this education in any college in England; until mid-century, all were closed to women.

In the 1690s both Mary Astell (*A Serious Proposal to the Ladies*) and Daniel Defoe (*An Essay Upon Projects*) had recommended the establishment of an institution of higher education for women, but the project was blocked by Bishop Burnet.[5] In 1775 Elizabeth Montagu's proposal to found and endow such a college was abandoned after Anna Barbauld refused the post of superintendent and denounced the project.[6] Barbauld later wrote in her *Legacy to Young Ladies* (1826): "A woman ought to have that general tincture [of academic subjects] which marks the cultivated mind. She ought to have enough of them to engage gracefully in general conversation. In no subject is she required to be deep. . . . "[7]

In prose and verse, Anna Barbauld consistently expressed very conventional views on women. We have already seen her poem "The Rights of Women."

In "To a Lady, with Some Painted Flowers," she employed traditional flower imagery to endorse what society then held to be women's true vocation: to please men.

> Flowers to the fair; to you these flowers I bring,
> And strive to greet you with an earlier spring.
> Flowers, sweet and gay and delicate like you,
> Emblems of innocence and beauty too.
>
> . . . .
>
> Gay without toil, and lovely without art,
> They spring to cheer the sense, and glad the heart.
> Nor blush, my fair, to own you copy these,
> Your best, your sweetest empire is—to please.[8]

Given the tenor of the times, Anna Barbauld's assessment of the issue was pragmatic; for nearly equal with education in importance to a young woman's future was her appeal to potential marriage partners. Education for display put first things first by making her attractive to her future suitors, rather than useful to her future husband.

In 1787, Mary Wollstonecraft's *Thoughts on the Education of Daughters* indicted this system of education for its extreme superficiality:

> Girls learn something of music, drawing, and geography; but they do
> not know enough to engage their attention, render it an employment
> of the mind. If they can play over a few tunes to their acquaintance,
> and have a drawing or two (half done by the master) to hang up in
> their rooms, they imagine themselves artists for the rest of their lives.

Wollstonecraft wanted girls to be taught to combine ideas, to be taught to think. She opposed very early marriages because they did not allow a young woman to attend to her soul, to cultivate her understanding, to struggle with the world, or to attain her full maturity. Furthermore, while she conceded that "no employment of the mind is a sufficient excuse for neglecting domestic duties," nevertheless she did not feel that intellect and domesticity were incompatible.[9]

Jane Taylor, second daughter in the famous Taylor family of Ongar, was nine years old when Mary Wollstonecraft's *Vindication* appeared.[10] As an adult, Jane Taylor agreed with Wollstonecraft about women's education and often expressed these ideas in her verse, which was sometimes light and entertaining, sometimes gentle and reflective, never strident or inflammatory. "On Intellectual Taste" (1824) is addressed directly to young women. The setting

of the poem is cozily domestic. Two sisters are waiting for their mother to arrive with the new trimming for their hats. One sister, Martha, is full of idle
chatter, while the other, Anne, is lost in intellectual contemplation of the
universe.

> Then roved her eyes from star to star,
> And soon her thought had fled as far,
> For thought has neither chain nor bar,
>   It ranges fair and free:
> And as she had not wings to fly
> Amid the starry realms on high,
> She marvelled that a mortal eye
>   Those distant worlds could see.

Notice that Taylor describes Anne's reverie in typical women's imagery of
chains and flight. Meanwhile, the girls' mother arrives and begins to trim the
hats.

> And there does eager Martha stand,
>   Suggesting this, approving that,
> And all her soul is in her hat
>   (Full large enough to hold it).

It is not that Anne is ungrateful—she thanks her mother for trimming the
hat—but that "her mind was braced with thought, / Some nobler happiness it
sought / Than 'ere, with nicest art, was wrought / With ribbon, pearl, or
lace."[11] In the poem's concluding stanza, Taylor urges young women to
prefer cultivation of the mind to decoration of the body.

Rather than blaming young women themselves for feminine flightiness, Jane
Taylor, like Mary Wollstonecraft, faulted the English system of education
wherein various bits and pieces of knowledge and accomplishment were
pieced together and presented to young women half at random, like a patch-
work quilt.

> Thus Science, distorted, and torn into bits,
> Art tortured, and frightened half out of her wits;
> In portions and patches, some light and some shady,
> Are stitched up together, and make a young lady.[12]

In Taylor's verse autobiography "The World in the House," she praises her
father for educating his own daughters with much "mental culture" and very
little "accomplishment" and discouraging them from pursuing the trifles and
frivolities that marred most girls' education.[13]

Subsequent writers decried also the superficiality of an education geared toward obtaining a husband (rather than toward making him a good wife). Few contemporary accounts of the intellectual bankruptcy produced by women's deficient education are at once more pathetic and more inspiring than that given by feminist Frances Power Cobbe in her autobiography, written in 1894. Cobbe described at some length her education at Brighton in 1836, with its emphasis on exterior accomplishments and its neglect of students' real potential. Though many of her classmates were clever, Cobbe recalled, and nearly all were well disposed, "all this fine human material was deplorably wasted. . . . Not that which was good in itself or useful to the community, or even that which would be delightful to ourselves, but that which would make us admired in society, was the *raison d'être* of each requirement. Everything was taught us in the inverse ratio of its true importance."[14] Cobbe managed to overcome this early miseducation and to educate herself, slowly and painfully acquiring knowledge and habits of mental rigor and self-discipline. How many less extraordinary girls did not?

Even conservative opinion leaders like Sarah Stickney Ellis and Elizabeth Poole Sandford came to criticize "the system of education which taught girls the wrong subjects and gave them the wrong standards."[15] Instead, however, they recommended domestic and moral training, preferably by the mother, in the home. The general view that a woman's proper education should prepare her for marriage and motherhood was only tentatively challenged by feminist writers before 1869 and was not challenged at all by most conventional writers.

Unlike Jane Taylor, Caroline Bowles (who married Poet Laureate Robert Southey when she was middle-aged and he was entering his dotage) was educated for marriage, not intellectual achievement. Mrs. Southey's autobiographical poem is "The Birthday," first published in 1836. According to this poem her mother taught young Caroline to read, and her father presented her with a copy of James Thomson's "Seasons" to encourage her versifying; but this can hardly be considered "mental culture." Furthermore, she was discouraged from her tomboyish habits and forced instead to acquire all the appropriate feminine accomplishments and skills. The one which she most despised was needlework:

> Unwelcome hour I ween, that tied me down
> Restless, reluctant, to the sempstress' task!
> Sight horrible to me, th' allotted seam
> Of stubborn irish, or more hateful length
> Of handkerchief, with folded edge touched down,
> *All* to be hemmed; ay, *selvidge sides* and all.
> And so they were in tedious course of time.[16]

Caroline Bowles' literary achievements might have been greater had she been able to spend more of her youth in pursuit of mental culture and less in training for future domestic duties.

But as Artemas Bowers Muzzey asserted in the 1843 courtesy book *The Young Maiden*, a woman's proper education was intended "to teach her to know her place, and her functions, to make her content with the one and willing to fulfill the other." Muzzey insisted on relegating woman to the role of helpmate: "Woman should be prepared to co-operate with [man] in the station he may fill, not openly and directly, but by a wise, gentle, and steady domestic influence."[17] In the same year, in *A Plea for Woman*, Marion (Mrs. Hugo) Reid attacked this "supposed power of female influence,"[18] a rationale for woman's subsidiary role which was by no means original with Muzzey, but which could be found in the writings of Mrs. Sandford, Mrs. Ellis, John Ruskin, and many others.

Lady Emmeline Stuart Wortley expressed the conventional notion of the power of "influence" in her poem "To Woman," which she published as editor of the *Keepsake* annual for 1840.

> From man shall conquering power expected be,
>   The sovereignty of will and of command,
> All the attributes of proud authority,
>   Since thus the steadfast laws of Nature stand.
>
> But by the graces, and their charmed gifts,
>   Still hath the Woman reign'd, and still *shall* reign. . . .
> So hath the angel in her aspect swayed
>   Throughout all time, and power and pride hath quelled.[19]

This poem indicates that although Lady Stuart Wortley evidently understood the way in which the theory of feminine influence combined the moral idealization with the practical subjugation of woman, she was not moved to protest. Of course, Lady Stuart Wortley was an aristocrat and a world traveller, an admirer of Byron and Napoleon. She may never have felt the theory's repercussions personally. Mrs. Reid, however, protested that since "the grand plea for woman sharing with man all the advantages of education is, that every rational being is worthy of cultivation for his or her own individual sake," it was unfortunate that it had become so much "the custom, even of the most liberal in these matters, to urge the education and enlightenment of women, rather as a means of improving man, than as, in itself, an end of intrinsic excellence."[20]

With the establishment in the late forties of the first colleges for women (Queens College, 1848, and Bedford College, 1849), the acceptable justification for educating women began to shift from merely preparing them to be pleasing companions and capable wives and mothers to recognizing and even valuing their independent intellectual potential. But the idea of higher education for women was regarded with skepticism and surrounded by controversy, as is perhaps best illustrated in *The Princess* (1847).[21] Although John Killham's study of Tennyson's poem concludes that it had been "a serious attempt, artfully disguised, to change an outworn attitude to an important human problem,"[22] nevertheless it was not so received. Furthermore, any such interpretation is undercut by the poem's conclusion, in which Princess Ida exchanges her dream of a women's university for marriage, however idealized, with the prince. Killham is clearly correct, though, in maintaining that *The Princess* incorporated numerous ideas then in the public consciousness.

Many passages which were at least faintly ridiculous in 1847 strike the modern reader as poignant. Consider, for example, in the prologue, Lilia's response to Walter's question about heroic and noble womanhood (a question accompanied, incidentally, by a pat on the head): "Where . . . lives there such a woman now?"[23]

> Quick answered Lilia, "There are thousands now
> Such women, but convention beats them down:
> It is but bringing up; no more than that:
> You men have done it: how I hate you all!
> Ah, were I something great! I wish I were
> Some mighty poetess, I would shame you then,
> That love to keep us children!
>
> (Prologue. 127-133)

Lilia's vehemence is mirrored in Princess Ida, who spurns men in establishing her women's university. Yet despite some obvious sympathy with Ida's goals and frustrations, Tennyson seems to present her as mistaken, finally, in her understanding of the relationship between the sexes. Where Ida had preached separation and equality, Tennyson apparently endorsed cooperation and complement. The final, conciliatory lines of the tale are given to the prince:

> My bride,
> My wife, my life. O we will walk this world,
> Yoked in all exercise of noble end,
> And so thro' those dark gates across the wild
> That no man knows. Indeed I love thee: come,
> Yield thyself up: my hopes and thine are one:
> Accomplish thou my manhood and thyself;
> Lay thy sweet hands in mine and trust to me.
>
> (VIII. 338-345)

Yet after hearing the story of Princess Ida, Walter has evidently changed his mind. He remarks, in the conclusion, "I wish she had not yielded."

The Princess is one clear example in nineteenth-century literature of the co-existence of old and new ideals of young womanhood. The new ideal, which would lead toward an acceptance of women as fully human beings with independent lives and even careers, was still in process of formulation. The establishment of Girton and Newnham Colleges at Cambridge (1869, 1871) and Somerville College and Lady Margaret Hall at Oxford (1879) marked not the culmination but only the first real momentum for later challenges to the Victorian idea that woman's sole true vocation was marriage.[24]

Meanwhile, the old ideal remained strong for most of the century, requiring from women certain different sets of desirable feminine characteristics. A young woman's position of subordinance, first to her father and eventually to her husband, required sweetness, docility, passivity, and obedience. Her status as an object of admiration, associated with her need to attract suitors, recommended beauty, softness, delicacy, and mastery of all the appropriate accomplishments: French, music, drawing, conversation, needlework, letter writing, etc. Finally, her destiny of marriage and motherhood necessitated, for the middle-class girl at least, some knowledge and experience with domestic skills such as ironing, cookery, and home management.

Rather like Alice in Wonderland (who was only about seven years old), the typical middle-class English girl was expected to assimilate these characteristics and cultivate these abilities in childhood, long before she was old enough to put them to use. One result was the child-woman, a popular figure in children's literature (e.g., Sylvie in Lewis Carroll's *Sylvie and Bruno* or Wendy in J. M. Barrie's *Peter Pan)* as well as a recurring character in the novels of Charles Dickens and others.[25] Unlike these examples, Mary Howitt's poem "Childhood, or the Triad" (published in 1835 when the Howitts' only daughter was eleven years old) is a relatively unsentimentalized portrayal of the English girl-child, but it is also one which clearly illustrates society's approval of the womanly little girl. The speaker in the poem is the doting mother of three young daughters—Jane, Rose, and Emily—each of whom is quite mature in her own individual way. The first daughter, Jane, is domestically inclined:

> Jane, my eldest, is sedate,
> Fit to be a Crusoe's mate;
> Quite a housewife in her way,
> Busily employed all day. . . .
> So correct, so kind, so sage,
> She's a wonder for her age. . . .

> Rose is quite a different child,
> Tractable enough and mild;
> But the genius of the three,
> The lady of the family.

Rose plays the piano and sings, writes poetry, and draws even better than her mother, "Though no little sum was spent / To give me that accomplishment." In short, Rose is precociously accomplished. Emily, the youngest, is a budding coquette or fashion plate:

> Oh, the little roguish thing!
> Now she'll dance, and now she'll sing,
> Now she'll put on modish airs
> Such as Mrs. Johnson wears;
> Shaking her rich curling tresses
> For the plumes with which she dresses.

All three children are sweet and docile. Even roguish Emily is "Loving yet and gentle still."[26] Among them, these three girls demonstrate household skills, accomplishment, and fashionable attractiveness—all the requisites of the ideal woman of seventeen or eighteen years of age.

In "The Birthday," Caroline Bowles Southey pointed up the differences between parental hopes for the boys and for the girls in her own (or any) family. Among the boys, there might be a future war hero, barrister, chancellor, or bishop:

> Thy sons will rove, as various fortune leads,
> Haply successful in their several paths,
> And, like thyself, in course of years, become
> The careful fathers of a hopeful race.
> Then will ambitious thoughts, and worldly cares
> Engross their hearts, and haply steal from thee
>   A portion of thy former influence—

No such thing will become of a daughter, however, whose future horizons are so limited that she can barely even expect to grow up:

> And little Annie—what will Annie be?
> The fair-haired prattler! she, with matron airs,
> Who gravely lectures her rebellious doll—
> "Annie will be papa's own darling child,
> Dear papa's blessing." Ah! she tells thee truth;

> . . . Thy blessing she will prove—
> The duteous prop of thy declining years.

Unlike the adult sons, whose family responsibilities encourage them to rely on their own judgment and no longer on their parents, Annie "will never change" despite the experiences of marriage and motherhood. Instead, her own children "will half renew again her infant days."[27] Thus did the sheltered nature of women's lives contribute to their infantilization. In "The Birthday," Caroline Southey apparently intended no irony; perhaps, as a woman of her own times, she was half unaware of the trivialization of women which she was depicting in her own autobiography.

With Jean Ingelow, it is less easy to be sure of her position. In "Laurance" (1867), Ingelow contrasts the worldly life of the young man Laurance with the sheltered existence of his beloved Muriel. Even Laurance himself is troubled about it:

> Because her girlish innocence, the grace
> Of her unblemished pureness, wrought in him
> A longing and aspiring, and a shame
> To think how wicked was the world—that world
> Which he must walk in—while from her (and such
> As she was) it was hidden; there was made
> A clean path, and the girl moved on like one
> In some enchanted ring.[28]

But why is Laurance troubled? Is it because the world is so irredeemably wicked, or because Muriel is so exaggeratedly pure? Does he really admire her enchanted ignorance? As the story develops, Muriel's lack of preparedness for life causes her great misery, while Laurance's worldly wisdom and restraint ultimately secure his (and her) happiness. Yet it is just her helplessness and purity which inspire him to strength of character. The innocence and dependency of feminine character provided the motive for masculine virtue.

On the other hand, one must be careful not to exaggerate the vapidity of young women's lives in the nineteenth century. Real life is not poetry, and real human beings are seldom so pure or so foolish as all that.[29] Besides, there was much opportunity for human interaction in the characteristically large early Victorian families. Young girls had brothers and, of course, girlfriends with whom to play and talk. There are even a few poems commemorating these relationships. Felicia Hemans' "Korner and His Sister" is a typical tribute to sisterly affection.[30] George Eliot's autobiographical poem "Brother and Sister" (written in 1869) recounts her childhood idolization of her older brother, Isaac. The latter poem ends on a sad note, however; the children are torn apart by school, never to regain "The childish world where our two spirits mingled / Like scents from varying roses that remain / One sweetness, nor can evermore be singled." In George Eliot's particular case the final estrangement from her brother was effected by the way she flaunted convention in her relationship with George Henry Lewes. She hints at this in the penultimate stanza of "Brother and Sister," with its harshness of tone and its mention of "divorce."

> . . . the dire years whose awful name is Change
> Had grasped our souls still yearning in divorce,
> And pitiless shaped them in two forms that range
> Two elements which sever their life's course.[31]

George Eliot's poem has the merits of intellectual tone and psychological acuity, whereas most women's poems about the brother-sister relationship were entirely sentimental. Since the brother figure might logically serve as a prototype of father, suitor, or husband, it is surprising to find relatively little poetry by women focusing on sisterly devotion to a brother.[32]

For that matter, there was also very little women's poetry exploring sisterly emotions of whatever kind—affection, admiration, jealousy—for a brother *or* a sister. Of the various possible relationships between women, only the mother-daughter theme was given real prominence. Most human relationships depicted in women's poetry were between women and men. Although female friendships, generated and endorsed by the homosocial culture of the nineteenth century, were often strong and enduring,[33] poems expressing this bond were relatively infrequent. A notable exception is the poetry of Fanny Kemble, whose many episodes of separating from women friends stimulated her to express her grief in poetry.[34] The depth and complexities of female friendship are expressed much more fully in personal documents such as letters and diaries.

Despite the consolations of family and friends, many young women certainly found their lives impoverished by their enforced innocence and isolation from "the world." The contributing phenomenon of "woman worship" incorporated the disembodied purity of angels[35] (and perhaps, to some extent, of the Virgin Mary) with the doctrine of female moral and religious influence to create the Victorian ideal woman in the popular imagination and therefore, of course, in poetry as well. Young middle-class women in the nineteenth century had continually to contend with that ideal. Some probably succeeded in approximating it, at least superficially, while others either failed to do so or chose not to try.

Those few who dared to reject the popular ideal faced animosity, ridicule, and excoriation. The *North British Review* devoted four full pages of Patmore's

1851 article on "The Social Position of Women" to a denunciation of the so-called emancipated woman who "has not thought the peculiar virtues of women worth cultivating."[36] In a famous series of essays in 1868 in the *Saturday Review*, Mrs. Eliza Lynn Linton continually and scornfully contrasted the scandalous, immodest, and misguided modern girl, "The Girl of the Period," with the "fair young English girl" of the recent past. Mrs. Linton clearly defined this dying ideal of womanhood:

> It meant a creature generous, capable, modest . . . refined . . . domes-
> tic . . . and graceful. It meant a girl who could be trusted alone if need
> be, because of the innate purity and dignity of her nature, but who
> was neither bold in bearing nor masculine in mind; a girl who, when
> she married, would be her husband's friend and companion, but
> never his rival . . . who would make his house his true home and
> place of rest. . . .

The modern girl, however, showed little regard for others' opinions, did not especially try to please men, and, according to Mrs. Linton, dressed like a common prostitute. "All men whose opinion is worth having prefer the simple and genuine girl of the past, with her tender little ways and pretty bashful modesties, to this loud and rampant modernization . . . talking slang as glibly as a man."[37] In a later chapter we will see how a few women writers chose to deal with this modern girl, or "New Woman," who began in the late sixties quite openly to challenge the constraints of the old ideal.

But nineteenth-century women poets most often represented the English girl as an innocent creature, in her middle or late teens, poised on the threshold of conventional womanhood. Often a natural setting and a symbolic season or time of day will reflect this girl's unspoiled beauty and anticipatory stage of life. The young woman in Mary Howitt's "The Morning Walk" (1833) possesses all the ideal qualities: a loving heart, an intent to please, a pure spirit, a secure faith, a beautiful face and form. She lives in a secluded country place, "A place of stillness and of shade, / As if for rural quiet made." The poem's narrator, an adult woman (possibly the girl's mother), addresses the younger woman, who is setting out for her morning stroll through the countryside. The birds are singing, the roses blooming, the trees glistening with dew. Yet age is also present "Where ancient woods have grown untrimmed . . . / And an old fountain's waters chime / All day as if they noted time." A constant movement in the poem between past, present, and future—both the girl's and the speaker's—carries the poem's theme: "Youth's visions are too fair to last."

Thought will grow sad, and care be strong,
And duties of a graver kind
Require from thee a stedfast mind.
And then, from those gone years of youth,
Thy mother's words of serious truth,
Forgotten else, will come to thee
From the clear depths of memory,
And guide thee through the shoals of life,
The thoughtful mother and the wife.[38]

Though written with some degree of artistic subtlety, "The Morning Walk" expresses an extremely conventional attitude.

Similarly in "Twilight" by Caroline Norton (1840), a young woman is advised by her mother to anticipate that life of "joy and sorrow blent" which, as we have seen, was woman's lot. The daughter, who is only sixteen, is soon to be married. The setting is summer twilight—lovely in its warmth and repose, and its swift descent into night. It is a time of beauty and transition. Watched by her widowed mother, the girl is deep in innocent slumber.

Beauty's perfection seem'd to make a pause,
And wait, on that smooth brow, some further touch,
Some spell from Time,—the great magician,—such
As calls the closed bud out of hidden gloom,
And bids it wake to glory, light, and bloom.

All at once she awakens from a romantic dream of love and marriage, saddened that real life can never measure up to the ideal. Her mother acknowledges "the long sacrifice of woman's days," but counsels her daughter to do God's will and accept her role as man's helpmate. This advice is expressed in the most conventional way:

"Sure it is much, this delegated power,
To be consoler of man's heaviest hour!
The guardian angel of a life of care,
Allow'd to stand twixt him and his despair!
Such service may be made a holy task;
And more, t'were vain to hope, and rash to ask."

The daughter pauses to absorb this information, then smiles and assures her mother that she has understood. "And from her mother's fond protecting side / She went into the world, a youthful bride."[39] For most of the nineteenth century, poetry about young womanhood simply took for granted the

desirability and imminence of marriage. As "Violet Fane" (Mary Montgomerie Lamb, Lady Currie) says in her much later poem, "Time":

> But the maid is a bride, and the bride a mother
>   (Bud, and blossom, and blown-out flower),
> And the new-born lives, one after another,
>   Are a-dance, like motes, in the sunlit hour.[40]

Generally speaking, the emphasis on youth and innocence in poems like
these reflects the fact that a girl's value as a bride depended not only on her
beauty, personality, accomplishments, and dowry, but on her chastity as
well.[41] Omnipresent floral imagery frequently alludes to virginity; the nineteenth-century preoccupation with chastity in women can be discerned also in
the numerous references (in both poetry and prose) to feminine "modesty,"
"virtue," "maidenliness," etc., and the abhorrence of the "bold," "forward,"
or "shameless" woman. Women poets treated the touchy subject of "defloration" infrequently and cautiously. Two sexually symbolic poems, each attach-
ing different significance to the event, will illustrate.

"The Purple and White Carnation" by Caroline Norton clearly invites
analysis with its subtitle "A Fable." In this mid-century poem, "Young Love"
mischievously shoots his arrow into the air in "Flora's bower," and it lands in
a white carnation. The vulnerable flower is "of virgin white . . . all snowy and
pure," with two little drops of an unidentified liquid (dew?) poised like tear-
drops just ready to flow. Usually, Cupid's arrow pierces the heart, and indeed
it is possible to read the following lines in that way. However, the sexual content of the passage is undeniable also.

> It rested, that dart; and its pointed tip
> Sank deep where the bees were wont to sip;
> And the sickening flower gazed with grief
> On the purple stains which dimmed each leaf,
> And the crystal drops on its leaves that stood
> Blush'd with sorrow and shame till they turn'd to blood.

From that day forth, the flower is blighted; the purple stains never disappear.
"Flora," who is very angry, curses the power of "Love" because "With whis-
pers and smiles he wins Beauty's ears / But he leaves her nothing save grief
and tears." Flora casts the ruined carnation from paradise.

> The floweret says, as it droops its head,
> "Alas! for the day when by love I bled;
> When my feathery flowers were pure and white,
> And my leaves had no earthly stain or blight."

The twice-stated moral of the poem is "what Love hath ruin'd must sink in decay." "Love" is thus the serpent, and the wounding of the flower symbolizes sin; it was the blossoms' "pride" which first caught Cupid's eye.

Leaving aside the problem of the author's conscious intentions, the impact of the poem is clearly sexual. Defloration, presented as a casually perpetrated rape, is a sickening and bloody event; Norton does not suggest that it is at all desirable. Instead, the flower yearns for paradise lost and bemoans her now inevitable death. And even Flora in her bower "wails and grieves . . . o'er that sad, lost flower."[42] Apparently, then, this is an unmarried girl seduced and betrayed by a lover. The nineteenth-century paradigm of the "fallen woman" will be explored more fully in a later chapter. The point here is to show the traumatic effect, as portrayed by Norton, when a woman's sexual initiation occurs in the wrong social context.

In contrast, "Maidenhood" by E. Nesbit (1898) is somewhat more positive about sexual initiation. Innocence is seen as a mixed blessing. It is beautiful, secure, and even visionary; yet it also veils the true colors and splendor of life from youthful eyes. "Love" in this poem is "the thorny crown" for which the maiden must soon exchange her "crown of lilies," perhaps suggesting that marriage is a kind of Christian martyrdom for women. The appeal of floral imagery (blossoms, lilies, the rose) is overpowered in the poem by the fear of thorns. It does not seem far-fetched to consider the flowers female and the pricking thorns phallic. The poem ends with an image of the virgin in a state of fearful anticipation.

> Yet in the mystery of her peaceful way
>   Who knows what fears beset her innocence,
> Who, trembling, learns that thorns will wound some day
>   And wonders what thorns are, and why, and whence?[43]

The initiated woman is to be relieved from this breathless anxiety and rewarded with wisdom; thus the state of experience at least offers compensations for lost innocence. The poem does not address the social circumstances of the event; given the publication date, and the unconventional private life of Edith Nesbit, we need not assume that the context implied is marriage.[44]

Conventionally, however, marriage did mark the boundary line between girlhood and maturity, as the daughter of the house exchanged the authority and protection of one man—her father—for that of another—her new husband. Let us conclude this chapter on young womanhood just as young womanhood itself so often concluded in the nineteenth century—with the bride's separation from her family. As might be expected, most women poets treated this event with sentimentality. Often there are tears of apprehension, loss, and nostalgia. "The Adieu" (1833) by Letitia Landon is written from the family's point of view. The daughter of the house has married and left the family circle to establish her new home. Though "glad the peal upon the air, / And gay the bridal throng," the bride wept to leave her beloved family. She and they will miss each other, reliving the good times only in memory now. Yet everyone involved recognizes that, despite the sadness of the parting, the young woman has taken the appropriate step.

> Loved, and beloved, her own sweet will
>   It was that made her fate;
> She has a fairy home—but still
>   Our own is desolate.
> We may not wish her back again,
>   Not for her own dear sake;
> Oh! love, to form one happy chain,
>   How many thou must break![45]

This is the final stanza of the poem. Note that the last image introduced is that of a chain—in the sense of a link, no doubt, but a chain nevertheless. Writing early in the century, Letitia Landon characteristically adopted a sentimental and melancholy tone, whatever her subject.

Augusta Webster, whose poetry appeared between 1860 and 1895, generally did not. She was known as a poet who "was not afraid of expressing herself in plain language on even the most delicate subjects."[46] When treating the subject of a young woman's commitment to marriage, however, she too lapsed into occasional sentimentality. Even so, "The Happiest Girl in the World" (1870) is a sensitive and intelligent exploration of the mingled innocence, apprehension, and hope of a sheltered English girl just recently betrothed. It is a dramatic monologue of over 350 lines, a prenuptial soliloquy by the bride, expressing her hesitancies and uncertainties about the true nature of love and marriage and about the substantiality of her affection for the groom. The poem ends on an optimistic note, as the young woman resolves to have faith in the fitness of whatever lies ahead:

> And I should fear I were too happy now,
> and making this poor world too much my Heaven,
> but that I feel God nearer and it seems
> as if I had learned His love better too.[47]

Mary Elizabeth Coleridge observed in 1888, "The borderland between Miss and Mrs., especially the extreme verge of the borderland, has an odd fascination . . . Sir Thomas Browne, we know, thought it a far more solemn thing than death. It is, at any rate, a crisis. . . . "[48] Indeed, it was perhaps *the* crisis of a young woman's life, and women poets were every bit as fascinated with it at the close of the century as they had been at the beginning. Mary Coleridge's three-stanza poem "Marriage," published in 1900, portrays the event as a solemn occasion of symbolic death and birth: the death of the English girl and the birth of the English matron.

MARRIAGE

No more alone sleeping, no more alone waking,
   Thy dreams divided, thy prayers in twain;
Thy merry sisters to-night forsaking,
   Never shall we see thee, maiden, again.

Never shall we see thee, thine eyes glancing,
   Flashing with laughter and wild in glee,
Under the mistletoe kissing and dancing,
   Wantonly free.

There shall come a matron walking sedately,
   Low-voiced, gentle, wise in reply.
Tell me, O tell me, can I love her greatly?
   All for her sake must the maiden die![49]

This little misgiving, possibly the groom's, will not, of course, forestall the wedding; for the "wanton" freedom of youth must still expect to give way, in 1900 as in 1800, to the demand of female destiny: marriage.

Throughout the nineteenth century, the polar stars of a girl's life were her education and her marriage. Perhaps because weddings appealed to sentiment more than schoolbooks could, women poets for the most part reinforced an ideology of English maidenhood that deemphasized genuine education and accentuated personal preparation for marriage. In the next chapter we shall see how women's poetry responded to current social ideas surrounding the institution of marriage and to the marital relationship itself.

3
Wives

Young womanhood was considered the appropriate time for middle-class girls to form an attachment and contract a prudent marriage. Indeed, the lack of acceptable economic and social alternatives to marriage forced young women and their families to take courtship, love, and marriage very seriously. A young woman's social status and her personal happiness both depended on her marrying, and marrying well. There would be no second chance.

Before exploring the women poets' treatment of marriage and the married woman, let us first examine the conventional representation of the ideal wife and the social context of that ideal: marriage in the nineteenth century. The popular courtesy books of the century consistently emphasized the virtue of wifely submissiveness. Women were reminded of both Old and New Testament authority for the husband's superiority over the wife—especially Paul's dictum "Wives, submit yourselves unto your husbands as unto the Lord" (Ephesians 5:22). Accordingly, *Woman As She Is, and As She Should Be*, which appeared in 1835, carefully prescribed the wife's proper behavior toward her husband: "With grace to bear even warmth and peevishness, she must learn to adopt his tastes, study his disposition, and submit, in short, to all his desires. . . . "[1] Mrs. Sarah Ann Sewell, in *Woman and the Times We Live In*, which appeared thirty-four years later in Manchester, was still telling young wives very much the same thing: "It is a man's place to rule, and a woman's to yield. . . . It is her duty to bend so unmurmuringly to his wishes, that the rest of the household will follow her example, and treat him with the due respect his sex demands."[2]

In her study of *The Early Victorian Woman*, Janet Dunbar summarizes the popular ideal of wifely perfection: "softness and weakness, delicacy and modesty, a small waist and curving shoulders, an endearing ignorance of everything that went on beyond household and social life."[3] Thus, besides submission to her husband's will, the wife was to cultivate not her intelligence, but her beauty and her domesticity. As we have seen, a woman's education was adapted not to developing her intellect but to perfecting her accomplishments and her household skills. Her horizons were effectively limited, and her outlook became mainly home centered. Her contribution to her husband's much fuller and more varied life was to provide him with a refuge from "the harsh competitiveness of the outside world of industry and commerce." In fact, the contrast between the workaday world of the Victorian man, with its ever-quickening pace, and the relative seclusion of his home has been advanced as one explanation for the prevailing emphasis on "the feminine virtues of gentleness and sympathy."[4] The woman was to create a home that would be a "bright, serene, restful, joyful nook of heaven in an unheavenly world."[5] Her sphere of activity was thus generally contained within (and, inevitably, subordinated to) her husband's; her main role in life was to please him.

Eliza Lynn Linton, in describing "ideal women," in 1868 asserted, "In general, their noblest virtues come out only in the quiet sacredness of the home, and the most heroic lives of patience and well-doing go on in seclusion, uncheered by sympathy and unrewarded by applause."[6] The nature of married women's real activities in the home can become lost for us in this kind of vague and idealized statement. But as Mrs. Linton was well aware, housewifery could be very hard work. According to Patricia Branca, "Reality for most middle-class women was that they spent all their days and most evenings in scrubbing, dusting, tending fires, for six to ten rooms in a three-to-four story home, in addition to the cooking, shopping, washing and sewing required for a family of seven. While the middle-class woman had assistance in her work, it did not save her from hard physical labor."[7] Although such a life was perhaps heroic enough, could it accurately be called "quiet"?

In return for all these various contributions to her husband's happiness, the wife expected to be honored, loved, and protected; if abused, she had virtually no recourse. Divorce was impossible for a woman until 1857, except by an Act of Parliament, which was very expensive and difficult to obtain. Even after 1857, the grounds for divorce were quite limited—and different for men and women. A woman had to prove cruelty, desertion, sodomy, bestiality, or rape. A man had to prove only adultery. Though successfully amended, divorce and separation laws were still unequal at the turn of the century. When a woman married, of course, she forfeited what few civil rights she had.

The wife's duty to her husband included a sexual obligation also. Victorian ambivalence about sex has been noted many times.[8] Though a proper wife was to be chaste, ladylike, and unprovocative—in other words, was to appear sexless—the Victorian family was generally quite large. William Acton, in

Functions and Disorders of the Reproductive Organs (1857), declared, "the majority of women (happily for society) are not very much troubled with sexual feeling of any kind. . . . As a general rule, a modest woman seldom desires any sexual gratification for herself. She submits to her husband's embraces, but principally to gratify him; and, were it not for the desire of maternity, would far rather be relieved from his attentions."[9] Over a century later, it may be difficult to accept that nineteenth-century women could see themselves so differently from women today. It is tempting to conclude that this (male-defined) ideal was only a convention, which women may have endorsed publicly, but which they must certainly have repudiated privately.[10] Nevertheless, ample evidence exists that the nonsexual woman was not merely a myth.[11] Indeed, as Nancy Cott has pointed out, the ideology of feminine "passionlessness" may even have served women's interests to some extent by replacing the "sexual/carnal characterization of women" in the late eighteenth and early nineteenth centuries with a "spiritual/moral" image, thus "allowing women to develop their human faculties and their self-esteem."[12]

On the other hand, when Acton's "modest woman" married, the sudden revelation and imposition of her conjugal duties could prove disastrous, since sex education for women was essentially nonexistent. Henry T. Kitchener, in his *Letters on Marriage* (1812), complained of "the neglect of mothers in not properly preparing their daughters for the marriage state." In his opinion, "many young women brought up in small families in retired situations . . . know nothing of the nature of the sexual commerce; and, when they marry, are terrified."[13] Havelock Ellis cited the case of a nineteenth-century Englishwoman in her thirties who, on her wedding night, was so shocked and disgusted by the revelation and the physical experience of the sex act that neither she nor the marriage ever recovered.[14] In March 1854, five years after her abortive marriage to John Ruskin, Euphemia Chalmers Gray wrote to her father, "I had never been told the duties of married persons to each other and knew little or nothing about their relations in the closest union on earth."[15] There must have been many other young brides whose mothers left the revelations of sexuality to the bridegroom;[16] at any rate, the shock of the wedding night ordeal probably contributed to many a Victorian woman's alienation from sexuality.

Yet the law reinforced the wife's obligation to accommodate her husband sexually on demand and to bear his children without complaint. Until 1884 she could actually be imprisoned for denying her spouse his "conjugal rights."[17] The result was that "married women usually spent many years in childbearing, and their expectation of life was not long."[18] Though in most cases the husband's regard for his wife probably forestalled abuse of his privileges, nevertheless the opportunity for such abuse was an integral part of the system. "The laws of England and their interpretation by the courts encouraged physical punishment of wives as deriving from a husband's responsibility for his wife's actions. In common law a man had the right 'to give his wife moderate correction . . . by domestic chastisement' just as he could his children."[19] John Stuart Mill was outraged: "The vilest malefactor has some wretched woman tied to him, against whom he can commit any atrocity except killing her, and, if tolerably cautious, can do that without much danger of the legal penalty."[20]

Additional oppression fostered by the legal system surrounding marriage stemmed from the man's absolute right to his wife's property. For instance, by law an engaged woman could not dispose of her own property without her fiancé's consent. The obvious reasoning was that the man looked forward to obtaining not only the woman herself, but her property as well, and should not be cheated out of his due after he had committed himself. The novels of the period are full of satiric depictions of the consequences of such reasoning. Marriage often operated as a business arrangement, and honest affection held second priority after commercial gain in matchmaking. This attitude toward marriage is clearly illustrated in an 1859 article in the *Saturday Review* titled "Queen Bees or Working Bees?" which rejected proposed marriage law reform.

> Married life is a woman's profession; and to this her training—that of dependence—is modelled. Of course, by not getting a husband, or by losing him, she may find that she is without resources. All that can be said of her is, she has failed in business, and no social reform can prevent such failures.[21]

In summarizing the position of the wife in nineteenth-century society, one must point to the home as the center of the woman's existence. Her clear duty was to maintain that home for her husband and to promote his happiness as best she could—through contribution to his material wealth, submission to his will, gratification of his sexual desires, and deference to his more thorough education and greater intellectual power.

Of course there were always those who refused to accept the appropriateness of this role, for themselves or for others. In 1846 Anna Jameson, later a co-founder of the successful feminist periodical the *English Woman's Journal*, summarized and rejected the conventional domestic ideal of "Woman's Mission and Woman's Position."

> *Domestic life* supposes as its primary element the presence, the cares, the devotion of woman. . . . In all the relations between the sexes, she

is the refiner and the comforter of man. It is hers to keep alive all those purer, gentler, and more genial sympathies . . . without which man, exposed to the rougher influences of everyday life, and in the struggle with this selfish world, might degenerate . . . into mere brutes. . . . All this sounds so very trite, one is ashamed of the repetition. Who has ever questioned the least of these truths, or rather truisms? No one;—the only wonder is, that while they are accepted, promulgated, taught as indisputable, the real state of things is utterly at variance with them; and they are but lying commonplaces at best.[22]

Once the "pernicious ideal of marriage," as Ray Strachey characterized it, "had begun to be questioned, the number of men and women who revolted against it rapidly increased. The only wonder, indeed, is that it should have been tolerated so long."[23]

By 1896 Georgiana Hill could write, "Viewed as a career, marriage holds a less important place than formerly. It is now only one among many choices open to women."[24] Still, if the role of wife-mother had ceased by the turn of the century to be the only choice, it nevertheless remained the preferred choice of most women. Therefore, we must view Victorian representations of married women in light of both the conventional ideas and the controversy about marriage in the nineteenth century.

Marriage was such an accepted fact of women's lives that it comes as no surprise to find that it occupied a very prominent place in literature. Furthermore, because the institution of marriage depended so heavily upon the conventional ideal of woman for its *raison d'être*, and because both that institution and that ideal were coming under attack, society, which always has a stake in maintaining its current institutions and ideals, responded vociferously. One such mode of response was extensive literary consideration of the husband-wife relationship and its implications, and especially of the woman's proper role within marriage.

In the literature of the period generally, the conservative view of the wife and her role was modified in some ways. Walter E. Houghton, in *The Victorian Frame of Mind*, summarizes the three most important formulations: the entirely submissive wife, "whose whole excuse for being was to love, honor, obey—and amuse—her lord and master, and to manage his household and bring up his children"; the "New Woman," an advocate of women's rights, revolting against woman's traditional role in the home and demanding equal privileges with men; and the "angel in the house" (of Coventry Patmore's poem) whose true function was "to guide and uplift her more worldly and intellectual mate."[25]

In *The Angel in the House* (1854-1856) one can trace the doctrine of benevolent feminine influence, the belief in the sacredness of the home, and the consequent worship of the woman as wife. Though the character of the husband in the poem seems sometimes credible enough, the character of the wife is never allowed to transcend the Victorian ideal and partake of reality.

There were, of course, significant exceptions to the general stereotyping of the wife figure; the women novelists of the day were depicting marriage rather differently: they generally set forth an ideal more respectful of the woman's individuality and human rights than the male novelists did.[26] Furthermore, a few important male writers (chiefly poets) began in the sixties and afterwards to depict the husband-wife relationship more realistically and to accord women's rights more sympathy.[27]

Dante Gabriel Rossetti's sonnet "Nuptial Sleep" (1870), for example, presented the sexual passion of the marriage bed with astonishing frankness:

> At length their long kiss severed, with sweet smart;
>   And as the last slow sudden drops are shed
>   From sparkling eaves when all the storm has fled,
> So singly flagged the pulses of each heart.
> Their bosoms sundered, with the opening start
>   Of married flowers to either side outspread
>   From the knit stem. . . . [28]

Of course, some readers of *The House of Life* found this particular sonnet objectionable. In his attack on Rossetti in "The Fleshly School of Poetry" (1871), Robert Buchanan insisted that such a realistic presentation of marital intercourse was profoundly indecent: "It is neither poetic, nor manly, nor even human, to obtrude such things as the themes of whole poems. It is simply nasty."[29] The sonnet was cancelled in 1872 and was not restored until William Michael Rossetti's edition of his brother's works in 1904.

Another male writer whose depiction of marriage was unconventional was George Meredith, whose *Modern Love* (1862) represents a much more subtle, more realistic, indeed more "modern" conception of the marriage relationship than does *The Angel in the House*. Meredith's narrator assigns responsibility for the failure of the marriage to husband and wife equally:

>   I see no sin:
> The wrong is mixed. In tragic life, God wot,
> No villain need be! Passions spin the plot:
> We are betrayed by what is false within.[30]

He also wishes that his wife had brought to their relationship "more brain" (Sonnet 48), not more devotion, nor more submission, nor yet more moral fiber. The view of marriage thus implied in *Modern Love*—that "marriage is false and dangerous if it sets out like a ship gliding over the depths of passion and guided by heavenly lights"[31]—was strangely out of step with the prevailing point of view; Meredith's poem was not generally well received.

At any rate, not until the 1860s it seems, when *Modern Love* and Robert Browning's *The Ring and the Book* (1868-1869) appeared, did respected male literary figures start openly questioning the state of the husband-wife relationship as it had been defined by society throughout the century.[32] Such a tradition did exist in the writings of women, but the Victorian public did not seem particularly attentive to its implications. As a possible explanation, John Reed has suggested that while "throughout the century women were seeking to establish a new image of themselves, . . . men in their literature and art were attempting to fix them in suitable types."[33]

In the best that women poets produced on the theme of marriage are numerous small pieces which, taken all together, provide a complex and multi-faceted perspective on women and marriage in the nineteenth century. Among the most important questions which these poems illuminate are: Why should one marry? What does it mean to "marry well"? Does a husband own his wife? Who is the ideal wife? the happy wife? What makes a satisfying home? What is the nature of female sexuality? of conjugal love? How does it feel when a virtually indissoluble marriage goes bad? What can a woman do about it? What is it like to be a widow or a divorcée? As a group, nineteenth-century women poets addressed themselves to all these social (yet personal) topics, and to many more besides.

A conflict between romantic and commercial motives for marriage occurs frequently in women's poems. Ordinarily, a girl does not question whether she should marry; it is understood that she will if she can. Her problem is to make the best match possible: preferably one which promises both genuine affection and financial security. When it is possible to find both, but not in one and the same man, the girl and her parents have to decide which is more important—love or money. According to Lawrence Stone, in *The Family, Sex and Marriage in England 1500-1800*, a preference for affectional marriage, which had been steadily growing for more than a hundred years, suffered a setback in the wake of revolutionary radicalism and had to be won all over again in the nineteenth century.[34] Women poets were part of that struggle; they were unanimous in recommending not the pragmatic but the sentimental choice: marrying for love.

In the poems which the melancholy Letitia Landon scattered throughout the popular annuals in the twenties and thirties are numerous representations of a woman's happiness destroyed by a fatally wrong marriage. Sometimes, as in "The Choice," the girl herself has allowed the lure of riches to betray the promise of love.

Now take thy choice, thou maiden fair,
  Of the gifts thy lovers bring;
The one has brought thee jewels rare,
  The other flowers of spring.

The maiden watched the rubies glow,
  And wreathed them in her hair;
But heavy they prest upon her brow,
  Like the weight of secret care.

. . . .

And ever an inward pulse would stir,
  When she saw a spring flower wave;
But never again did they bloom for her,
  Till they bloomed upon her grave!

She was borne to her grave with purple pall,
  And scutcheon, and waving plume;
One followed—the saddest one of all—
  And threw flowers over her tomb.[35]

The woman's very self is identified with the life, beauty, and springtime promise of the flowers. The jewels, though beautiful and bright, possess a sinister power which drains her vitality and sends her to an early grave. In other words, true love invigorates and loveless wealth enervates the spirit. The woman's reunion with the flowers after her death seems merely ironic, rather than a presage of life or love to come. At the funeral, the "saddest one of all" is the rejected lover, whose flowers of love provide a last pathetic contrast with the expensive trappings of the husband's cold regard. When a woman marries for money instead of love, Landon tells us, it is the death of her best self.

Another article of belief inherited from the eighteenth century held that although nothing justified a girl in marrying without her parents' consent, at the same time "a parent ought not to force a child into a marriage repugnant to her, and . . . a child is justified in passively resisting such tyranny."[36] Sometimes, then, the girl's parents are to blame when a marriage goes wrong. Perhaps the bride has been pledged against her will to a man wealthier than the one she loves; or she may be too young to be in love at all and they marry her to a man she will never be able to care for, as in "Marriage and Love" by Caroline Norton:

The mother hoped and prayed—her prayer was granted,
A lordling came—the very thing she wanted—
"Oh! what a match, my dear!"—and Laura sighed

> And hung her head, and timidly replied,
> "She did not love,"—"What put it in your head
> That it was needful?—you are asked to *wed*—
> Romantic love is all a childish folly,
> So marry, dear! and don't look melancholy;
> Besides, you cannot always live at home—
> Another year your sister's turn will come—
> And you will be *so* rich!"

Laura marries the lord, falls in love with her husband's brother, elopes with him, and ends up seduced and abandoned. Her lover marries another woman. "But hapless Laura, where is *she* the while? / The light gay form is mouldering in the grave."[37] The moral is clear: where love and marriage do not coexist, misery results.

Lest we be too harsh on the mother whose protective interference in match-making frustrates the hopes and desires of her daughter, Augusta Webster gives us a somewhat similar situation from the mother's point of view in "A Mother's Cry" from *A Woman Sold, and Other Poems* (1867). In this poem, the mother believes that her daughter's choice is a bad one, that the man she loves is a libertine and a phony. Because her true love has been forbidden, the daughter begins the customary pining away toward death. In anguish, her despairing mother pleads for the understanding, forgiveness, love, and trust of her estranged daughter. Most of all, she begs her not to die. Yet she still believes that "the lonely cold home beneath the sod / Than his had been better for you." By way of justifying her decision, the mother offers a rationale which will be familiar to any woman whose youthful misplaced enthusiasm was ever pitted against her mother's more mature judgment.

> Ah! surely if you had learned
> By bitter taste the ill that I dread
> You would think, "Did my mother sleep,
> Or did her love, that she yielded her child
> To one whom it was but a curse to wed?
> Yes, she has held my happiness cheap,
> For *I* by my young heart's love was beguiled,
> But *she* must surely have discerned."[38]

Of course, the dispute here is over morals, not money. Even so, to depict the exercise of parental veto at all sympathetically is highly unusual in women's poetry, where romantic love is generally presented as adequate justification for marrying.

The idea (or hope) that love for her husband would develop during the course of a woman's marriage is often stated in poetry by parental figures eager to see their daughters marry well and is shown to be false about as often as it is shown to be true. In Jean Ingelow's "Laurance" (1867), the husband's considerate nature and genuine love for his bride successfully woo her from thoughts of a false former lover. In *Denzil Place* by "Violet Fane" (1875), however, the young heroine's marriage to a kindly, considerate man much older than herself is turned to chaos when the woman falls in love not with her husband, but with their handsome young neighbor.[39] In both cases, the risk of unhappiness with such a match is recognized by the author, if not by the characters in her story, from the very beginning. Again, when a woman marries where she does not truly love, she is only inviting unhappiness.

Occasionally, a heroine's love is not returned—her beloved may even have married someone else—yet for social and economic reasons, the heroine still must marry. This melancholy circumstance gives women poets an opportunity to exploit the pseudo-Gothic theme of the reluctant bride.

> Yet she, too, at the altar gave up her wan cold hand,
> That shudder'd as they circled it with an unwelcome band;
> Ah! crime and misery both. . . .

This passage is from "Remembrance" by Letitia Landon, who concludes the poem with the assertion that "Such is a common history, in this our social state, / Where destiny and nature contend in woman's fate."[40] The premise that marriage was woman's only appropriate goal (and one which she should attain as quickly and as profitably as possible) led women poets to explore the unhappy possibilities of marriage for the wrong reasons.

Women poets did not always approach this latter topic with sentimentality; sometimes they treated it with sarcasm or cynicism. In "Cupid's Arrow" by Eliza Cook, Vulcan restores Cupid's latterly ineffectual weapon to its former potency—by weighting it with gold. "The urchin shot out, and rare havoc he made; / The wounded and dead were untold: / But no wonder the rogue had such slaughtering trade, / For the arrow was laden with *gold*."[41] "The Heiress's Wooer," from Webster's *A Woman Sold*, is an eligible young heiress's caustic rejection of the suit of a false lover who pursues her only for her money:

> Love! What is love to beings like to thee?
> An idol, glaring blank through jewelled eyes,
>   Its soulless framework garnished round with gold;
> A stair to mount thee to a high degree;
>   A tinsel gewgaw fashioned to be sold,
> Whose little value must be glozed with lies.

This man has abandoned the poorer woman who truly loved him. Like hapless Laura, she "plains it now among the mouldering dead." The heiress, who knows the whole sordid story, dismisses the suitor: "I buy no lover, I. Waste no more care. / I pray thee seek thyself some fitter prey."[42] This poem appeared somewhat later than most of the others we have noticed. Perhaps the anger and contempt it expresses about the economic aspect of marriage represent the reverse side of the sorrow and morbidity which pervaded women's more sentimental treatments of that same theme. Yet in either type of treatment, the poet's attitude is clearly critical.

Once a marriage occurred—for whatever the reason—the newly created wife became, as we have seen, the sole responsibility, the virtual property (body and spirit) of her husband. This bald fact of ownership could be poetically dressed up, as it was in Frances Havergal's "Only for One" (1869); but even so, the sentiment expressed seems excessively exclusionary today.

> I have a love for all who care
> Aught of its warmth to claim or share,
>   Free as the sun;
> But I have a love which I do not hint,
> Gold that is stamped with my soul's imprint,
> A wealth of love, both mine and mint,
>   Only for one![43]

The speaker is, of course, a wife. Each of the two images—the sun and the gold coin—is meant to represent a valuable kind of love. The former is warm, open, accessible; the latter is hidden, exclusive, rare. Yet the image of gold cannot escape the additional connotations of greed, miserliness, and commerce.

Another poet whose works are often ambiguous is Dinah Craik. In her poem "Plighted" (1859) on the same subject as "Only for One," it is the husband who speaks:

> Mine to the core of the heart, my beauty!
> Mine, all mine, and for love, not duty. . . .
> Give to a few friends hand or smile,
> Like a generous lady, now and awhile, . . .
> But thy heart of hearts, pure, faithful, and true,
>   Must be mine, mine wholly, and only mine.
>
> Mine!—God, I thank thee that Thou hast given
> Something all mine on this side of heaven. . . .

The words "my" and "mine" appear nineteen times in this thirty-two-line poem, as the husband smugly compares himself with the master of the goodliest chambers or the high priest of the holiest sanctuary. In the final apostrophe to God, he concludes sanctimoniously, "Two to the world for the world's work's sake— / But each unto each, as in Thy sight, one,"[44] invoking God's blessing on the mutuality of the marital commitment. Yet in light of the speaker's revealed egotism and possessiveness, if he and his wife are one, clearly that one is *he*.

It is difficult to know whether Dinah Craik intended her readers to infer criticism of this husband. A very conservative poet, Craik generally portrayed women in the most traditional ways. Yet she also wrote passionately in favor of female friendship and supported single women's right to self-dependence and "something to do."[45] Her occasionally startling use of tropes may have been accidental or unconscious; or it may have been the most conscious and purposeful artistry. In Craik's fiction, Elaine Showalter believes, she "excelled at the peculiar combination of didacticism and subversive feminism, which at much more developed levels of intellect, characterized the novels of Charlotte Brontë and George Eliot."[46]

Consider the sexual implications of the male speaker's diction in "To a Beautiful Woman" (1859).

> I marvel, who will crown you wife, you grand
> And goodly creature! Who will mount supreme
> The empty chariot of your maiden heart,
> Curb the strong will that leaps and foams and chafes
> Still masterless, and guide you safely home
> Unto the golden gate, where quiet sits
> Grave matronhood, with gracious, loving eyes.[47]

The bride is at once a queen and a spirited animal to be broken like a horse. The husband will achieve this mastery by "mounting" the "maiden chariot" and subduing the "leaping, foaming, chafing" body of the animal that draws it. The point of the encounter, frankly stated, is to "curb the strong will" of the woman and to transform her into an ideal English wife and mother—grave and submissive. Craik's attitude remains difficult to locate. Today, one hundred years later, we must perhaps evaluate her male speakers' reveries for what they reveal to us and leave the question of the author's intention alone. But one thing is certain: when Dinah Craik wrote this poem, a woman's conjugal duty to her husband was expressly spelled out by the law; she had no right to refuse him.

Nowhere in women's poetry can we find a poem to match Dante Gabriel Rossetti's "Nuptial Sleep" for frankness or sensuality. Possibly the closest is a difficult and allusive classical poem by "Michael Field" (Katherine Harris Bradley and her niece Edith Emma Cooper) on the subject of "Tiresias" (the

Greek prophet who lived seven years of his life as a woman). In the moment of his transformation, Tiresias discovers a finer sensitivity to life than he had had as a man.

> When womanhood was round him thrown:
> He trembled at the quickening change,
> He trembled at his vision's range,
> His finer sense for bliss and dole,
> His receptivity of soul.

So far this is clearly in line with conventional thought about the innate differences between men's and women's sensibilities.

> But when love came, and, loving back,
> He learnt the pleasure men must lack,
> It seemed that he had broken free
> Almost from his immortality.

This, on the other hand, is surprising. Tiresias steadfastly maintains that the pleasure which women receive from sexual love exceeds that which men receive. In an age when medical doctors were debating whether women received any sexual pleasure at all, here is a striking affirmation of female sexuality. Bradley and Cooper go on to extol "the mystic rapture of the bride."

> When man's strong nature draweth nigh
> 'T is as the lightning to the sky,
> The blast to the idle sail, the thrill
> Of springtide when the saplings fill.
> Though fragrant breath the sun receives,
> From the young rose's softening leaves,
> Her plaited petals once undone
> The rose herself receives the sun.[48]

Like "Nuptial Sleep," "Tiresias" is an extraordinary poem. *Works and Days,* the journal which "Michael" and "Field," as they styled themselves, maintained jointly for more than ten years, shows that these two women had a very different apprehension of sexuality from the average Victorian woman as she is usually represented. Their entries reveal a sensual appreciation and a sexual understanding of one another and of other women which may be attributable to the unusual physical closeness of their own relationship.[49] Jeanette Foster has concluded that Bradley and Cooper were a lesbian couple.[50] Whatever the reason, their poetry is neither typically Victorian nor conventionally feminine. Indeed, women's poetry which offered any description at all of female sexuality was unusual in the nineteenth century.

Women poets much more frequently addressed the theme of feminine submission and masculine dominance, either obliquely, as Dinah Craik did in the 1850s, or more openly, as the century wore on. The sixties was the decade of Mill's *The Subjection of Women* and Robert Browning's *The Ring and the Book*, both stressing the potential for tyranny and oppression within marriage. The terminology of master and slave to characterize the marriage relationship became more common in women's poetry around this time also. This is not to say that all such poems were bluntly critical of marriage. For instance in Jean Ingelow's "A Morn of May," the topic is treated quite playfully.

> Quoth the Sergeant, "Work is work, but any ye might make me
> If I worked for you, dear lass, I'd count my holiday.
> I'm your slave for good and all, an' if ye will but take me,
> So sweetly as ye carol upon this morn of May."
>
> "Medals count for worth," quoth she, "and scars are worn for honour,
> But a slave an' if ye be, kind wooer, go your way. . . ."
>
> "Beauty, when I said a slave, I think I meant a master;
> So sweetly as ye carol all on this morn of May."
> Shy, she sought the wooer's face, and deemed the wooing mended;
> Proper man he was, good sooth, and one would have his way:
> So the lass was made a wife, and so the song was ended.
> O! sweetly did she carol all on the morn of May.[51]

We are supposed to be amused by the girl's sense of the rightness of things, and we do not fear that her gentle Sergeant will abuse her. Nevertheless, the burden of the poem is that women prefer to be men's slaves.

Twenty years or so later, "The Slave Turned Tyrant" by "Violet Fane" is not lighthearted in the slightest. The poem openly deplores the contemptuous attitude toward women and marriage which turns an adoring suitor into a tyrannizing husband.

THE SLAVE TURNED TYRANT

> Should you despise her for that,—born to sway
>   She serves instead;—at your beloved feet
>   Meek and obedient, that she takes her seat,
> And,—as you frown or smile,—is grave or gay;—
> A word,—a look,—can darken all her day
>   Or make night glorious,—but, as thus you mete,

> Conscious of might,—alternate bitter and sweet,
> Careless of what you do, or what you say,—
> Think, Master mine! not thus, in by-gone days
>   Dared your hand smite her, or your accents check
>   The love you craved for! . . . Hers has been the fault
>   Who raised her slave to sit above the salt,
>   And so, she may not chide, but only prays
>   For mercy,—with your heel upon her neck.[52]

According to "Violet Fane," woman herself is partly to blame for her own condition of oppression. By her slavish attitude of worship, she has invited it and must suffer the consequences. However, it is the male reader who is addressed and who ought to be shamefaced for taking advantage of his wife's devotion.

The male speaker in Ingelow's "Wedlock" (1867) realizes the sacrifice of liberty which his recent bride has made in order to marry him; he even generates a few tears about it before reflecting that all is just as (society says) it should be:

>   "O love!
> A little while thou hast withdrawn thyself,
> At unaware to think thy thoughts alone:
> How sweet, and yet pathetic to my heart
> The reason. Ah! thou art no more thine own.
> Mine, mine, O love! Tears gather 'neath my lids,—
> Sorrowful tears for thy lost liberty,
> That yet, O love, thou wouldst not have again.
> No; all is right. But who can give, or bless,
> Or take a blessing, but there comes withal
> Some pain?"[53]

It is clear from the rest of the poem that this newlywed husband thoroughly loves his wife. Perhaps Ingelow felt that a man who could thus empathize with his wife's painful renunciation of freedom for his sake was no oppressor at heart. (Perhaps, too, he anticipates regretfully his own diminished freedom as a married man.) When a husband truly loves his wife, such poems imply, his love goes a long way toward compensating her for the sacrifices and trials of marriage and motherhood.

Somewhat wistfully, Caroline Norton, whose marriage was stormy almost from beginning to end, rhapsodized about the "True Love" of a husband for his wife. Yet she could not resist a turn of the screw in the poem's last line.

TRUE LOVE

To look upon the fairy one, who stands
Before you, with her young hair's shining bands,
And rosy lips half parted;—and to muse,
Not on the features which you now peruse,—
Not on the blushing bride,—but look beyond
Unto the aged wife, nor feel less fond:
To feel, that while thy arm can strike them dead,
No breathing soul shall harm that gentle head:
To *know*, that none with fierce and sudden strife
Shall tear thee from her, save with loss of life:
To keep thee but to one, and let that one
Be to thy home, what warmth is to the sun;
To gaze and find no change, when time hath made
Youth's dazzling beauty darken into shade,
But fondly—firmly—cling to her, nor fear
The fading touch of life's declining year;—
This is true love, when it hath found a rest
In the deep home of manhood's faithless breast.[54]

Norton's poetry characteristically reflected her disillusionment with society's promises of financial and emotional security in marriage. Her own husband's greed, malice, and physical abuse nearly ruined her, both socially and financially.[55] Norton often used her verses, many of which appeared in popular magazines and annuals, as propaganda for her cause.[56]

I have quoted rather extensively from these poems about marriage in order to represent the true flavor of women's poetry on the subject. For the most part, it is not nearly so saccharine as we might have anticipated. In a few poems there is genuine passion, anger, or even sexuality. The poetry of "home," however, seldom contradicts the Ruskinian notion of the home as sanctuary, especially for the world-weary husband and father. The wife and mother's own exhausting day of household labor goes unmentioned. Instead, women's poetry sentimentally represents the home as the world's one secure refuge, the abode of stability, tranquility, and love. Dora Greenwell's popular little poem "Home" captures the contemporary ideal which was cherished by all.

HOME

Two birds within one nest;
Two hearts within one breast;
Two spirits in one fair

Firm league of love and prayer,
Together bound for aye, together blest.

An ear that waits to catch
A hand upon the latch;
A step that hastens its sweet rest to win;
   A world of care without,
   A world of strife shut out,
A world of love shut in.[57]

In fact, the serenity and stability of English domestic life were a matter of some national pride. Felicia Hemans' poetry in particular was acclaimed for its patriotic and sentimental treatment of home in such poems as "The Graves of a Household," "The Spells of Home," "The Homes of England," "The Voice of Home to the Prodigal," and "The Forsaken Hearth." As one admiring critic wrote, "Her household gods go with her wherever she goes. . . . The element of her poetry was the warm air of the fireside. The faith, the trust, the fear, the love, even the anguish, of a woman's heart sustained her. . . . It is the poetry of the household, the poetry of the heart."[58] In the opinion of Cora Kaplan, "For all her faults, Mrs. Hemans ought to be read at length before trying any of the great woman poets of the nineteenth century."[59] Certainly Felicia Hemans' idealized treatment of home and hearth enjoyed great popularity because it precisely answered the expectations of the poetry-reading public.

When, in 1836, Caroline Norton wished to plead for humane treatment of England's poor, she used the pride and sentimentality attached to the English idea of home in order to touch the public conscience.[60] In *A Voice from the Factories*, she contrasted the genteel homes of the middle class with the hardship and squalor of the lives of the impoverished lower classes.

"The happy homes of England!"—they have been
A source of triumph, and a theme for song;
And surely if there be a hope serene
And beautiful, which may to Earth belong,
'Tis when (shut out the world's associate throng,
And closed the busy day's fatiguing hum),
Still waited for with expectation strong,
Welcomed with joy, and overjoyed to come,
The good man goes to seek the twilight rest of home.[61]

Among the poor, however, it is not only the father who must toil all day, but the children who must go to the factory or the mill and come home so tired they have hardly enough strength to eat. The hovel to which they return is a travesty of the beloved English "home." Women in the homes of the poor are household angels no longer, but only drudges and breeders of misery.

In addition, the lower-class wife, it was sometimes admitted, was subject to physical abuse from her husband. Jean Ingelow's "Brothers, and a Sermon" (1863)[62] contains a direct reference to wife beating, as does Louisa Bevington's "Bees in Clover" (1882).[63] Women poets did not treat the darkest side of married and home life among the middle and upper classes with quite so much frankness as in their occasional representations of the lower classes. But the delicate balance of male/female relations within marriage, where the husband legally held all the power, did educe some poems about marital discord—even including wife abuse, separation, and divorce.

Louisa Bevington's puzzling sonnet "One More Bruised Heart" (1882) certainly seems to commiserate with an abused woman, perhaps a youthful bride who, like Pompilia in *The Ring and the Book*, has suffered at the hands of a tyrannizing husband.

ONE MORE BRUISED HEART

One more bruised heart laid bare! one victim more!
    One more wail heard! Oh, is there never end
    Of all these passionate agonies, that rend
Young hopes to tatters through enslavements sore?
So long, pale child, your patient spirit bore
    Its wrong in secret, ere you sought a friend!
    And yet, what love of mine can ever mend
Again for you the veil your tyrant tore?

Oh, there are woes too bitter to be shown!
    Oh, there are tears too burning to be seen!
    Yet purest sympathy, select and clean,
May feel the agony its very own.
Sweet slave-child, whom your voiceless griefs oppress,
I cannot cure; I may in part express.[64]

The speaker, apparently the poet herself, is impotent to rectify the wrongs. She can only express them to the public, in the form of this poem. The secrecy in which the child's griefs must be endured seems to imply a sexual dimension to the abuse, as does the last line of the octave. Perhaps it is a poem about the sexual abuse of a child, rather than a wife. At any rate, it evidently refers to domestic misery of some kind, because it is the child's heart, not just her body, which is bruised, and the speaker, though sympathetic, is helpless to intervene. The language of "tyrant" and "slave" and the reference to a veil irrevocably torn support the conclusion that the context of the suffering in this poem is indeed marriage. Bevington's recognition that it is her function as a poet to express her fellow woman's grievances explains the way she places the child victim's pathetic dilemma within the context of the many, many others like her who, helpless and ashamed, hide their mistreatment from the largely unsympathetic society in which they exist.

This anguished portrayal of domestic unhappiness was not the norm; sometimes women poets even made sport of marital squabbles. Yet in disparaging humor, there is almost always a grain of truth. Two poems, one from the husband's point of view and one from the wife's, will illustrate the lighthearted treatment of the subject. Helen Selina Sheridan, Lady Dufferin, the older sister of Caroline Norton, wrote poetry mainly to amuse her friends and family and to entertain in polite society. "The Charming Woman" (1835) was set to music and circulated around English drawing rooms, where it was enthusiastically sung after dinner for years. In the poem, prospective husbands are warned against marrying a charming woman, lest she prove immodest, flirtatious, strong-willed, politically inclined, imprudent with money, or even a bit "Blue." A couple of sample stanzas will convey the tone of this poem: ridicule.

> Yes, indeed, she's a charming woman,
>   And she reads both Latin and Greek,—
> And I'm told that she solved a problem
>   In Euclid before she could speak!
>
> And her shoulders are rather too bare,
>   And her gown's nearly up to her knees,
> But I'm told that these charming women
>   May dress themselves just as they please!
>
> She can chatter of Poor-Laws and Tithes,
>   And the value of labour and land,—
> 'Tis pity when charming women
>   Talk of things which they don't understand!
>
> O young men, if you'd take my advice,
>   You would find it an excellent plan,—
> Don't marry a charming woman,
>   If you are a sensible man.[65]

The opposite of the Victorian ideal wife, the much maligned "charming woman" might be said to represent a link between the eighteenth-century Bluestocking and the nineteenth-century New Woman.

Caroline Southey's poem "The Hedgehog," published with "The Birthday" in 1836, outlines ways of coping with a grumpy and loquacious husband. The best strategy from the wife's point of view is emphatically *not* to argue too well, for she might win the debate and make him grumpier than ever. Nor should she simply "suffer like a martyr / In silent sweetness," because her husband will keep on picking a fight until he has the chance to argue his point. Like a prickly hedgehog, a husband cannot be successfully forced or entreated into a good humor. Mrs. Southey's tongue-in-cheek recommendation for pacifying an angry husband is still a familiar bit of advice today:

> And to effect such change benign
>   In *human Hedgehog*—saint or sinner—
> To smooth his bristles—soothe his rage—
> There's not an argument so sage,
> Or so prevailing, I'll engage,
>   As a good dinner.[66]

But while this prescription for domestic peace might cure a marital problem that was essentially superficial, it would scarcely work if the problem was conceived to inhere in the structure of marriage itself.

Women poets later in the century were more likely than Lady Dufferin or Mrs. Southey to perceive the potential not for comedy but for tragedy in Victorian marriage mores. "Xantippe" (1884) by Amy Levy portrayed the frustration and despair of the neglected wife of Socrates, in order to dramatize the devastation of female intellect and the sacrifice of female self-respect which the institution of marriage had implied ever since ancient Greece. On her death bed, Xantippe recalls her life with the great philosopher, who went to his own noble death some years before. In her youth, Xantippe scorned "the merry mockeries" of "maiden labour" and yearned for knowledge and enlightenment.

> Then followed days of sadness, as I grew
> To learn my woman-mind had gone astray,
> And I was sinning in those very thoughts—
> For maidens, mark, such are not woman's thoughts—
> (And yet, 'tis strange, the gods who fashion us
> Have given us such promptings). . . .

Because she can achieve her desire for education only through a man, Xantippe agrees to marry Socrates; she even learns to love him, though he is old and wrinkled and she is young and lovely. She prays that he will guide her, with wisdom and love, toward intellectual fulfillment. Sadly, Socrates cannot seem to see her as she truly is, but only as he believes all women to be—frail, unintelligent, and incapable of coping with the strain of applied study or the intoxication of sudden knowledge.

One afternoon, as Socrates is instructing Plato, Xantippe, who is bringing the men some wine, overhears an arrogant remark about feminine ignorance. Overcome with rage, she speaks out eloquently in behalf of her sex, but her indignation is received with mockery and cold contempt. In a fury, she flings the wine skin onto the marble floor and runs from the room. This incident is the turning point in Xantippe's career; it is the true sentence of her death, for it vanquishes all her best hopes and dreams forever. The red wine which gushes from the broken wine skin symbolizes the violence of the assault on her spirit. Immediately afterward, she tells us, she went through the various stages of reaction to death: grief, curses, anger, hopelessness, despair, and finally acceptance. For her own cup of hemlock, she quenched her previous thirst for knowledge by sinking her spirit in the womanly chore of the loom, savagely reducing herself to the level she once had scorned: "I spun until, methinks, I spun away / The soul from out my body, the high thoughts / From out my spirit." Her bodily death, occurring so many years after her spiritual suicide, is almost anti-climactic. Suddenly the dying woman's sight begins to fail. Xantippe's last words symbolize the tragedy of her life: she begs, "give me light!"[67]

"Xantippe," which appeared in the *University Magazine* and in a collection of verse published at Cambridge, was much more ambitious in scope and tragic in import than most women's poetry in the nineteenth century. Oscar Wilde dubbed Amy Levy "a girl of genius." In 1889, at the age of twenty-eight, she committed suicide, apparently in despair over family bereavements and encroaching deafness. She had never married.[68] Amy Levy's tragic vision of womanhood was different from the rueful acceptance of "woman's lot" or, alternatively, the passive decline into death which characterized so much of women's poetry earlier in the century. In Levy's poems, women engage in an active, even heroic, struggle with their destiny.

There is another poem, by E. Nesbit, which, by its title at least, represents the tragic effect of masculine notions about womanhood upon the happiness of married life. "A Tragedy" is a double soliloquy dramatizing the failure of communication between husband and wife which has forever blighted their lives. The wife believes that her husband, buried in his books, does not love "his silly stupid wife," who, unbeknownst to him, is deathly ill. After her death, he reveals that all his labors were for her sake and that he loved her very much. But the patronizing attitude which prevented him from expressing his love arose from his mistaken, conventional belief in her essential childishness, her sexual blankness, and her passive contentment with her life.

Thank God, your child-heart knew not how to miss
    The passionate kiss,
Which I dared never give, lest love should rise
    Mighty, unwise,
And bind me, with my life-work incomplete,
    Beside your feet.
You never knew, you lived and were content.

For her part, the wife made no attempt to tell him how she really felt. Now, of course, it is too late.

    My one chance went;
You died, my little one, and are at rest—
    And I, unblest,
Look at these broken fragments of my life,
    My child, my wife.[69]

The real tragedy here (or perhaps the pathos) is the unnecessary sacrifice of marital joy caused by mistaken ideas of wifely propriety and masculine superiority.

    The misery of married lovers who have been parted by distance, death, or—worst of all—discord was a popular subject with women poets in the nineteenth century—especially with those who had endured that kind of misery themselves. Caroline Norton published numerous poems about abused wives and aggrieved husbands, of which "The Two Pictures" (1834) is a clear though uninspired example.[70] Fanny Kemble's "Paolo and Francesca," on the other hand, rises far above the level of "The Two Pictures" in rendering the grief of separated lovers.

There be, who wandering in this world, with heart
Riveted to some other heart for ever,
Past power of all eternity to sever,
The current of this life still drives apart,
Who, with stained eyes, and outstretched arms, and cry
Of bitterest longing, come each other nigh,
To look, to love, and to be swept asunder,
The breathless greeting of their agony
Lost in the pitiless world-storm's ceaseless thunder.[71]

Fanny Kemble was divorced five years after the poem's publication.
    In "Divided," "Violet Fane" depicted the gulf of uncontrollable circum-

stances and disparate aims which could open between even the most devoted of husbands and wives. He is a statesman, she a poet. Each encourages the other toward success, but the pursuit of fame urges them into separate paths. They never quarrel; they only drift apart, until "it came to pass, / These two, that once were one, are two again, / And she is lone in spirit." The poem refrains from judgment; yet it seems clear that had the wife abandoned her own work in order to further her husband's (as Sarah Stickney Ellis would have recommended), the two might have remained close. The effect of their division upon the wife's poetry is especially significant in light of the general tenor of poetry by women as we have observed it to be:

> Thus all her songs are sad—of withered leaves,
> And blighted hopes, and echoes of the past,
> And early death. . . . [72]

Evidently the professional pursuit of poetry did not well accord with married life in the nineteenth century. In its general atmosphere of gloom, women's poetry may sometimes have been responding to the marital unhappiness which women poets' unlady-like ambition could generate.

Jean Ingelow, too, wrote a poem titled "Divided." First published in 1863, it was one of her best loved pieces. The image is of a couple walking on opposite sides of a streamlet which becomes ever wider and faster, until it divides them forever. The natural descriptions in this poem are among her loveliest, and the emotional quality of the gradual separation has great authenticity. "Divided" is one of the poems that led her biographer, Maureen Peters, to conclude that in her youth Ingelow must have suffered the loss of a sweetheart at sea.

Be that as it may, Ingelow wrote numerous poems on the theme of separation. One of her most interesting and unusual treatments is "Katherine of Aragon to Henry VIII" (1850), in which she confronts the subject of divorce. Addressing the Prince, on learning of his intention to divorce her, Katherine retains her dignity and her pride. Yet she pledges continuing devotion to her husband: like a ring of Saturn, her love will encircle him wherever he may wander. Having delivered herself of this speech, she collapses with grief: "Look back no more, since all is lost— / Forget—forget, my soul!"[73] The nineteenth-century divorcée—a very rare individual—might certainly have felt the same way, for of course divorce was a social and economic catastrophe.

Widowhood could also be disastrous, and it was a far more frequent event than divorce. Women were dependent upon their husbands for so much—financial security, social status, love and affection—that the death of one's husband was a bitter loss indeed. The poetry of widowhood characteristically expresses the devastation of the widow, who may be represented as a recent bride, or the mother of a family, or a sick, elderly woman. Unless she is left independent economically, her loss is irremediable. In this case, if no one comes to her aid—a parent, a former suitor, a clergyman, or perhaps a grown son or daughter—she will probably follow her husband to the grave. Felicia Hemans' "Madeline" traces the decline of a recent bride widowed on her honeymoon voyage of emigration to America.

>   —Oh! but ill,
> When with rich hopes o'erfraught, the young high heart
> Bears its first blow!—it knows not yet the part
> Which life will teach—to suffer and be still,
> And with submissive love to count the flowers
> Which yet are spared, and through the future hours
> To send no busy dream.[74]

The young widow lapses into illness and is revived only when, from over the ocean, her beloved mother arrives to raise her head and reclaim her life.

When a widow bears her loss with courage, faith, and fortitude, she is cited as a woman of extraordinary strength. Unlike the corresponding figure in fiction, the widow in women's poetry is virtually never represented as the butt of jokes or the object of various new suitors' attentions. Rather, she dedicates her remaining years—be they five or fifty—to the service of others and the memory of her departed husband.

> She brings the books they chose together
> And reads the verse he liked the most;
> And here, as softly as a ghost,
>   Comes gliding through the winter gloom
>   To say her prayers beside the tomb
> Of him she loves and never lost.[75]

This stanza, from "The Widow" by Agnes Mary Frances Robinson, captures the sentimental ideal of love that transcends even death. Mary Robinson (Mrs. James Darmesteter) was herself widowed in 1894 after six years of marriage; by 1901 she had remarried. Thus, as we have seen, women's poems sometimes expressed their own innermost emotions and sometimes only rehearsed the expected sentiments. It is difficult to evaluate the authenticity of poems where the two overlapped. Furthermore, originality of thought neither guaranteed nor precluded beauty and originality of expression.

What does seem certain is that women poets in the nineteenth century recognized a discrepancy between the social and poetic ideal of marriage and the reality. In the narrative poetry, there are far fewer model wives and far more delinquent ones than we might have expected. The number of representations of ideal marriage is balanced by references to marital strife, alienation, abuse, and even divorce. While women poets were perhaps cautious in revealing attitudes and depicting situations which criticized marriage, the home, and female innocence, the overall impression one receives from reading this poetry is surprisingly unsettling. As an institution, marriage is presented as overly commercial, with little accommodation for feminine self-determination. Sexuality is too embarrassing to discuss, and the marital relationship in itself implies the opportunity for tyranny, estrangement, frustration, or despair. Yet marriage is also the only alternative which offers a woman the chance of financial security, sexual fulfillment, and respectability. Thus, women writing poetry were able to detect and describe many of the problems with their current system; but for most of the century their imaginations were not engaged in offering visions of a better future.

4

Mothers

Motherhood in the nineteenth century was extremely serious, often a life-and-death matter. Accordingly, in the poetry written on the subject by women, motherhood was generally treated with great solemnity, intensity, and respect. One's own mother was represented as an ideal being to be emulated and adored. Furthermore, most young women could look forward to assuming the role of mother themselves, with all its attendant duties, trials, and obligations, almost immediately after they were married. For while the newly married woman was still struggling to achieve the wifely ideal, on the one hand, and to cope with the revelations of sexuality, on the other, she frequently found herself pregnant.

Although birth control information was available in the nineteenth century, it was not widely circulated in England until the 1880s.[1] Not only was contraceptive advice, even from doctors, often incorrect or even unhealthful,[2] but the whole subject was regarded with horror by most respectable women. "Birth control was condemned as immoral, disgusting, unnatural, injurious to the health, and damaging to the family and therefore to society as well."[3] Consequently, as Dr. R. T. Trall wrote in 1866, "the health of a majority of women in civilized society is seriously impaired and their lives greatly abbreviated by too frequent pregnancies."[4] The average number of children per couple was, in the 1860s, between five and six,[5] and frequently a woman suffered numerous miscarriages and much discomfort between successful pregnancies.

With just a few exceptions, women poets did not address the issue of family size, which became controversial only late in the century. However, in one of the songs from her prose fantasy *Phantasmion* (1837), Sara Coleridge expressed the popular view that a mother's love was infinite, so that each of her many successive children could expect an undiminished share of attention and affection:

Deem not that our eldest heir
Wins too much of love and care;
What a parent's heart can spare,
   Who can measure truly?
Early crops were never found
To exhaust that fertile ground,
Still with riches 'twill abound,
   Ever springing newly.[6]

To express parental resources in terms of productive, fertile ground was certainly an appropriate comparison at a time when most parents were quite prolific indeed. On the other hand, Sara Coleridge's own family was relatively small. The only daughter of Samuel Taylor Coleridge, she had two brothers who survived infancy. During her marriage (to a cousin, Henry Coleridge), Sara gave birth to four children, only two of whom survived.

In the 1890s, by which time some respectable women had begun consciously limiting the size of their families,[7] a few poems appeared which refused to glorify the joys of bearing and rearing a large brood of children. *Mother and Daughter,* a sonnet sequence which Augusta Webster left unfinished at her death in 1894, reflects this relatively new point of view. Sonnet 25 is an exact repudiation of the sentiments expressed in Sara Coleridge's poem.

You think that you love each as much as one,
   Mothers with many nestlings 'neath your wings.
   Nay, but you know not. Love's most priceless things
Have unity that cannot be undone.
You give the rays, I the englobed full sun;
   I give the river, you the separate springs:
   My motherhood's all my child's with all it brings—
None takes the strong entireness from her: none.[8]

The idea of infinitude and inexhaustibility expressed in the earlier poem has here been replaced by the idea of unity and exclusivity. The mother of many is depicted as a sort of brood hen. Her maternal love is no longer represented as capable of increasing with each new child who demands his or her share. Rather, the love available to each child must grow less and less with every new arrival, as the finite amount of the mother's time, attention, and emotional capacity is divided again and again. The mother of only one, however, loves with a complete and entire devotion that may be more fully satisfying.

In the preceding Sonnet 24, Webster acknowledges the advantages to a mother of a larger family: more love and attention to receive while the children are young, less devastating grief to suffer should a death occur, more companionship to anticipate when she grows old. Yet this sonnet also concludes with an expression of contentment in being the mother of only one child.[9] Of course, extreme parental devotion to an only child was not new to poetry, fiction, or real life. But it was somewhat unusual to imply that a small family might be a matter of individual right and preference, rather than a manifestation of God's will. In both of these paired sonnets, the hint of contempt for the blithe and selfish mother of many contrasts sharply with the sentimental idealization of that figure in poems like Sara Coleridge's.

In a similarly unsentimental vein, Alice Meynell's "Parentage" (1896) went so far as to question the social rationale for motherhood. The legend of the poem reads, "When Augustus Caesar legislated against the unmarried citizens of Rome, he declared them to be, in some sort, slayers of the people." Meynell responds, "Ah no! not these! / These, who were childless, are not they who gave / So many dead unto the journeying wave." Rather, it is fathers and mothers who, in the very act of giving life, condemn also to inevitable death the progeny they engender: "And she who slays is she who bears, who bears." The poem identifies war and death with patriarchy ("But those who slay / Are fathers. Theirs are armies. Death is theirs—").[10] Yet we must resist the temptation to make of the poem a feminist protest against the breeding of cannon fodder. After all, Alice Meynell herself gave birth to eight children. "Parentage" is probably better understood as a philosophical reflection upon the futility of human existence rather than as an anti-motherhood poem.

Unlike many women in the nineteenth century, for whom the careers of wife and mother were virtually simultaneous, Alice Meynell survived the rigors of her numerous pregnancies and lived to be seventy-five years old. Complications of childbirth claimed many women's lives, especially during the epidemic of "puerperal fever," which reached its worst proportions between 1860 and 1885.[11] Even Sarah Stickney Ellis, who stressed resignation and patient suffering, warned that childbirth represented "the possibility of near and awful death, . . . an event which in many cases has proved but a short passage to the grave."[12]

Contemporary literature tended to reflect this growing awareness of the hazards of parturition. In her study of childbirth in the English novel, Madeline Riley found that it was treated with less cheerfulness and greater reserve in the nineteenth century than in the eighteenth. Nineteenth-century novels "have the most unhappy, bleak confinements: deaths abound and are less casually treated than formerly. The impression is that childbirth is a difficult, secret, exclusively feminine affair. Anxieties have increased—fear of death, money worries; the health itself of the women before and after childbirth is more delicate and precarious."[13] Because of the conventions of plot, fictional representations of childbirth could hardly be avoided. Novelists had to deal with it somehow, and they generally tended to get as much dramatic impact from it as possible.

In poetry, however—especially nonnarrative poetry—it was certainly possible and probably seemed desirable to ignore or gloss over those aspects of pregnancy and childbirth which Queen Victoria referred to as "so very animal."[14] This is precisely what most contemporary poets—including women poets—chose to do. The sonnet "Motherhood" by Mathilde Blind is thus extraordinary for its straightforward rendition of the pangs of childbirth:

> From out the font of being, undefiled,
>   A life hath been upheaved with struggle and pain;
>   Safe in her arms a mother holds again
> That dearest miracle—a new-born child.
> To moans of anguish terrible and wild—
>   As shrieks the night-wind through an ill-shut pane—
>   Pure heaven succeeds; and after fiery strain
> Victorious woman smiles serenely mild.

However, this description is balanced by a mystical identification of the new mother with Mary, the mother of Christ:

> Yea, shall she not rejoice, shall not her frame
>   Thrill with a mystic rapture! At this birth,
> The soul now kindled by her vital flame
>   May it not prove a gift of priceless worth?
> Some saviour of his kind whose starry fame
>   Shall bring a brightness to the darkened earth.[15]

The diction and rhythm of the octave create a triple series of contrasts between the harsh and difficult process of labor and the relief and calm after delivery, so that the sound and sense of the poem correspond. For example, the third such contrast is between "after fiery strain" and "smiles serenely mild." The referent of both is, of course, "Victorious woman." In the sestet, the tone established through biblical diction, inverted word order, and parallel structure prepares the reader for the revelation of the last two lines.

The "font of being" is clearly the mother's womb. But whether it is the womb or the new life which is "undefiled" is ambiguous. If the former, then this mother is the Virgin Mary herself; if the latter, then the poem stands in defiance of the doctrine of original sin. "Motherhood" appears in *The Ascent of Man* (1889), Mathilde Blind's ambitious attempt to reconcile the theory of evolution with the mythology of religion, to integrate Genesis and geology.[16]

Consequently, the sonnet may be read as an attempt to translate the myth of the Madonna into the experience of the ordinary woman. Following this interpretation, we can see that every mother's womb is "undefiled," the sacred locus of new life; and every new life is likewise "undefiled," innocent at birth. Each newborn child is cause for rejoicing—a potentially perfect, a humanly divine individual.

A second theme of the poem is human perfectibility through evolution. The woman is Mother Earth herself, who, with upheaval and struggle and pain, may at last give birth to perfected humanity, with the capacity to "bring a brightness to the darkened earth." At any rate, on the literal level the poem expresses the trauma and joy of childbirth and the new mother's eager hopes for her child; it is one of the very few nineteenth-century poems to do so.

Besides the prevailing reticence about female physical functions, the prolonged pain and the risk of death which often accompanied pregnancy probably explain why so few women (even mothers) wrote celebrations of the experience of childbirth. For the average Victorian woman, little time elapsed between marriage and the first pregnancy; in fact, many women died around the age of menopause or earlier. Dr. Trall lamented that thousands of women "are brought to their graves in five, ten, or fifteen years after marriage, and rendered miserable while they do live,"[17] as a result of constant pregnancy. But while neither the joys of a successful delivery nor the horrors of a fatal one found much direct representation in women's poetry, maternal death was an important theme during the entire course of the century. Most poems about the death of a mother, though sentimental in tone, convey a genuine emotion which does justice to the subject.

The mother who died giving birth was a sadly real figure in the nineteenth century. "The Dying Mother to Her Infant" (1830) by Caroline Bowles captures the pathos of such an untimely death.

> My baby! my poor little one! thou'st come a winter flower,—
> A pale and tender blossom, in a cold, unkindly hour;
> Thou comest with the snow-drop—and, like that pretty thing,
> The power that called my bud to life, will shield its blossoming.

The conventionality of the poem's opening—the floral image, the reliance on divine protection—gives way shortly to a more realistic representation of the speaker's thoughts. She is, after all, a woman on the verge of an unwelcome, even a frantic death. Little by little, as her wandering monologue unfolds, we discover the details of her life. She is barely nineteen years old and married only a year; this child is her first. The marriage has been thorny, and her husband unfaithful. She has, in fact, wished for death, but now she would live on if she could, for the sake of the child and of the maternal love just opening in her heart: "all the love—the mighty love for thee, / That crowded years into an hour of brief maternity." She envisions the child's future stepmother usurping her place in the household and in the child's heart. "And hast thou not one look for me? those little restless eyes / Are wandering, wandering everywhere the while thy mother dies."[18] The poem ends with a Wordsworthian sentiment that the newborn child may yet be in communion with the angels and may thus meet her mother's spirit as the one passes into life and the other into death.

Just as death in childbirth remained a terrible reality, poetry which dealt with that event remained current throughout the nineteenth century. In 1897, Mary Elizabeth Coleridge's short poem "Shadow" characterized a father's mixed feelings toward the child whose birth was the cause of his mother's death:

> Child of my love! though thou be bright as day,
>   Though all the sons of joy laugh and adore thee,
> Thou canst not throw thy shadow self away.
>   Where thou dost come, the earth is darker for thee.[19]

Evidently, the older children in the family ("the sons of joy") do not share their father's ambivalence. Often, as in this poem, the mother's death did not occur with her firstborn, at age nineteen or younger, but after a family was already formed. If she then died before the youngest had matured, she might leave quite a few children motherless. In "Crippled Jane" (1865) by Caroline Norton, a dying mother expresses particular anxiety about the fate of her third child, a lame girl with an ugly face and form and a difficult temperament. "God have mercy upon her! God be her guard and guide; / How will strangers bear with her, when, at times, even *I* felt tried?" In representing the mother as less than enchanted with one of her own children, "Crippled Jane" is somewhat unconventional. It might be laid alongside Wordsworth's "The Idiot Boy" for the contrasting attitudes of two mothers of imperfect children. Norton's poem ends with a note of pathos struck in a Wordsworthian manner: "I die—God have pity upon her!—how happy rich men must be!— / For they said she might have recovered—if we sent her down to the sea."[20]

A seven-stanza poem from Sara Coleridge's *Phantasmion* expresses a child's grief for her dead mother in conventional imagery of nesting birds, sheltered flowers, and beaming sunlight. In the penultimate stanza, the bereft child rejects the varied experiences of life, yearning instead for the comfort of the womb, or perhaps for immersion in the eternality that the sea often represents for nineteenth-century poets.

O, what to me are landscapes green,
With groves and vineyards sprinkled o'er,
And gardens where gay plants are seen
To form a daily changing floor?
I dream of waters and of waves,
The tide which thy sea-dwelling laves.[21]

This poem typifies women's poetry on the theme of maternal death in the way it breaks through its conventional imagery and sentimental tone to express authentic, individual grief.

Many of the children brought into the world with so much risk and pain did not survive to adulthood. Between 1850 and 1880, the child mortality rate in the middle classes ran at about 25 percent, and the middle-class mother was herself considered largely responsible.[22] In the midst of her distress over the death of her child, she might turn to the pages of, say, the *British Mother's Journal* and read that her mismanagement of the child's diet and health care were probably to blame. (Yet mothers were given very little accurate information or professional guidance about how to correct these errors.) She might also find in the pages of the same or some other women's magazine a poem written in response to the bitter loss of a child. "The infant deathbed scene so popular with the religious writers, the grief of a bereaved mother at the loss of her child, which was a regular feature in many of the women's magazines, reflected grim reality."[23]

The poetry which depicted the death of a child and the grief of its mother was probably written and published in order to comfort bereaved parents and to purge their grief. Often the deathbed is described in detail and the pathos of the situation is stressed, provoking the reader to tears. Then the poem offers religious consolation, to the parents and to the empathizing reader. Many of these poems were written, of course, to commemorate actual children's deaths, and their quality varies greatly. Mary Ann Browne's "The Departed," written on the death of a seven-year-old child, is very trite: "A faded flower, a bud of beauty blasted; / A broken lute, a precious diamond shattered . . . / To which shall we compare thee, gentle child?"[24] Fanny Kemble's " 'Tis an Old Tale and Often Told" is better, emphasizing not the child but the young mother devastated by repeated losses:

—perishing by her side
The children of her bosom drooped and died;
The bitter life they drew from her cold breast
Flickered and failed;—she laid them down to rest,
Two pale young blossoms in their early sleep;

And weeping, said, "They have not lived to weep."
And weeps she yet? no, to her weary eyes,
The bliss of tears her frozen heart denies;
Complaint, or sigh, breathes not upon her lips,
Her life is one dark, fatal, deep eclipse.

Paradoxically, the mother, in her deep depression, is more death-like than the dead children. They are drooping, sleeping flowers. She is cold and still, without tears and almost without breath. Furthermore, we learn that she is homesick and that her husband's love has apparently failed. In her misery, she almost prays for death. Extreme though this tale of woe may appear, it is, Kemble assures us, "The hourly story of our every day, / Which when men hear they sigh and turn away. . . . "[25]

A set of three poems by Jean Ingelow dramatizes the effect of such multiple losses, even on parents who are more mature, who are devoted to one another, and who have other children. The poems are "Henry, Aged Seven Years," "Samuel, Aged Nine Years," and "Katie, Aged Five Years," dated October 15, October 29, and November 3, 1849, and commemorating the deaths of three children in the family of Jean Ingelow's friend, the Reverend Edward Harston.[26] The Harstons were stunned by the three rapid losses. In "Katie," Ingelow predicts that the bereaved mother will mourn her lost children for the rest of her life.

Only daughter—Ah! how fondly Thought around that lost
    name lingers,
Oft when lone your mother sitteth, she shall weep and
    droop her head,
She shall mourn her baby-sempstress, with those imitative
    fingers,
        Drawing out her aimless thread.
. . . .
Be Thou near, when they shall nightly, by the bed of
    infant brothers,
Hear their soft and gentle breathing, and shall bless
    them on their knees;
And shall think how coldly falleth the white moonlight
    on the others,
        In their bed beneath the trees.[27]

Ingelow's trilogy is sad but philosophical in tone, offering Christian consolation, while at the same time recognizing that the parents' loss is essentially inconsolable. "Katie" concludes with a vision of blessed reunion when the far-off Day of Judgment shall come. Maureen Peters, who believes the poem is too morbid and sentimental for modern tastes, pronounces it "a perfect example of the emotional values of the age."[28]

Despite intermittent periods of anxiety, mourning, and depression when one of her children died, the average middle-class mother in the nineteenth century led a busy, active life. Though of course she had at least one servant to help her, she had her hands full with her household to run and her many surviving children to rear. Furthermore, servants or no, there were numerous responsibilities which, as a good and conscientious mother, she was expected personally to fulfill. From the 1790s and even earlier, courtesy books, religious addresses, and handbooks offered both inspirational and practical advice, stressing the mother's duty to instruct her children in religion and morality as well as to provide them with useful knowledge and skills. As a genre, the mother's guide began with a reminder to mothers of the importance, even the sanctity, of their calling, then proceeded to give practical advice on how to instill the children with piety and virtue, educate them effectively, and best attend to their physical, as well as moral and intellectual, well-being. In the flurry of directives for mothers coming down to them from various authorities—religious, medical, and professional—women's own perceptions and personal experiences of motherhood tended to be de-emphasized or overlooked. Thus, despite the Victorian reader's apparent appetite for domestic poetry and fiction, the everyday duties and emotions of mothers were seldom the focus of women's poems.

Of course, there were exceptions. In 1865, for instance, Caroline Norton edited an illustrated table book of domestic verse called *Home Thoughts and Home Scenes* with poetry by herself, Jean Ingelow, Dora Greenwell, Dinah Craik, and others.[29] "Affection," a poem of Caroline Norton's published in *Friendship's Offering* for 1833, expresses a mother's anxieties about what may befall her children.[30] To the 1834 volume of this same annual, Norton contributed "To My Child," an effusion of mother-love and partiality:

> Art thou not beautiful?—I hear thy voice—
> Its musical shouts of childhood's sudden mirth—
> And echo back thy laughter, as thy feet
> Come gladly bounding o'er the damp spring earth.
> Yet no glaze follows thee but mine. I fear
> Love hath bewitched mine eyes—my only dear.[31]

The following year, Caroline Norton's husband deprived her of her children, as by law he had a right to do. Her long and bitter struggle to regain her children resulted in the 1839 amendment of English child custody laws. However, her youngest son died before he and his mother could be reunited.[32] Literarily, Norton's domestic poems were often prosaic, but the sentiments and fears she expressed in them were genuine enough.

The impulse to express maternal feelings was often fulfilled by the composition of verses for children, an area which lies outside the realm of our attention here. E. Nesbit, however, published a number of "baby poems" which, according to popular opinion, were "very sweet."[33] These were poems addressed to, but not exactly written for, infants. They included lullabies, assurances of maternal love, and, most interesting, short passages about mother and child interaction. Despite their cooing tone, these poems represent some of the day-to-day activity of mothering. The following excerpt is from a "Song" in "The Moat-House," published in Nesbit's *Lays and Legends* (1886).

> Oh, baby, baby, baby dear,
> We lie alone together here;
> The snowy gown and cap and sheet
> With lavender are fresh and sweet.
>
> . . . .
>
> We are so tired, we like to lie
> Just doing nothing, you and I,
> Within the darkened quiet room.
>
> . . . .
>
> Soft sleepy mouth so vaguely pressed
> Against your new-made mother's breast,
> Soft little hands in mine I fold,
> Soft little feet I kiss and hold,
> Round soft smooth head and tiny ear,
> All mine, my own, my baby dear![34]

In 1892, Alexander Japp correctly described E. Nesbit's poetry as "very apt at giving voice to many of the indefinite yearnings of womanhood towards higher ideals, a fuller development, a wider sphere."[35] But the baby poems she wrote expressed also the joy which could be found in motherhood, restricted though it might be.

Augusta Webster's *Mother and Daughter* sonnets, too, were expressions of the varied moods and experiences of motherhood. When they appeared in 1895, William Michael Rossetti felt compelled in his introduction to defend the validity of the theme. "Nothing certainly could be more genuine than these Sonnets. A Mother is expressing her love for a Daughter—her reminiscences, anxieties, and hopeful anticipations. The theme is as beautiful and natural a one as any poetess could select." Even so, Rossetti wondered why

Mrs. Webster had not, like so many other women poets, been "forestalled in such a treatment. But," he concluded, "some of the poetesses have not been mothers."[36]

More often, women's poetry about mothers and mothering responded not to everyday experiences, but to the high ideals promulgated by the various authorities in the popular press. Moral instruction, by precept and example, was held to be an especially significant component of the ideal mother-daughter relationship. Obsessive concern with the religious aspect of education, typified by the formation of Maternal Societies "to unite godly and praying mothers" and "to awaken the careless to a sense of their duties and position as mothers of immortal souls,"[37] began around mid-century to shade into a more general concern for national character building and practical education.[38] Mothers were encouraged "to generate beings who, as women, may tread the footsteps of their mothers, or, as men, may excel in the higher virtues" which the mother herself, on account of her sex, could never attain.[39] Mrs. Ellis, believing that, "In order to raise the character of a people, it is necessary that mothers should form a high estimate of the importance of their own efforts," pointed out that mothers have the training of boys, as well as girls, in their care, a fact which, she thought, "might sometimes startle them into a consciousness of the vast amount of responsibility resting upon them," for all the men of the next generation "will have received, as regards intellectual and moral character, their first bias, and often their strongest and their last, from the training and influence of a mother."[40] Here is the familiar idea of woman's limitless influence over the men to whom she is related. Even after her sons have left her care and tuition, their conduct reflects on her.

By 1851, as women's complaints about their situation in England began to be heard, the acerbic *North British Review* rested the case for male inculpability (and therefore inability to remedy discomfort) upon this phenomenon of female influence:

> If . . . women are sufferers from the caprice and tyranny of men, it must be remembered that they themselves have taught and trained the tyrants. Their very sufferings are their own work; for by exerting their full influence as mothers in a right direction, they might have trained a race of men with truer feelings, and a keener apprehension of justice.[41]

Thus if English women as a class were ill treated by their society, they had only their own ineptitude to blame; as mothers, they had obviously failed to cultivate the appropriate moral sensibility in their sons.

Inculcation of morality, if most important, was just one of the middle-class mother's many responsibilities. Additionally, she was expected to supervise the activities of the nursery, to tutor the children, to provide for their physical and material needs, to discipline them when necessary, to love them at all times, and to ensure their general happiness and well-being. And, of course, *only* the mother could (or should) perform certain duties. "The mother is the natural protectress of the children when they are young and need her guidance—she is naturally fitter to guide and cherish them than the father."[42] She ought to breast-feed them if she could, turning them over to wetnurses[43] or "bringing them up by hand" (artificial feeding) only if she found she was "not endued with the powers of constitution requisite" for performing this "first of the parental duties which nature points out to the mother." Mothers who chose "spontaneously to transfer to a stranger" this important office were admonished as being selfish and "unnatural."[44] The charge of "unnatural motherhood" was most often leveled against women who, like Becky Sharp in *Vanity Fair*, failed to demonstrate an appropriately self-sacrificing love and concern for their children. Amelia Sedley Osborne, with her single-minded devotion to young Georgy, represented the high point of Victorian motherhood; Becky Sharp represented the nadir. Obviously, the actual behavior of ordinary middle-class mothers fell somewhere in between.

Aristocratic mothers had more freedom, of course, because they had more assistance in the form of governesses and servants. Impoverished women, on the other hand, had fewer and less-appealing alternatives—including sending their children out to notoriously dangerous "baby farms." Some resorted to abortion or even infanticide (as did seduced and abandoned women in the "respectable" ranks of society),[45] but these various contradictions to the prevailing ideology, though known, were seldom explored within the thematic reference of motherhood (though they were addressed in other contexts, as we shall see).

Certainly, women poets did not give the subject of unnatural mothers anything like the effort and attention they expended on delinquent wives. Really, only Felicia Hemans gave this aspect of motherhood much notice at all; and her several poems dealing with such subjects as child neglect, infanticide, and maternal suicide-murder generally illustrate the (Romantic) excess of some noble emotion and take place in an exotic foreign clime or in ancient or medieval legend.[46] For example, in "The Parting Song," based upon a legend of medieval Greece, an unnatural, unloving mother lives to regret her neglectful treatment of her youngest son, whose farewell song gives her a "late repentant pang." Hemans makes no attempt to justify maternal neglect. Instead, she stresses that the mother *should* have loved her son: it was his "birthright."[47] As a rule, women poets simply did not question the middle-class ideal of motherhood in the same way that they had examined and judged the institution of marriage. The "natural" duty of primary devotion to one's child was seldom rejected.

Adherence to the sentimental ideal of mother-love appears even in the ideology of prominent feminists of the day. For example, in her lecture series on *The Duties of Women* (1881), Frances Power Cobbe urged mothers to provide for their children a love so pure and thoroughgoing that it becomes the paradigm of divine love, assuring the child from the start that "there is such a thing as perfect love in the universe."[48] In this she echoes Mrs. Ellis, for whom the mother must be a guardian spirit, an angelic being whose "instinct of maternal love," like the miracle of divine love, "is of that kind which cannot fail."[49]

Jean Ingelow made this similarity between divine and maternal love expressly clear in "To Katie, Asleep in the Daytime" (1847). In a direct biblical allusion, Katie's mother's love for her daughter is described as "love that passeth knowledge."[50] The self-sacrificing (Christ-like) nature of that love is often represented in women's poetry. Letitia Landon's "The Sailor," for example, portrays a widowed mother who continues to endure only for God and for her sailor son. When the son is wounded in battle and brought home to die, she spends all her savings to nurse him. The day after his funeral, she is found dead with the tear-stained family Bible in her lap.[51] Mothers like this, who live only for their children's welfare and ascend to Heaven when their earthly task of guardianship and intercession is ended, are frequent figures in nineteenth-century poems.

Mother-love itself is represented as an overwhelming force, possibly the strongest type of human love that exists. A mother who denies that love or who thinks to forgo it for some greater happiness (for herself or for the child) conventionally finds the anguish she suffers as a consequence to be intolerable. In Adelaide Procter's "The Sailor Boy," for example, a widowed peasant woman has renounced her son in order to marry a wealthy earl. Yet she visits the boy from time to time, unable to admit she is his mother, but equally unable to give him up entirely. She is in constant distress, describing herself as "a poor woman mad and wild, / Who coined the life-blood of her child, / And, tempted by a fiend, had sold / The heart out of her breast for gold."[52] All the earl's love and all his money cannot compensate her for the renunciation of her son, nor can the heir she bears the earl replace her first-born child in her affections. After about five years of torment, she is dead.

This kind of unquenchable love was represented as the maternal norm, and only a very few voices of objection were raised. Augusta Webster's was one such voice. *Mother and Daughter* is itself mainly an expression of maternal love, but it also contains several sonnets which contradict the notion of woman's love as unfailing.

'Tis men who say that through all hurt and pain
   The woman's love, wife's, mother's, still will hold
   And breathes the sweeter and will more unfold
For winds that tear it and the sorrowful rain.
So in a thousand voices has the strain
   Of this dear patient madness been retold,
   That men call woman's love.[53]

Of course, as we have seen, it was women as well as men—at least in poetry—who glorified the constancy of woman's love. In Webster's opinion, maternal love, though it might never die of natural causes, could certainly be killed by excess of sorrow and pain:

   . . . methinks, sad mothers who for years,
Watching the child pass forth that was their boast,
Have counted all the footsteps by new fears
Till even lost fears seem hopes whereof they're reft
And of all mother's good love sole is left—
   Is their Love, Love, or some remembered ghost?[54]

A love that persevered unchanged through long years of assault or neglect—as woman's love reputedly did—might be called "mad," or ghostly, or even divine, but it could not be considered a normal, humanly attainable state of emotion. Like any healthy love, mother-love must be returned in order to stay strong. But Augusta Webster's sensible point of view, articulated during the last five years of the century, was a departure from the prevailing nineteenth-century opinion of mothers and mother-love as near divine.

   Thus, the ideal of motherhood throughout the century was an extremely elevated one. Mrs. Ellis felt compelled to distinguish between woman as mere wife, who should place herself in a secondary position, and woman as mother, in which role, she explained, "I do not see how it is possible for her to be too dignified, or to be treated with too much respect."[55] For Tennyson, the mother outshone the angels in the scale of being:

No angel, but a dearer being all dipt
In Angel instincts, breathing Paradise,
Interpreter between the Gods and men,
Who look'd all native to her place, and yet
On tiptoe seem'd to touch upon a sphere
Too gross to tread, and all male minds perforce
Sway'd to her from their orbits as they moved,

And girdled her with music. Happy he
With such a mother!

(*The Princess*, VII. 301-309)

This transfiguration of woman was doubtless effected partly by the juxtaposition early in the century of motherhood with religion and the theory of feminine influence.

In any event, the sanctification of the mother occurs in poem after poem, by women as well as men, in the nineteenth century. Sometimes, as in "Encouragement" by Emily Brontë, it is the mother's death which transforms her into a supernatural being. Like so many dead mothers, this one becomes a guardian angel. One orphaned sister tells the other:

Remember still, she is not dead;
  She sees us, sister, now;
Laid, where her angel spirit fled,
  'Mid heath and frozen snow.

And from that world of heavenly light
  Will she not always bend,
To guide us in our lifetime's night,
  And guard us to the end?[56]

Felicia Hemans' "The Image in Lava" commemorates the discovery at Herculaneum of an image of Madonna and Child—that is, of a woman clasping a baby to her bosom—preserved in molten lava in the moment of catastrophe. In a poem filled with religious allusion, Hemans celebrates the image as an emblem of the sanctity and immortality of mother-love.

Immortal, oh! immortal
  Thou art, whose earthly glow
Hath given these ashes holiness—
  It must, it *must* be so![57]

Concerning the Madonna image, Eric Trudgill has suggested in his figure study *Madonnas and Magdalens*, "For the Victorian idealist frightened by sex, devoted to motherhood, and troubled by religious doubts the Virgin Mother, as a feminine archetype, combined immaculate sexual purity, perfect motherly love and a vehicle for pent-up religious emotions."[58] But it is interesting to speculate for a moment on a different possible explanation of mother-deification in women's poetry: the nature of the child-mother relationship in the nineteenth century. To her child—especially to a daughter—the nineteenth-century mother was the almost exclusive source of nourishment, comfort, discipline, and security. In this role, she must have appeared truly godlike to the unsophisticated understanding of a child.

Emily Pfeiffer's "The Lost Eden" (1881) relates the loss of innocence which accompanies a child's first recognition of her mother's mortality. Wistfully looking back, the adult narrator of the poem recalls her childhood faith in the power of her mother:

> For me there can be never found again
> A fortress so impregnable to pain,
>   So sovereign a seat,
>   So sweet, and soft, and balmy a retreat
>   Against all harms,
>   All influence malign and vague alarms,
> Mother, as that which, when a child I knew,
> Rapt, shielded from the alien world by you.

The "sovereign," protective mother has become a virtual deity to the child:

> For me you were immortal in those days,
> Too high for question, and too good for praise;
> I think, indeed, a being uncreate,
> Beyond the touch of time or reach of fate.[59]

All too soon the child in this poem discovers that even her mother must die one day. Her childhood security is shattered, but her adoration of her mother lives on. In just this way, a child's belief in her mother's omnipotence might be destroyed but the impulse to worship could persist in the form of an extreme idealization of motherhood itself. At any rate, women poets in general tended to reinforce the conventional image of motherhood or else not to depict mothers at all.

In thus endorsing the sanctity and significance of motherhood, women poets were in step with their times, for as we have seen, even outspoken feminists concurred. Allegations in the 1860s that emancipated women would neglect their husbands and children[60] were met with assurance to the contrary. For example, Emily Davies, "one of the most redoubtable of the pioneers of sex equality, admitted [in 1866] 'that home duties fall to the lot of almost every woman, and nothing which tends to incapacitate for the performance of them ought to be encouraged.' "[61] Even into the nineties, feminists continued to assert, as Mary Wollstonecraft had done a hundred years earlier, that emancipation would make women better, not worse, mothers.

Indeed, one woman who published much affecting poetry idealizing motherhood was the feminist Eliza Cook. The best known of her many poems about her own beloved mother's death was the most sentimental and least worthwhile: "The Old Arm-Chair" (1836), which in 1930 made its way in excerpt into *The Stuffed Owl: An Anthology of Bad Verse*.[62] But her other verses on this theme are "Lines Written at Midnight, in the Anticipation of a Dreaded Bereavement," "The Mourners," "The Star of My Home," and "I Miss Thee, My Mother," each of which can still touch a receptive reader's heart.[63] While these poems may be conventional enough in imagery and tone, when read as a group they resonate with genuine emotional force. A sample stanza, from "The Star of My Home," will serve to illustrate the point.

> I remember the days when the tear filled my eye,
>   And the heaving sob often disturbed my young breast;
> But the hand of that loved one the lashes would dry,
>   And her soothing voice lull my chafed bosom to rest.
> The sharpest of pain and the saddest of woes,
>   The darkest, the deepest of shadows might come;
> Yet each wound had its balm, while my soul could repose
>   On the heart of a Mother, the Star of my Home.[64]

Eliza Cook was essentially a journalist, not a poet. The quality of her verse is almost uniformly poor. But in writing about her mother's death, she both rose above her usual poetic standard and expressed a species of grief and respect that many of her readers could and did share.

Thus, the belief in the extreme importance of mothers to society and the consequent faith in an ideal of motherhood scarcely diminished during the course of the nineteenth century. Only the nature of the maternal function and the lineaments of the maternal ideal changed somewhat in the popular consciousness. The mother's religious significance decreased as her practical duties increased in importance. While the ideal qualities of devotion, diligence, patience, fairness, and personal circumspection remained more or less constant, piety gradually gave way to practical efficiency, mildness to the exercise of (benevolent) authority, and humility to self-cultivation, both moral and intellectual. With very few exceptions, women's poetry failed to register even this amount of change. Ignoring the more secular emphasis of the new ideal, women poets continued to deify motherhood, to recommend self-sacrifice, and to accept the seemingly inevitable tragedies of maternal and infant death with patient sorrow and religious resignation.

5
The Fallen Woman

The middle-class woman who was *not* related to a man (often through no fault of her own), either as a chaste, obedient daughter or as a virtuous wife and mother, risked finding herself still essentially "relative" to men, but in an uglier way, and with an inescapable and disastrous loss of respect and class standing. For the converse of the ideal wife and mother was, during much of the nineteenth century, the "fallen woman," who aroused both fear and pity in middle-class women and who endured overt censure and covert exploitation by upper- and middle-class men. She exemplified the woman who had failed in her vocation to guide men and to uplift society. Even worse, she had violated the rigid social code of female sexual conduct, thereby endangering not only national morality, but also male property and paternity rights. Any woman who thus jeopardized male prerogatives consequently forfeited the right to male protection, which was, as we have seen, necessary to her well-being, sometimes even to her very survival.

Therefore, as convention would have it, the fallen woman was inevitably discovered and turned penniless from her father's or her husband's door. A forlorn and persistent figure, this "ruined" woman haunted the pages of nineteenth-century social essays, newspaper reports, novels, stories, moral tales, and poems. In some ways, she became for Victorian literature what the Wandering Jew had been for Romantic: a recurring symbol of human frailty, guilt, and inability to atone. For it was understood—among the middle classes, at least—that society did not forgive, forget, and reclaim its fallen women. Before turning to literary analysis, it will be helpful to review contemporary ideas about seduction, adultery, and prostitution and to recognize the atmosphere of controversy in which varying beliefs were professed.

The double standard of sexual ethics, reinforced by English laws and customs surrounding marriage, divorce, wife beating, women's property rights, and prostitution, and fostered by the belief in women's lack of sexual desires, was chiefly responsible for society's staunch intolerance. Until about 1850, "courtesy books and similar literature . . . [took] the double standard more or less for granted as a convention of society, telling wives to bear their husbands' immorality with patience and even cheerfulness."[1] But through the forces of Evangelical Christianity and middle-class respectability, the double standard began thereafter to draw more and more criticism, concurrent with a growing sense of alarm about the apparently undeniable national escalation of prostitution. Moral leaders like Josephine Butler urged a new sexual restraint among husbands, while at the same time fighting against the institutionalization of prostitution. The emphasis on female chastity, however, showed little sign of lessening among the middle classes before the turn of the century.[2]

Although the fallen, or unchaste, woman was not necessarily identical with the prostitute, she was believed to have taken the fatal first step toward a life of total degradation. In his influential sociological treatise on prostitution in England (*Prostitution*, 1857, 1870), William Acton worried that "By unchastity a woman becomes liable to lose character, position, and the means of a living; and when these are lost is too often reduced to prostitution for support."[3] In other words, by over-zealous condemnation, Victorian society was fostering the very crime it supposedly sought to eradicate. What have we done for the women and children who might have been our own? asked Elizabeth Chapman in her essay "The New Godiva."

> We have taught them that a first downward step is irretrievable, and stamps upon them a brand which nothing can efface. . . . We have herded them together in one outcast class. . . . We have hardened them, often in periods incredibly short, unsexed them, made of them drunkards, blasphemers, tempters, fiends in human form.[4]

In a sixty-page discussion of prostitution in the *Westminster Review* for July 1850, W. R. Greg pointed out that if the standard applied to women were applied also to men, that is, "if young men, who commit one act of unchastity, were compelled to feel that all their prospects in life were in consequence blighted forever, and that their position was lost, hopelessly and irrecoverably—society would be infested with, and almost made up of, desperadoes."[5] By making desperadoes of fallen women, the double standard operated to encourage prostitution perhaps nearly as much as to prevent it.

Adding to the problem was the role of prostitution in sustaining the ideal of chaste womanhood, a connection which did not go unrecognized at the time. W.E.H. Lecky described this paradox quite vividly in 1869:

> . . . there has arisen in society a figure which is certainly the most
> mournful, and in some respects the most awful, upon which the eye
> of the moralist can dwell. . . . Herself the supreme type of vice, she is
> ultimately the most efficient guardian of virtue. But for her, the
> unchallenged purity of countless happy homes would be polluted, and
> not a few who, in the pride of their untempted chastity, think of her
> with an indignant shudder, would have known the agony of remorse
> and of despair.[6]

This exploitative situation evoked impassioned protest from Josephine Butler
and her followers, who sought to rescue and rehabilitate fallen women. Butler
led the successful campaign to repeal the notorious Contagious Diseases Acts
of 1864, 1866, and 1869, which had officially sanctioned prostitution, more
or less, by requiring health inspections of suspected prostitutes and enforced
detention and treatment of those determined as diseased.[7] She objected that
"Even if we could admit . . . that a man could at the same time practise
debauchery and cherish an honourable love, even then we would refuse to acquiesce in the sacrifice of one of the lowest of these women, who . . . we hold
to be our sisters; even then we would turn away in disgust from the thought
of a family life whose purity is preserved at the price of her degradation."[8] Actually, all of these totally pessimistic depictions of the fate of the fallen woman
represented only one side of the case, as we shall shortly see.

Nevertheless, it was apparent to everyone that the incidence of women
turning to "vice" was rapidly increasing. For obvious reasons, no reliable estimate of the number of women engaged in prostitution in nineteenth-century
England has been achieved, despite numerous attempts. The problem of prostitution was, of course, inherited from previous centuries. In 1797 Dr. Col-
quhoun placed the number of prostitutes in London alone at fifty thousand.[9]
The following year, Mary Wollstonecraft remarked upon "the shameless
behavior of the prostitutes, who infest the streets of this metropolis, raising
alternate emotions of pity and disgust."[10] Henry T. Kitchener, in 1812,
decried "the enticements of common prostitutes, and the great increase in
their numbers. There is not a city or large town in the kingdom that does not
abound in them. . . ."[11] By 1839, the estimate had reached eighty thousand
in some reports.[12] By mid-century, prostitution was acknowledged as a major
national problem.

Numerous studies attempted to come to grips with the causes and conditions of prostitution in England so as to devise appropriate remedies.[13] During
the eighteenth century, many women with cottage-industry jobs lost them to
industrialization and could not compensate for their lost income from the
financial resources of husbands or fathers. In 1799 Mary Ann Radcliffe pre-

dicted that the consequence of men engrossing women's occupations would be widespread prostitution, and maintained that "the frailty of female virtue more frequently originates from embarrassed circumstances, than from a depravity of disposition."[14] In 1870 Acton suggested that prostitution followed the economic law of supply and demand. The late marriages imposed on middle-class men by considerations of money and status, coming into conflict with their natural sexual energies, created the demand for prostitutes. Female poverty and lack of alternatives created the supply. Acton also indicted seduction, successful not only through male exploitation of female innocence, as the stereotype went, but also through male financial temptation of female financial distress.[15]

Not surprisingly, in light of Victorian assumptions about sexuality, prostitution was rarely attributed to female sexual desire. Bracebridge Hemyng, who investigated prostitution for the fourth volume of Henry Mayhew's *London Labour and the London Poor* (1862), acknowledged its economic basis but also postulated certain personality factors as possible causes of the lax morality among "female operatives" (lower-class working women): "natural levity" and "love of dress and display, coupled with the desire for a *sweetheart*" (emphasis mine).[16] Thus, like most contemporary writers, these early sociologists virtually ignored female sexuality, imposing their own middle-class bias on the lives of working-class women.

On the other hand, virtually everyone who analyzed prostitution agreed that the overwhelming poverty of the lower, working classes, caused by low wages and unemployment, was the real key. Housing accommodations, both private and public, were so overcrowded that the poor of all ages and sexes generally slept together, a situation which promoted youthful sexual experience, incest, and rape and made the strict sexual morality of the middle classes appear farcical.[17] Furthermore, the hunger, drabness, and general deprivation of the lives of lower-class working women made their enlistment in the ranks of prostitution if not tolerable, at least comprehensible. In the workshops, factories, mills, and mines, men, women, and children slaved for twelve-hour days, side by side, often half naked. Perhaps scandalized by the indecency as much as affected by the piteousness of the lives of the working class, Victorian reformers addressed the condition-of-England question with great fervor.

Along with legislation to improve the housing, education, and working conditions of the poor, other remedies were also attempted. Acton proposed making men legally and financially responsible for *all* their children and supported assisting unwed mothers during pregnancy and lying-in.[18] Magdalen homes for rescuing prostitutes and reintegrating them into society (though not as marriageable women) sprang up all around England. By 1860 there were more than forty such refuges. The age of consent was raised from twelve to thirteen in 1875 and then to sixteen in 1885, partially in response to a sensational series of articles by W. T. Stead in the *Pall Mall Gazette* during July 1885. "The Maiden Tribute of Modern Babylon" was an exposé of white slavery and child prostitution.[19] Thus many different steps were taken during the century both to alleviate the misery and to suppress or control the practice of prostitution, as the public became more sensitive to the condition and more aware of the numbers of its "fallen women."

In the course of informing the English middle class, the reformers, sociologists, and writers (novelists and poets included) inevitably tended to exaggerate. It became the conventional wisdom that the path of the fallen woman led only downward—from seduction through ostracism, poverty, pregnancy, and prostitution to a miserable, untimely death. Now of course venereal disease was a real occupational hazard (no one had yet found a way to control the epidemic),[20] but the actual health and life expectancies of prostitutes may not have differed much from those of the rest of the female population. Asserted Acton, "we shall seldom find that the constitutional ravages often thought to be necessary consequences of prostitution exceed those attributable to the cares of a family and the heart-wearing struggles of virtuous labor." Additionally, he believed, "the great mass of prostitutes in this country are in course of time absorbed into the so-called respectable classes," frequently through marriage.[21]

Acton's different perspective was widely publicized, but not always credited. The missionary reformer William Logan, for instance, called Acton's theory of the transience of the prostitute "absurd" and insisted that once her career had begun, a prostitute's remaining life expectancy was reduced, on the average, to a mere six years.[22] Indeed, the controversy about the actual conditions of prostitutes in nineteenth-century England continues today and may never be resolved.[23] Because sociological methods were in an early stage of development during the critical period, statistics are unreliable and contemporary accounts are random and impressionistic. Furthermore, the biases and social goals of the investigators undoubtedly influenced their conclusions.

Likewise, public opinion was diverse, varying according to class, gender, political philosophy, and personal experience. Poetic and fictive treatments of the "ruined" or "fallen" woman helped both to establish and to repudiate the cautionary stereotype. In so doing, they ran a course parallel with increasing public awareness, concern, and responsiveness on the issue.[24]

A succinct and classic example of the initial stereotype in literature is John Clare's "A Maid's Tragedy." The fallen heroine has been turned out of her father's home during a bitter cold rainstorm. She makes her way to her lover's house, but he refuses to take her in. Their illegitimate child dies:[25] " 'Love's tender pledge within my arms / Is numbed and breathes no more.' " Still she pounds desperately on her false lover's door, until "Benumbed with cold, her heart did break; / She sat her down and died."[26] This poem was written during the first third of the century, at a time when most poets—men and women alike—were portraying the fallen woman strictly according to convention, if at all.

During the middle decades of the century, however, literature underwent a gradual shift in emphasis from depicting the fallen woman as miserable and irretrievably lost, which was calculated both to prevent other women from sinning and to create sympathy and forgiveness for those who sorely needed them, toward depicting the fallen woman as less inexorably doomed and degraded. Novelists and poets thus helped to secure for the fallen woman a greater degree of sympathy and toleration on the part of the general public.

Despite the limitations of the prevailing stereotype, female poets approached the subject of the fallen woman with greater frequency and more emotional commitment than male poets did, at least before about 1860. They delved more deeply into both the causes of a woman's lapse and the details and varieties of the suffering and punishment she might endure as a result.

On the issue of who was to blame, women poets did not generally seek to absolve the woman herself of the primary guilt, nor were they likely to arraign the marriage system *per se* as even a contributing cause. *Denzil Place*, by "Violet Fane," which blames the custom of premature, money-motivated, arranged marriages, is a notable exception; however, it did not appear until 1875. *Denzil Place* very nearly allows Constance, the adulterous wife, to marry her lover, Geoffrey, and live happily ever after; however, her death in childbirth prevents this. In the epilogue, the narrator specifically asks her readers to forgive Constance and assures us that the other characters in the story have already done so.[27] In refusing to condemn Constance for her adultery, "Violet Fane" was out of line with the general stance of nineteenth-century women poets. That her poem could have been well received shows how far public opinion had advanced by 1875.

On the other hand, most women's poetry throughout the century did assign at least partial blame either to the male seducer or to the destitute condition of the woman (or both). Yet even when they represented the male seducer as being equally culpable with the woman morally, women poets demonstrated the strength of the double standard by punishing the woman harshly and the man lightly or not at all. Caroline Norton's early poem "The Sorrows of Rosalie" (1829) is a good example.[28] The naive young Rosalie is seduced, impregnated, and abandoned by her lover, who repudiates her in order to marry a woman with money. When confronted with his sick and hungry child, the man simply turns away. In order to feed her child, Rosalie becomes first a beggar, then a thief. She is caught and thrown into prison, where the child dies of starvation. After her release, Rosalie makes her way to her father's home, from which she had eloped years before, only to find that the house has been sold and her father is dead. Poor, sorrowing Rosalie lingers beside the graves of her father and her child, awaiting her own death. In its horrific rendition of the dire consequences of seduction (for a woman, that is), this poem is relentless. Although we pity Rosalie and despise her seducer, it is *she* who suffers in this corrupt world, while *he* is rewarded.

In an odd little poem in *Phantasmion* (1837), Sara Coleridge represents a maiden attempting to defend herself against seduction. All the while that the prince (with "ardour" and "passionate prayers") tries to seduce Iarine, she resists, singing over and over again a few incantatory verses which her mother had taught her for just such an occasion:

> Newts and blindworms do no wrong,
> Spotted snakes from guilt are clear;
> Smiles and sighs, a dang'rous throng,
> Gentle spirit, these I fear;
> Guard me from those looks of light,
> Which only shine to blast the sight.

The grotesque and sometimes phallic imagery in this stanza (blindworms, spotted snakes) recurs in the poem's other two stanzas as well (serpents' tongues, beetles, spiders, etc.). Besides its appropriateness as a metaphor for sexual threat, this kind of imagery also conjures up a suggestion of witchcraft. Iarine is trying to protect herself by uttering a magic spell and invoking a guardian spirit (perhaps her mother's). She is also trying to block her own responsiveness, by banishing the prince from her awareness. For those who may wonder how it all turns out, here are the next two sentences from *Phantasmion:*

> As the prince drew nearer to the damsel, she pressed closer to the door, trembling all over, and singing more and more earnestly, and at last she knelt down, wrapping the silken garment round her head and face and her whole figure, till she was completely enveloped. Thus baffled and utterly disappointed, Phantasmion stood still. . . . [29]

As it happens, the prince's intentions are honorable, but Iarine doesn't know that yet.

Writing in the waning years of the Romantic tradition she inherited from her father, Sara Coleridge dealt with sexual passion rather more openly than would later be acceptable—especially for a woman—as Victorianism took firmer hold of England. Strangely enough, however, the inclusion of (more or less disguised) seduction scenes like this in literature considered suitable for children in the nineteenth century was not unusual. What else is the import of Mary Howitt's "The Spider and the Fly," for instance?

It comes as no surprise, of course, that women poets did not depict female passion more frankly, even in their representations of fallen women. Given the current ideology about respectable womanhood, they could not reasonably have been expected to do so. Nevertheless, they did occasionally reveal greater acknowledgment of female sexual motivation and give greater credence to passion as the cause of sin than male sociologists like Acton and Hemyng were willing to postulate. Partly, perhaps, because it wasn't possible to be very direct about it, women poets tended to accord the sexual aspect of seduction and prostitution only a cursory treatment and to concentrate instead on other motivations and on the ensuing distress.

When a woman was tempted to illicit sexual relations not only by love or passion, but also by poverty and destitution, resistance became doubly difficult. Numerous women's poems all throughout the nineteenth century depict women whose prostitution was virtually forced upon them by circumstance.

> I had no friends, no parents. I was poor
> In all but beauty, and an innocence
> That was not virtue—failing in the trial.
> Mine is a common tale, and all the sadder
> Because it is so common: I was sought
> By one that wore me for a time, then flung
> Me off; a rose with all its sweetness gone,
> Yet with enough of bloom to flaunt awhile,
> Although the worm was busy at its core.
> So I lived on in splendour, lived thru' years
> Of scorning, till my brow grew hard to meet it;
> Though all the while, behind that brazen shield,
> My spirit shrank before each hurtling arrow
> That sang and whistled past me in the air.

This passage is from "Christina" by Dora Greenwell (1851).[30] The narrator can look back on her career as a prostitute with relative detachment, because she is speaking from a Magdalen home, where she awaits death in peacefulness and a state of grace. The representation of society's scorn as a flurry of arrows against which the prostitute must raise a "brazen shield" recalls the defensive, "hardened" attitude Hemyng found in many of the women he interviewed for *London Labour and the London Poor*.

The use of "worm in the bud" or "blasted rose" imagery to describe sexual ruination was conventional in the nineteenth century. For example, "A

Simile," by Joanna Baillie's literary protégé Anne Hunter, vividly depicts the physical devastation and other dreadful consequences of blighted virtue.

A SIMILE

I saw the wild rose on its parent thorn
   Half clos'd, soft blushing, thro' the glitt'ring dew,
Wave on the breeze, and scent the breath of morn;
   Lelia, the lovely flow'r resembled you.
Scarce had it spread to meet the orb of day,
   Its fragrant beauties op'ning to the view,
When ruffian blasts have torn the rose away;
   Lelia—alas! it still resembles you!

So, torn, by wild and lawless passion's force,
   From every social tie, thy lot must be;
At best oblivion shades thy future course,
   And still the hapless flow'r resembles thee![31]

Initially Lelia is represented as an unspoiled flower of perfect maidenly innocence. The violence of her defloration, during which she is "torn" by the "ruffian" winds, suggests a rape more than a seduction. And of course it is the feminine flower and not the masculine gust of wind which has suffered irreparable damage and must endure the consequences. Clifford Bax and Meum Stewart interpret "A Simile" as "a dainty lyric about a wanton . . . presumably a girl of the Regency."[32] But Lelia seems less a "wanton" than a victim—whether of her own "lawless passion" or of someone else's. In what way does a real rose attract or provoke the winds which destroy it?

   Returning to the subject of society's collusion in the fallen woman's fate, we observe that in some women's poems, the prostitute's motivation is entirely financial, a matter of exhausted alternatives and "embarrassed circumstances," as Mary Ann Radcliffe put it, or of outright destitution. This is the direct message of such poems as "The Homeless Poor" by Adelaide Procter (1862)[33] and "The Scapegoat" by Mary Robinson (1884)[34] which clearly imply that society is hypocritical for driving women into sin and then penalizing them for it. "The Dying Child" by Letitia Landon represents a woman "in abject misery—that worst of poverty, which is haunted by shame," whose vision of life is so grim that she refuses to allow medical assistance to her dying daughter:

How could I bear to see her youth
   Bow'd to the dust by abject toil,
Till misery urged the soul to guilt
   From which its nature would recoil?[35]

This poem is essentially sentimental, and Letitia Landon knew next to nothing personally about the circumstances she was describing. Yet "The Dying Child" represents a relatively early, if unsophisticated, mixture of sympathy and sociological analysis in its depiction of the figure of the prostitute.

The companion poems "Judgment" and "The Heart of the Outcast" by Mary Howitt contrast the two opposing viewpoints about the fallen woman which had formed in the public consciousness by about mid-century: the "just" and the merciful. The speaker in the first poem, who represents society's more stringent attitude, is cruel, arrogant, and hypocritical:

> Lives like hers the world defile;
>   Plead not for her, let her die,
>   As the child of infamy,
> Ignorant and poor and vile,
>   Plague-spot in the public eye;
>   Let her die![36]

In the second poem, the outcast herself pleads for mercy, not from society, but from the "God of love."

> Therefore will I put my trust
>   In thy mercy: and I cleave
>   To that love which can forgive. . . . [37]

The humility and sincerity of the outcast's prayer expose the essentially un-Christian self-righteousness of a society which would take God's judgment into its own merciless hands. Mary Howitt deplored the social system which condemned a fallen woman while letting her seducer or exploiter go scot free. In repeatedly portraying the sufferings of betrayed girls and social outcasts and emphasizing the injustice of their terrible fate, she was typical of women poets generally.

Of the many dreadful consequences which seduced women suffer in women's poetry, the mildest is the mental anguish of the parents, husbands, or children whom they truly love and from whom they are forever separated. They also have to endure social rejection and disgrace, often for the rest of their lives. Sometimes, because they have lost their "character" and cannot find respectable employment, they are forced to become common prostitutes and to endure unspeakable degradation of body and spirit. Often there is an illegitimate child, whose suffering and death give the mother more exquisite pain than her own personal agonies ever could. Women who survive all of these trials may then be confronted with imprisonment, the death of their loved ones, or their own early death. But they are never forgiven for their sins and welcomed back, as whole and virtuous women, into society. Those few who are reclaimed and redeemed, by a Magdalen home or by an individual rescuer, spend the rest of their lives in penitence and atonement, and usually they, too, die young.

The sorrow her defection causes to her family is presented as a very affecting grief, though one the woman often recognizes only after it is too late. In poetry by women, betrayed husbands and abandoned children seldom forgive their wayward wives and mothers. But surprisingly enough, fathers often do. By offering his blessing to the prodigal daughter, the forgiving father becomes a symbol of divine love and mercy. In "True Love" by Mary Howitt, a father recounts the story of his fallen daughter Jane, "a thing of sin and shame," who was betrayed by a wealthy neighbor. This and other sorrows have stolen away youth, beauty, and joy from Jane's mother. Only regard for his wife has prevented the father from wreaking vengeance upon Jane's seducer, at the probable cost of his own life. Yet in spite of all this, he still hopes for the erring daughter's return:

> Let the betrayer live, wife;
> > Be this our only prayer,
> That grief may send our prodigal
> > Back to the father's care.[38]

Similarly, in "The Prison Chaplain" by Caroline Norton, the father beholds his daughter, a penitent "Magdalen," on her knees before God, and, with a sign, he too blesses and forgives her.[39] The name "Magdalen," which was synonymous with "prostitute" in the nineteenth century, comes from the New Testament story of Christ's forgiveness and acceptance of the repentant Mary Magdalene (Luke 7:37-50). The forgiving father provided one of the very few positive moments in the life of the fallen woman as portrayed by women poets.

The Christian context of any appeal on behalf of the fallen woman was thoroughly conventional. In "Brothers, and A Sermon" by Jean Ingelow, the preacher urges his congregation, in the name of Christ's mercy to Mary Magdalene, to have pity upon the poor "castaway" in their own neighborhood and to convert their scorn for her into compassion:

> I say that there was once a castaway,
> And she was weeping, weeping bitterly;
> > . . . if any neighbours had come in,
> They might have seen her crying on her knees,

And sobbing "Lost, lost, lost!" beating her breast—
Her breast for ever pricked with cruel thorns,
The wounds whereof could neither balm assuage
Nor any patience heal—beating her brow,
Which ached, it had been bent so long to hide
From level eyes, whose meaning was contempt.[40]

Of course, speeches from the pulpit are noted for hyperbole, but Ingelow was obviously making a serious point in this poem. Today, such extremity of despair over a lost reputation may seem absurd. But the ostracism of society was deadly for a middle-class woman, even as late as 1863, and the "Christian" community in the poem probably will not forgive the castaway. Ingelow goes on to suggest that the fallen woman may find solace and refuge in Christ, but *not* in nineteenth-century English society.

For rudimentary shelter and a location in which to ply their trade, the most degraded of London prostitutes resorted to Hyde Park.

There the lost victim, on whose tarnished fame
A double taint of Death and Sin must rest,
    Dreams of her village home and Parents' blame,
And in her sleep by pain and cold opprest,
Draws close her tattered shawl across her shivering breast.[41]

This was the last stop for the poor village girl who had lost her reputation and been banished from her home. In these five short lines of verse from *The Child of the Islands* (1845), Caroline Norton expresses the essence of the fallen woman myth: seduction, expulsion, destitution, sin, and death. The real women whom this poem represented sometimes resorted to suicide.

Indeed, a sentimental tradition developed around the theme of the suicide of a fallen woman in nineteenth-century poetry by men. Such poems sometimes commemorated actual deaths, as did William Bell Scott's "Rosabell" (1837) and Thomas Hood's "The Bridge of Sighs" (1844). Hood's well-known poem deals quite graphically with the suicide by drowning of "One more Unfortunate, / Weary of Breath."[42] Those who pull her body from the river are urged to "Take her up tenderly, / Lift her with care. . . . Touch her not scornfully; / Think of her mournfully, / Gently and humanly" (5-6, 15-17). Hood also attempted to prick the consciences of his male readers, who might well be responsible for a sad situation similar to that in the poem.

In she plunged boldly,
No matter how coldly
The rough river ran,—

> Over the brink of it,
> Picture it—think of it,
> Dissolute Man!
> Lave in it, drink of it,
> Then, if you can!

(72-79)

"The Bridge of Sighs" was an undisguised attempt to direct public sympathy and attention toward the fallen woman's plight.

Surprisingly, most women poets eschewed the convention of suicide, despite the opportunity for pathos and sentimentality which it presented. Instead, they generally allowed their fallen heroines to die in a more Christian way, perhaps because it was difficult to reconcile the hope of heaven with the choice of a sinful death. At any rate, in women's poetry there are very few suicides, except insofar as the loss of the will to live or the conventional pining away into death may be considered suicidal.

An exception is "From Out of the Night" (1881) by Emily Pfeiffer. This poem is a suicidal monologue, spoken by a poor, orphaned working girl (apparently a seamstress) whose lover has acceded to his father's wish that he marry a richer woman. The heroine commits suicide in the traditional way—by drowning. In Pfeiffer's own words, the poem is an attempt to "exhibit *dramatically* a young mind pervious to all the influences of beauty, love, joy and sorrow, which, having lost its hold upon The Unseen, drifts, in the first tempest of life, upon destruction."[43] The diction of the poem is especially revealing. The innocent young woman's sexual "awakening" to a "hidden self," a "sweet shame," is described in natural terms: "the yet folded blossom that softly is seeking its way / To the full, rounded life which the sun is at work to complete."[44] The floral image is, of course, conventional, but the gentleness and the sweet inevitability of the process contrast sharply with, for instance, Anne Hunter's "A Simile." There seems to be nothing sinful or shameful in the sexual union of the lovers. The fallen girl's despair is not a consequence of her sexual ruin but of the social necessity that pledged her lover's hand to another woman. Her suicide is, as Pfeiffer says, a result of her lack of faith in God's will. In fact, "From Out of the Night" resists both the self-righteous and the condescending attitudes toward the fallen heroine, and her suicidal death seems, for once, an exertion of free will, rather than an inevitable punishment for an unforgivable crime.

Most of the fallen women in nineteenth-century women's poetry, though not suicides, do die young, as Logan and others believed that their social counterparts did, rather than complete a normal life span, as Acton had tried to insist. The early death was part of the myth; it was the necessary, the ultimate punishment. Poem after poem concludes with the fallen woman's actual or imminent death, including most of the ones we have already examined.

One final piece is Fanny Kemble's "The Death-Song," recounting the agonies of a ruined maiden who seems literally to be dying of passion, shame, and unrequited love:

> Mother, mother! the bitter shame
>   Eats into my very soul;
>   And longing love, like a wrapping flame,
>   Burns me away without control.

This poem too is a monologue, as the dying girl repeatedly calls out to her mother for comfort and protection. The mother herself is only a shadowy figure in the poem, unable to preserve her child from death. In fact, she may not even be present except in the daughter's mind.

The girl begs, "Do not frown on your own poor child. / Death is darkly drawing near." But, again, the maternal disapproval may be only a projection of the girl's guilty imagination. At any rate, whether because the mother is a hallucination or because the daughter is too near death to respond to stimuli, the mother takes no action which the dying girl can perceive. "Mother, mother! sing me [a] song," she cries, but it is all in vain:

> Mother, mother! I do not hear
>   Your voice—but his—oh, guard me well!
>   His breathing makes me faint with fear,
>   His clasping arms are round me still.

There is perhaps an echo of Samuel Coleridge's "Christabel" here. In both poems, the guardian spirit of the mother which the endangered daughter invokes is powerless to protect her child from a sinful embrace. The mother in "The Death-Song" cannot compete with the force of passion and must resign her daughter to the grave.

The poem ends with two completely traditional images in an unfortunate mixed metaphor:

> Mother, mother! unbind my vest,
>   Upon my heart lies his first token;
>   Now lay me in my narrow nest,
>   Your withered blossom, crushed and broken.[45]

Despite the sentimentality of the last stanza, we as readers do feel genuinely sorry for this ruined, dying girl and frustrated with the mother's inability to help her; the poem emphasizes the vulnerability of female passion and the inefficacy against it of the maternal spirit.

Kemble's "The Death-Song" illustrates the way women poets—along with many other writers in the nineteenth century—contrived to generate sympathy for the fallen woman while outwardly conforming to the stereotype, thus fulfilling their readers' expectations but at the same time directing those readers' emotions more toward pity than toward contempt.

In fact, since the saintly woman was already an accepted convention, in the figure of the angel wife and mother, it was relatively easy for novelists and poets alike to emphasize the essentially womanly nature of even the most destitute and degraded woman and therefore to ennoble and redeem rather than to condemn her. Nina Auerbach finds in Victorian literature generally a "dual perspective" on the fallen woman: "an explicit narrative that abases the woman, [and] an iconographic pattern that exalts her."[46] As the process went on, a curious and somewhat awkward affinity emerged to replace the previous antipathy between the Madonna and the whore.

In women's poetry, however, motherhood and sexual sin were seldom complementary. More often, one cancelled out the other. In "The Lady of the Castle" by Felicia Hemans, for example, the fallen woman has essentially resigned her right to motherhood by abandoning her daughter in favor of her lover. This shocking decision places her in the category of "unnatural" mother. Hers is presented as a defection almost too unmaternal to be credible:

> She fell!
> That mother left that child!—went hurrying by
> Its cradle—haply not without a sigh,
> Haply one moment o'er its rest serene
> She hung—but no! it could not thus have been,
> For *she went on!*—forsook her home, her hearth,
> All pure affection, all sweet household mirth,
> To live a gaudy and dishonour'd thing,
> Sharing in guilt the splendours of a king.

Motherless, the child Isaure matures into a lovely young woman "full of thought and prayer, . . . tender still and meek, . . . pale and pure," etc., but also sadly unable to love. When, after a decade's absence, the mother returns and throws herself in humility and despair at her daughter's feet, Isaure shrinks from her touch:

> —t'was but a moment—yet too much
> For that all-humbled one; its mortal stroke
> Came down like lightning, and her full heart broke

At once in silence. Heavy and prone,
She sank. . . .
Dead lay the wanderer at her own proud gate.[47]

The child's rejection of the repentant mother is, obviously, the mother's own fault. According to Hemans, an adulterous mother cannot hope to regain the height of motherhood from which she has fallen. A chaste mother may sometimes forgive an erring daughter, as in Hemans' "The Penitent's Return,"[48] but never the reverse.

On the other hand, a woman whose motherhood is the direct result of her sin may find in the child an ennobling principle which, while the child lives, partly redeems the mother from sin and despair.

> Yea, for this cause, even SHAME will step aside,
>   And cease to bow the head and wring the heart;
> For she that is a mother, but no bride,
>   Out of her lethargy of woe will start,
>   Pluck from her side that sorrow's barbed dart,
> And, now no longer faint and full of fears,
>   Plan how she best protection may impart
>   To the lone course of those forsaken years,
> Which dawn in Love's warm light though doomed to set in tears.

This stanza is from "The New-Born Child" by Caroline Norton. Though the mother thus depicted has regained the will to live, it is not for the sake of her own survival, but only for the child's. In the same poem, Norton acknowledges the grim possibility of an opposite response to the birth of an illegitimate child: infanticide.

> The dread exception—when some frenzied mind,
>   Crushed by the weight of unforeseen distress,
> Grows to that feeble creature all unkind,
>   And Nature's sweetest fount, through grief's excess,
>   Is strangely turned to gall and bitterness;
> When the deserted babe is left to lie,
>   Far from the woeful mother's lost caress,
> Under the broad cope of the solemn sky,
> Or, by her shuddering hands, forlorn, condemned to die.[49]

Such an inversion of maternal love as infanticide was, as we have seen, not unknown in the nineteenth century. It was the act of a social desperado.

Caroline Norton recognized also the cruelty of society toward the innocent illegitimate child. In "The Creole Girl," she depicts the loneliness and early death of a "love-child" rejected by society and by her own father because her deceased mother had been unchaste. "Poor mother, and poor child," Norton comments, "unvalued lives! / Wan leaves that perish'd in obscurest shade."[50] In her approach to the fallen woman as mother, Norton saw the possibility of redemption and reclamation as well as the likelihood of persecution and desperation for the outcast mother and her fatherless child.[51] However, women poets did not generally conceive of motherhood and prostitution as compatible, but found the literary and cultural affinity between the Madonna and the whore uncongenial.

More often, they represented the agent of the fallen woman's salvation as spiritual, and depicted the redemption of the Magdalen as a religious conversion experience. The "hardened" prostitute in "Christina" is rescued (in the name of Christ) by the love and faith of her former best friend (*Christina*). Dora Greenwell may have named this compassionate and saintly woman character after Christina Rossetti, whom she greatly admired. During the 1850s Christina Rossetti was a frequent and popular visitor at the St. Mary Magdalen Home for fallen women at Highgate. At any rate, two women characters in the poem serve as foils to illustrate the contrast between the joy of the pure and the misery of the impure woman. The poem details not only the progress of the harlot's sinful past life but also the process of her religious awakening. In diction and tone, it resembles a sermon more than an autobiography, and it belongs as much to the Victorian literature of conversion as to the controversy over prostitution. But the imminent death it assigns to the redeemed Magdalen is very much in the fallen woman tradition.

E. Nesbit's "Refugium Peccatorum" (1888) is a very similar poem to "Christina," in tone, emphasis, and import. A prostitute wanders into a Catholic church one day, drawn by the visions of her happier youth which the singing evokes. She hears the priest tell of the love, bounty, sorrow, and mercy of the Virgin Mary, and she vows then and there to reform. Like Greenwell, Nesbit emphasizes the contrast between the two women—the chaste and the unchaste—in this instance, literally the Madonna and the whore:

> O Mother-maiden—what a woman-face!
> Sordidly sensual, unlovely, base,
> Scored with coarse lines burnt in by years of wrong,
> Stamped with the signet of the vile and strong;
> Hopeless, impure, with eyes unwashed by tears
> Through many soulless, desecrated years,
>
> She sat there stupid, broken, lost, defiled,
> Before pure mother and ideal child.

The priest accepts her confession and resolution, and he promises that on the morrow he will help her begin a new life. But during the night, in silent, penitent prayer, the fallen woman is "saved," by being gathered to Mary's breast (i.e., she dies). In the morning, the priest finds her dead at the foot of the statue of Mary, and the contrast is reemphasized:

> The morning sunshine glorifies the face
> Of Mary, Mother of ideal grace,
> Touches the poor soiled face that has grown grey
> Through rouge the tears have but half washed away;
> She does not weep now—does not breathe or stir,
> The Maiden Mother has had pity on her.[52]

Nesbit does not seem to have intended irony in this conclusion. The modern reader may feel that the prostitute's death carries more of judgment than of mercy, and that the living woman, however sinful, was preferable to the inanimate statue, however pure. But the figure of Mary is meant to represent divine grace, and the prostitute has perhaps achieved a greater peace in death than she would have done in life, even as a sinner redeemed.

For, in literary accounts at least, even the most sincere of these repentant sinners did not completely regain her lost status and begin a truly "normal" life. What was required of her, instead, was continuing penance, humility, and gratitude. Furthermore, Magdalen homes were often, in reality, austere, regimented, and conventual. Amy Levy's "Magdalen" (1884) repudiates the sudden religious conversion of the prostitute and instead conveys her understandable dissatisfaction with the asceticism of the "refuge," which frequently drove "redeemed" women back onto the street in search of a little life:

> The bare, blank room where is no sun;
> The parcelled hours; the pallet hard;
> The dreary faces here within;
> The outer women's cold regard;
> The Pastor's iterated "sin";—

Totally disillusioned, the woman turns neither to God nor to the other women in the refuge for comfort or inspiration. When her doctor warns that she will die, she responds, "It may be so, yet what care I? . . . / I have no faith / In God or Devil, Life or Death." Throughout her soliloquy, this woman is preoccupied only with her own pain. The poem virtually throbs with it. "Nothing is known or understood," she asserts, "Save only Pain."[53] Amy Levy thus contradicted the notion that every common prostitute was psychologically, spiritually, and emotionally ready for renunciation, redemption, and death.

If Amy Levy's "Magdalen" was a protest against the sentimentalization of the fallen woman, Adelaide Procter's "A Legend of Provence" (1858) represented the apotheosis in women's poetry of the fallen woman redeemed. Based on the same thirteenth-century tale about a runaway nun as John Davidson's "A Ballad of a Nun" (1895), Procter's verse narrative elevates the redeemed castaway, through God's grace, into a veritable saint. The original legend tells of a convent sister who, pining for life and love, flees the cloister in order to experience "the world." Years later, a fallen woman, she returns to the convent to beg for readmittance and finds that, miraculously, the Virgin Mary has occupied her place, in order to preserve for her the love and respect of her sisters.

In Procter's version, the erring nun has lived in the convent all her life and scarcely knows what she embraces when she steals away with a young knight. When she returns, in "chill remorse / And black despair," she hopes only to be allowed to die surrounded once again by the protective convent walls. To find not only forgiveness, but reinstatement and even glorification, is more than she could ever have dreamed. Mary tells her, "Only Heaven / Means *crowned*, not *vanquished*, when it says 'Forgiven!' " In light of nineteenth-century attitudes toward the fallen woman, this total reclamation is "miraculous" indeed.

In the poem's conclusion, Procter expresses an optimistic faith in the realization of human aspiration to the Good:

> Have we not all, amid life's petty strife,
> Some pure ideal of a noble life
> That once seemed possible? Did we not hear
> The flutter of its wings, and feel it near,
> And just within our reach? It was. And yet
> We lost it in this daily jar and fret,
> And now live idle in a vague regret.
> But still *our place is kept*, and it will wait,
> Ready for us to fill it, soon or late:
> No star is ever lost we once have seen,
> We always may be what we might have been.[54]

Adelaide Procter had converted to Roman Catholicism in 1851, and the religious inspiration of "A Legend of Provence" is obvious throughout. In depicting the fallen woman as redeemable through the grace of God, Procter was not breaking new ground. On the other hand, her assertion that "We always may be what we might have been," when applied to the fallen woman, was extraordinary.

Between 1853 and 1890 the fallen woman in virtually any form became generally acceptable in literature. (Perhaps that is one reason she began to disappear from the poetic scene: aside from her obvious function as a vehicle for sentimentality, the appeal of such a figure must surely lie also in the suggestion of the illicit.) In *The Idylls of the King*, between 1859 and 1885, Tennyson gave the fallen woman, personified by the adulterous Queen Guinevere, her fullest poetic statement as a destructive force in society. In "The Defence of Guenevere" (1858), William Morris suggested that a woman might have a right to act on her own emotions, to be true to her own lights, even to the point of committing adultery. In 1866, Thomas Hardy wrote a poem depicting the fallen woman with humor. A country girl unexpectedly encounters an old acquaintance, now living in town. " 'And whence such fair garments, such prosperi-ty?' " she asks. Comes the reply: " 'O didn't you know I'd been ruined?' said she." This poem, "The Ruined Maid," was not published, however, until 1901.[55]

The prostitute could even be depicted with something approaching realism, as in the controversial poem "Jenny" (1870) by Dante Rossetti. The narrator of "Jenny" contends at one point in his long soliloquy that if compassionate Englishwomen could only see, for once, the true plight of Jenny and her sisters, they would take up her cause. "But that can never be," he laments, for the prostitute is "Like a rose shut in a book / In which pure women may not look."[56]

Like many another woman poet, Augusta Webster also hoped to use her poetry to gain public sympathy for the fallen woman. The distinction of her work is that, like Dante Rossetti, she chose to do so by shedding light on an obscure subject, presenting the prostitute in a singularly straightforward and realistic, rather than a sentimental, manner. Webster's "A Castaway" (1870) is a lengthy poem (about six hundred lines) ranging widely over the whole complicated issue of prostitution. The speaker, an urbane, high-class prostitute, defends her profession and her life but at the same time betrays her feelings of loneliness and regret.

Born into the middle class, Eulalie was unexpectedly cast upon her own (nonexistent) resources when both her parents died. For a time she worked as a governess, but discovered she knew no more than her pupils did and (foolishly, as she now thinks) resigned in frustration. Next she became a housemaid, since she was not sufficiently skilled with a needle to earn a living as a seamstress, dressmaker, or milliner. Had she married, she thinks, "how content: / my pleasure to make him some pleasure, pride / to be as he would have me, duty, care, / to fit all to his taste, rule my small sphere / to his intention; then to lean on him, / be guided, tutored, loved—.''[57] But no one offered marriage and so, in short, she fell.

Several times she tried to redeem herself. An appeal to her brother met with scorn and a five-pound note. The Magdalen home she entered for a week drove her to the brink of suicide by its "dreary hideous room, coarse pittance, prison rules" (p. 45), and the despair provoked by isolation. The infant for whose sake she "might have struggled back" (p. 53) died after only a few hours, and she spurned the cash settlement its father offered to give her. What were her options?

> and if I rambled out into the world,
> sinless but penniless, what else were that
> but slower death, slow pining shivering death
> by misery and hunger? Choice! What choice!
>
> (p. 46)

Still, she thinks, "if some kind hand, a woman's—I hate men— / had stretched itself to help me to firm ground, . . . / I could have gone my way not falling back" (p. 46). But it was not to be. Eulalie portrays herself as diverted by circumstance into the role of prostitute and trapped there by "the prudent world / that will not have the flawed soul prank itself / with a hoped second virtue, will not have / the woman fallen once lift up herself. . . . / lest she should fall again" (p. 57).

This summary of her life and her reflections about it presents only one side of Eulalie's character as revealed in the poem. She is also proud, cynical, so-phisticated, self-possessed: "I have looked coolly on my what and why, / and I accept myself—" (p. 41).

> And what is that? My looking-glass
> answers it passably; a woman sure,
> no fiend, no slimy thing out of the pools,
> a woman with a ripe and smiling lip
> that has no venom in its touch I think,
> with a white brow on which there is no brand;
> a woman none dare call not beautiful,
> not womanly in every woman's grace.
>
> (p. 36)

She denies the notions about her necessary coarseness, drunkenness, disease, early death, etc. Furthermore, she refuses to concede that her "traffic is any less honorable than that of lawyers, preachers, doctors, journalists, tradesmen," all of whom "feed on the world's follies, vices, wants" just as she does (p. 39). As for the injured wives, with their "shrill, carping virtues. . . . / How dare they hate us so? what have they done, / what borne, to prove them other than we are? / What right have they to scorn us—glass-case saints, / Dianas under lock and key—" (p. 40).

Where, finally, does Eulalie place the blame for her "castaway" state? She is something of a fatalist:

> Yours the blame,
> and not another's, not the indifferent world's
> which goes on steadily, statistically,
> and count by censuses not separate souls—
> and if it somehow needs to its worst use
> so many lives of women, useless else,
> it buys us of ourselves, we could hold back,
> free all of us to starve, and some of us,
> (those who have done no ill and are in luck),
> to slave their lives out and have food and clothes
> until they grow unserviceably old.
> Oh I blame no one—scarcely even myself.
> It was to be.
>
> (p. 59)

Yet, for all her cynical banter, she cannot tell whether she is about to laugh or to cry about her situation. Fortunately, at that moment the doorbell rings and she needn't do either. Her long soliloquy ends, "Oh, is it you? / Most welcome, dear; one gets so moped alone" (p. 62).

"A Castaway" is a realistic, courageous poem, in both content and style; Robert Browning, Augusta Webster's acknowledged mentor, admired it very much. Mackenzie Bell, who generally found Webster's poetry too "virile" and not sufficiently beautiful, nevertheless admired "A Castaway" and recognized its originality.[58] Vita Sackville-West praised it as "the vigorous expression of a woman . . . deeply concerned with the lot of women throughout her life."[59] And B. Ifor Evans noted that Augusta Webster's feminism gave her poetry "a strength, sometimes even a corrosive quality, which distinguishes her work from that of imitators and mere versifiers."[60] In other words, "A Castaway" was to women's poetry what "Jenny" was to men's: the century's fullest and finest direct confrontation with the reality and the tragedy of prostitution.

One additional poem, "A Study" (1875) by Alice Meynell, illustrates the artistic use which could be made in the seventies of the theme of the fallen woman. "A Study" is also a monologue—or rather a series of three monologues, with interruptions. We follow one woman through the course of a single, crucial day in her life, from pre-dawn to nightfall. The exact circumstances of the poem are left unclear, but we know that she has walked from her lonely cottage to a nearby seaport in order to glimpse her only child for the last time and then walked back home. It seems that the child, from whom she has been forcibly separated for five long years, has inadvertently discovered, among his guardian's papers, evidence of the great, secret crime in his mother's past life and has determined to leave the country and never to see her again.

The guardian, whose exact relationship with the child and his mother is also unclear, represents masculine betrayal, judgment, and punishment of the erring woman. A stern man, he does not even pity her, but remarks that he has done his duty to both mother and child, and condemns her to "home and hidden life, . . . absence and perfect silence until you die."[61] She takes the dismissal with great outward calm but also with great inward pain and returns to her home in "sorrow for ruined and for desolate days," both past and future (p. 65). It seems apparent that the "crime" was sexual in nature, probably adultery or even prostitution. Her repentance is sincere, her loneliness acute, but, "Who would believe me, knowing what I am?" she asks (p. 60).

The true interest and artistic merit of the poem lie not in the pathos of the familiar story, however, but in the intricacy of the heroine's thoughts and emotions and in her relationship to her only real companion: the natural world. The first monologue, "Before Light," begins:

> Among the first to wake. What wakes with me?
> A blind wind and a few buds and a star.
> With tremor of darkened flowers and whisper of birds,
> Oh, with a tremor, with a tremor of heart—
> Begins the day i' the dark.
>
> (p. 58)

As she gropes her way toward consciousness, she remembers the significance of the day: she will see her beloved son again. She predicts:

> The morning will awake,
> Like to the lonely waking of a child
> Who grows uneasily to a sense of tears,
> Because his mother had come and wept and gone.
>
> (p. 58)

Though she does not know, but only suspects it, this is precisely how the encounter with her son will turn out. Similarly, she projects the day on into the evening hours:

And one will come with secrets at her heart,
Evening, whose darkening eyes hide all her heart,
And poppy-crowned move 'mid my lonely flowers,
And shall another, I wonder, come with her,—
I, with a heavy secret at my heart?

(pp. 58-59)

The heroine's close relationship with nature is at once mystical, pantheistic, and Christian:

—A little life, O Lord, a little sorrow.
And I remember once when I was ill
That the whole world seemed breaking through with me,
Who lay so light and still. . . .

(p. 59)

This affinity with nature, established in the poem's first movement, continues throughout. It is her isolation from human affection which has brought about the heroine's immersion in the natural world, where she finds both companionship for her loneliness and solace for her grief. In the final lines of the poem, the voice suddenly shifts to an unidentified third person omniscient narrator, who describes the forlorn woman's tedious journey home:

She therefore turned unto the Eastern hills,
Thrilled with a west wind sowing stars.
            . . . There she felt the earth
Lonely in space. And all things suddenly
Shook with her tears. She went with shadowless feet,
Moving along the shadow of the world,
Faring alone to home and a long life,
Setting a twilight face to meet the stars.

(p. 66)

The motif of light and shadow, day and night, defines the very structure of the poem. The lyrical beauty with which Meynell handles this concept is perhaps unmatched in Victorian literature except by Tennyson's *Maud*.

"A Study" contains also a great deal of religious imagery which, though not orthodox in its Christianity, is more or less conventional in its presentation. The other major image pattern by which the heroine reveals her state of mind is purely female: recurring metaphors of childhood, motherhood, and pregnancy. One simile we have seen already, the morning awakening like a lonely child. The deprived mother is understandably preoccupied—this day of all days—with her child and with herself as a mother. Thus, for example, she describes her renewed, her penitent self in these terms:

"The world is full of endings for me, I find,
Emotions lost, and words and thoughts forgotten.
Yet amid all these *last* things, there is one,
But one Beginning, a seed within my soul.
                                    . . . day by day
A little innocent life grows in my life,
A little ignorant life i' the world-worn life;
And I become a child again with a world to learn,
Timorous, with another world to learn,
Timorous, younger, whiter towards my death."

(p. 61)

In the modern idiom, we might say that here is "a woman giving birth to herself." In the third monologue, "At Twilight," this imagery mingles again with the imagery of time and nature, as the heroine embraces her sole consolation:

For my absent child God gives me a child in Spring;
New seasons and the fresh and innocent earth,
Ever new years and children of the years,
Kin to the young thoughts of my weary heart,
Chime with the young thoughts of my weary heart,
My kin in all the world.

(p. 65)

In this interweaving of various appropriate images to reveal the speaker's mind and heart lies the poem's greatest merit. "A Study," included in the 1875 *Preludes*, was for some reason omitted from the *Collected Poems of Alice Meynell* in 1913.[62] Yet, in retrospect, it appears to have been one of her more sustained poetic efforts. By contrast especially with "A Castaway," it seems also to have been a much more consciously artistic use of the fallen woman theme than had previously been attempted.

Thus were the literary (and polemical) possibilities in the figure of the fallen woman greatly expanded in the sixties and seventies. As this change occurred, the single pattern of the seduction, betrayal, and inevitable punishment of the fallen woman lost its earlier rigidity. Those few women poets who chose to take a different approach were, after about mid-century, operating within a well-established counter-tradition. By the 1880s some writers—though not women poets—were even allowing the fallen woman to redeem herself through marriage. By the end of the century, the original literary stereotype of the fallen woman had more or less ceased to exist.

6
The Spinster

Beside the fallen woman stood another female figure whose shadowy existence violated nineteenth-century expectations: the spinster. Although eminently respectable, the unmarried woman of a certain age (generally understood to be thirty) was in many ways as much a social outcast as the whore. Especially if she were neither wealthy nor "protected" by a father, brother, or brother-in-law, she found herself without a serious and socially acceptable purpose in life and frequently even without the means to live out her exile in comfort and security. While her legal rights were greater than those of married women, her opportunities for employment and for social contact were, especially early in the century, extremely limited.

Contemporary opinion tended to write her off as an anomaly, one of the few but inevitable failures in the matchmaking business. However, as the century wore on, the number of English women who would never assume the expected role of wife and mother showed a steady and alarming increase, and the figure of the spinster loomed correspondingly larger in the popular (and literary) imagination. Partly as a result, social attitudes became more tolerant, and work opportunities became more open. By the close of the century, the popular image of the "old maid" pretty much gave way to the less pitiable and more controversial figure of the "New Woman."[1]

By 1851, the rapidly growing number of single women aged fifteen and over had already reached 2,765,000, and it increased by 16.8 percent over the next twenty years.[2] In 1862, W. R. Greg calculated that the number of women who were spinsters not from choice or disposition, but "in consequence of social disorders or anomalies of some sort" was 750,000. Thus, he envisioned three quarters of a million surplus women, women for whom, statistically, no husbands existed. These women "who in place of completing, sweetening, and embellishing the existence of others, are compelled to lead an independent and incomplete existence of their own" were, to use Greg's terminology, "redundant."[3] The rather large disparity between the numbers of males and females in England at mid-century has been attributed partly to different mortality rates and partly to male emigration. Apparently it reflected a significant change from conditions in the previous century.

In the eighteenth century, when, presumably, marriage came easier, the spinster was generally represented as a ridiculous figure, a fair target for contempt: Tobias Smollett's Tabitha Bramble is a perfect example of the type.[4] The first step in rehabilitating the spinster was to change public opinion about her. In 1785 William Hayley published *A Philosophical, Historical, and Moral Essay on Old Maids,* intending "to redress all the wrongs of the autumnal maiden, and to place her, if possible, in a state of honour, content, and comfort." The attempt was something of a failure, since Hayley's premise was that all women would marry if they could, and that the old maid is naturally quite miserable. She is "not only a solitary fly, but as a fly in those cloudy and chilling days of autumn, when the departure of the sun has put an end to all its lively flutter, and leaves it only the power of creeping heavily along in a state of feebleness and dejection." The effect of Hayley's essay is to replace scorn and derision not with honor, but with pity. "To sneer at the ancient virgin, merely because she has a claim to that title, is . . . a piece of cruelty as wanton and malicious as it is to laugh at the personal blemishes of any unfortunate being, who has been maimed by accident, or deformed from his birth."[5] In other words, the old maid is a grotesque social cripple.

In his *Enquiry into the Duties of the Female Sex* (1801), Thomas Gisborne emphasized the pathos of the wasted lives of unmarried ladies:

> They are persons cut off from a state of life usually regarded as the most desirable. They are frequently unprovided with friends. . . . Sometimes they are destitute of a settled home; and compelled by a scanty income to depend on the protection, and bear the humours, of supercilious relations. Sometimes in obscure retreats, solitary, and among strangers, they wear away the hours of sickness and of age, unfurnished with the means of procuring the assistance and the comforts which sinking health demands. Let not unfeeling derision be added to the difficulties, which it has perhaps been impossible to avoid, or virtue not to decline.[6]

Gisborne's last remark, suggesting that the spinster was not necessarily to blame for her unhappy state, prefigured the nineteenth-century tendency to regard the increasing numbers of single women as victims of circumstance.

In 1851, the *North British Review* responded to the first statistical revelations about the appalling increase in single women, by lamenting "the disrespect cast . . . on single life," when so many women simply could not expect to marry:

> How unwise . . . to stigmatize as dishonourable a state of life to which any woman may be compelled, and that without any fault of her own! . . . How much better would it be to educate women with a feeling of self-dependence and moral strength, which would enable them, if left unchosen, to feel sufficient self-respect to bear the sneers of the world, and to pursue their own occupations cheerfully, having in view the high end to which they were born.[7]

Thus, even the more conservative opinion makers of mid-Victorian society felt called upon to suggest a constructive remedy for the situation: in this case Coventry Patmore endorses educating women for self-dependence.

Other reactions to the single woman's dilemma ranged all the way from urging her simply to cheer up, to calling for the opening of all professions and trades to women workers. Dora Greenwell, in an 1862 article on "Our Single Women," recommended that the traditionally feminine area of social work become more accessible to organized women volunteers.[8] Indeed, such work did become a serious occupation. Eventually, activities like sick-nursing, visiting the poor, and teaching were upgraded, compensated, and professionalized, although not without a struggle.

Meanwhile, the controversy settled around two alternate approaches to the single woman's problem, as Frances Power Cobbe explained:

> 1st. We must frankly accept this new state of things, and educate women and modify trade in accordance therewith so as to make the condition of celibacy as little injurious as possible; or,—

> 2nd. We must set ourselves vigorously to stop the current which is leading men and women away from the natural order of Providence. We must do nothing whatever to render celibacy easy or attractive; and we must make the utmost efforts to promote marriage by emigration of women to the colonies, and all other means in our power.[9]

Cobbe, who was herself a spinster, endorsed the first alternative; W. R. Greg and others insisted on the latter. Greg's scheme for transporting four hundred thousand superfluous women to the Antipodes, though it attracted a few enthusiasts, failed because it was short-sighted and unfeeling and because it did not take into account numerous practical, economic, and political obstacles.[10] Instead, women made slow gains in various fields and levels of employment during the latter part of the century, so that, by the advent of the "New Woman," spinsterhood was no longer the social or economic tragedy it had been a hundred years before.

Of course, the skewed ratio of women to men was only one of a variety of explanations for the increase in spinsterhood. Greg cited the tendency, in the economic turmoil of the nineteenth century, for status-conscious middle-class men to postpone marriage until they felt financially secure and noted a complementary tendency among middle-class girls to reject suitors who could not establish for them households comparable to those their fathers had built up over perhaps twenty or thirty years.[11] Furthermore, if a young woman was needed at home, then of course her duty as a daughter took precedence over her desire for a husband. "Many a girl," wrote Eliza Cook, "the only child of an otherwise lonely parent, the sole prop of a widowed father or mother, the solitary light of a fast decaying life, has given herself up with the noble devotion of woman, to cheer the last hours of those to whom she owed her life."[12] Such a vigil might extend throughout the courtship years, leaving the middle-aged woman all alone when the "aged parent" finally died. Some women, no doubt, missed marrying because of individual circumstances. One thinks of Jane Austen, for example, or of Elizabeth Barrett who, at age thirty, was most assuredly a spinster, by virtue of her own invalidism and her father's protective mania. Susan Gorsky mentions also "the inability of a woman to marry because of unrequited love or the loss of her lover through unfaithfulness or death."[13]

Despite the prevailing belief that "no woman is single from choice,"[14] some women undoubtedly preferred celibacy. Some were disillusioned with the state of marriage as an institution. Cobbe pointed out that "the knowledge of the risks of an unhappy marriage (if not the risks themselves) has become more public" through the operation of the divorce court, which, "in righting the most appalling wrongs to which the members of a civilized community could be subjected, has revealed secrets which must tend to modify immensely our ideas of English domestic felicity."[15] Others, though mid-Victorian society would hardly have believed it, chose to devote their lives to their work rather than to a man and his children. Florence Nightingale, for example, rejected what her friends and family felt was a perfect match in order to apply herself primarily to her nursing. And, of course, some women simply were not asked to marry, because potential suitors found them ugly or unpleasant, or because they were poor, or because, like the Brontë sisters, they lived modest young women's lives of virtual isolation from eligible young men.

Despite contemporary opinion, it is clear that spinsterhood offered more compensation and satisfaction than it might superficially appear to do. In her autobiography, Harriet Martineau remarked, "I am, in truth, very thankful for not having married." She continued, "I can easily conceive how I might have been tempted—how some deep springs in my nature might have been touched . . . but as a matter of fact, they never were; and I consider the immunity a great blessing. . . . My taste and liking are for living alone."[16] Certainly, some of the most respected and influential women of the nineteenth century were, like Harriet Martineau, unmarried: Frances Power Cobbe, Florence Nightingale, Emily Davies, Mary Carpenter, and Mary Russell Mitford, to name only a few. That there were not many, many more such prominent women, since spinsters were becoming so numerous, was due to poor education for women, social pressures against female achievement, and, perhaps, lack of encouragement from within the family.[17]

Most of the women poets who are the subjects of this study were either spinsters, or middle-aged brides, or in some other way unmarried during their careers: widowed, separated, or divorced. Research conducted by Elaine Showalter reveals that "of women writers born between 1800 and 1900, a fairly constant proportion—about half—were unmarried." Furthermore, many of those who married did so late in life, after their professional reputations were already established, and consequently had few or no children.[18] Women who were spinsters generally found that more time was available to them for serious work than was available to married women. Cobbe observed, "No great books have been written, or works achieved by women while their children were around them in infancy. No woman can lead the two lives at the same time."[19] Furthermore, Cobbe made the astonishing assertion that "the 'old maid's' life may be as rich, as blessed, as that of the proudest of mothers. . . . She feels that in the power of devoting her *whole* time and energies to some benevolent task, she is enabled to effect perhaps some greater good than would otherwise have been possible."[20]

Even single women without some great life work were not necessarily pathetic and useless, as the stereotype insisted. The maiden aunt, for instance, a purely domestic old maid, was a beloved and useful figure in many a large Victorian household. Eliza Cook described "the old maiden aunts round whom the children cluster for picture-books and gingerbread, who are looked for so anxiously by the nephews and nieces at festivals, and merry-makings, and holidays. . . ."[21] Or, if not domestically inclined, the single woman might be "an exceedingly cheery personage, running about untrammelled by husband or children; now visiting her relatives' country houses, now taking her month in town, now off to a favourite *pension* or Lake Geneva, now scaling Vesuvius or the Pyramids."[22]

Thus the spinster's existence, despite the ignominy, *could* be independent, comfortable, and productive, whatever her talents and interests might be. The crucial factor was, of course, money. By the late years of the century, as women's increasing wages and opportunities made it possible to earn an income sufficient to ensure respect, the social prejudices which made the single woman's life dreary and monotonous, and made the woman herself a ridiculous or pitiable figure, began gradually to fade away.

The literary fortunes of the spinster were somewhat slow in keeping up. In *Eliza Cook's Journal* for October 1850, she deplored the popular literary representations of the old maid: "If you happen to see an engraving of an old sour-faced lady in close companionship with a pug dog, two cats and a parrot, you may be sure that it is meant for an old maid. If you happen to hear of an ancient dame who occupies her whole time in scandalizing and damaging the fair fame of her neighbors, be certain that the story is fated to end with the circumstance that she is an old maid. If you read of a prude, who is so squeamish that she cannot bear to hear of the slightest friendship between the sexes, you may at once make up your mind that she belongs to the sisterhood of old maids." Cook felt that the "unprotected condition" of spinsters "ought to shield them from, rather than expose them to, the prejudices of which they are made victims,"[23] especially since, as she had previously observed, the single women of her acquaintance were generally "active, cultivated, energetic, judicious, [and] widely benevolent."[24]

By 1862, when Cobbe asserted that the potential "utility, freedom, and happiness of a single woman's life" had been socially acknowledged,[25] the literary stereotype was just making the transition from derision to pity. Dora Greenwell, herself a popular poet, noted the changing image of the single woman in literature from "the withered prude" of William Hogarth and William Cowper to "the gentle, dovelike Old Maid, of smooth braided silvery hair and soft speech and eye, generally . . . dressed in grey, who is supposed to have some tender secret buried in her heart, . . . but who, ever serene and cheerful, flits in and out between the scenes, listening, consoling, cheering, at all times ready to take up a little of existence at second hand."[26]

With the possible exception of Tennyson ("Mariana," "The Lady of Shalott," *The Princess)*, nineteenth-century poets did not, as a rule, expend much energy on the spinster. When the poetic subject is an old maid, it is usually clear that the author of the poem either disapproves of her or pities her or both. A perfect example is Arthur Symons' "The Unloved." Written in 1896 and published in 1900, it is, at the end of the century, as stereotypical a depiction of the pathetic old maid as any in literature:

These are the women whom no man has loved.
Year after year, day after day has moved
These hearts with many longings, and with tears,

> And with content; they have received the years
> With empty hands, expecting no good thing;
> Life has passed by their doors, not entering.[27]

As "The Unloved" illustrates, the poetic image of the spinster failed through-out the entirety of the century to keep pace with the changing social reality of the single woman.

We might expect that women poets, many of whom were themselves un-married, would have represented the nineteenth-century spinster more realis-tically than male poets did; and such was occasionally, though not generally, the case. Much of the popular poetry written by and for women reflected the two conventional attitudes: ridicule and pathols. On the other hand, whether satiric or sentimental in method, these poems usually deplored, even while they de-picted, the low social status of the "old maid"; and a few writers tried to chal-lenge it by depicting the figure in some alternative manner.

Two poems published in 1837, the year of Victoria's accession, will serve to illustrate the satirical and sentimental modes of representing the spinster. The first, Lady Emmeline Stuart Wortley's "I Am Come But Your Spirits to Raise," depicts a woman sinking into spinsterhood. It is a satiric poem with two female targets: the aging spinster and the hypocritical socialite. The latter is the speaker of the poem; she delivers her catty monologue during a social call on her friend Jane, whose father has just died. Protesting, "I came but your spirits to cheer," the visitor comments on Jane's faded appearance and re-minds her of all the fun she is missing while observing the obligatory period of mourning.

> To be sure, since your poor father's death,
>   You've been locked up and blocked up at home,
> Like a sword left to rust in the sheath,
>   Like a plant left to pine in the gloom.
>
> . . . .
>
> Now your hair always hangs out of curl,
>   All unconscious of riband or wreath;
> You are grown quite a different girl,
>   Since your poor gouty father's sad death.

Neither Jane nor her visitor is perceptibly moved by the death. Jane's air of sadness is attributable to the fact that her friend has stolen her beau, protesting all the while that she has encouraged him only for Jane's sake. A couple of stanzas will demonstrate how this feat has been accomplished: through subtle criticism of Jane in implicit contrast with herself.

Now he swears you wear loads of false hair,
  And I vow to him, love, 'tis your own,
And assure him that sorrow and care
  Have now mixed some grey hairs with the brown.

He protests, too, you rouged—so I say
  That if ever you did, you don't now—
For your colour is quite gone away,
  And like parchment your cheek and your brow.

And he says "women ne'er should use art,"
  (And I own that I think that is true);
Then I ask—ever taking your part—
  "Why, now, what *are* poor women to do?

My sweet Jane's not so young as she was;
  Thirty-two she'll see never again,
And beauty and freshness will pass—
  Ay—even from my exquisite Jane!"[28]

The speaker continues in this vein for nine more stanzas. Because the humor in the poem derives from the cleverness of the hypocritical friend, the frustrated spinster Jane becomes the butt of the joke. However, the malice of her tormentor is equally reproachable, and she, too, is a target of the satire. Lady Stuart Wortley has thus manipulated two feminine stereotypes—the spinster and the flirt—for humorous effect. Although the humor is of the variety that exploits the rivalry between women and deprecates female character, the poet saw fit, in this instance at least, to attack the attacker as well as the victim.

Turning to the sentimental vein, we find representations of the spinster which suggest a nobility of spirit behind her pathetic failure to marry. In "The Secret Discovered" by Letitia Landon, also published in 1837, the heroine Elinore relinquishes her long-time fiancé to her younger sister Minna because she has discovered that the two are in love. Although she pretends to be relieved by her broken engagement, Elinore never marries, but devotes herself to her aged parent.

     . . . beside their lonely hearth,
      She cheered her father's age,
  And made, for him, life's last dark leaf
      A sweet and sunny page.
      Did never other lovers come?
      They did—but came in vain;
  A heart like hers, when given once,
      Is given not again.[29]

Elinore adopted a life of self-denial, as the sacrifice of the first marriage opportunity usually implied in nineteenth-century literature. It is to be hoped that
in real life she might have accepted one of her later suitors. In its portrayal of
the gentle, self-sacrificing old maid, this poem, though sympathetic, is entirely
conventional.

Adelaide Procter's "Three Evenings in a Life" (1858), on the other hand,
takes a more critical stance, not on the nobility, but on the necessity, of such
extreme self-sacrifice. The three evenings are successive Christmas Eves in the
life of the spinster Alice. On the first, Alice declines an offer of marriage
because in her girlhood she had promised her artist brother she would devote
her life to his happiness and his career, a decision which costs Alice a great deal
of pain in carrying out. After her disappointed suitor leaves, Alice feels "a
strange and wild regret" for the love, home, and children she has renounced.
She even wonders, "What right had she to banish / A hope that God had
given?"[30] The struggle within her soul resolves itself in a redoubled affection
for her brother.

A year later, we discover that Alice's brother has married. It soon becomes
obvious to Alice that her sacrifice was unnecessary: her brother no longer
needs her, and his wife is jealous of their closeness. On this Christmas Eve,
brother Herbert lies dying; with his last breath he commends his wife Dora into Alice's care. She gives her solemn promise: "To Dora's life hencefor-
ward / She will devote her own" (p. 309).

In the third movement of the poem, Alice once again learns the uselessness
of selfless devotion. On Christmas Eve, Dora marries Alice's former suitor and
Alice wanders out "forlorn" from her dead brother's home.

> Forlorn—nay, not so. Anguish
>   Shall do its work at length;
> Her soul, passed through the fire
>   Shall gain still purer strength.
> Somewhere there waits for Alice
>   An earnest, noble part;
> And meanwhile God is with her—
>   God, and her own true heart!
>
> (p. 315)

Certainly this conclusion is optimistic about Alice's future. At least she
doesn't join Herbert in the grave, an event we might reasonably have anticipated in a nineteenth-century poem. Whether she will marry after all or
devote herself to some other worthy cause is not revealed, but in any event,
her life is far from over, and her faith in the virtue of self-sacrifice has been ef-

fectively challenged. The open-ended, hopeful conclusion to "Three Evenings in a Life" constitutes an unconventional representation of the spinster as an independent and useful woman.

In the same volume, Procter portrayed another self-sacrificing spinster, this time the victim of a long engagement. "Philip and Mildred" is a serious analysis of the damage done to love and to individual human beings by the middle-class tendency to delay marriage on account of finances and masculine ambition. On the day which should have seen the lovers' wedding, they are instead "rent asunder, and her heart must learn endurance, / For he leaves their home, and enters on a world of work and strife."[31] Endure she does: Mildred avoids all change and growth, keeping herself for Philip just as she was on the day he left her. He, on the other hand, matures, gains knowledge, and wins success. When at last they are financially able to marry, Mildred finds that Philip's "heart and soul and mind / Were beyond her now" (p. 277).

Why did this discrepancy occur? Procter tells us Mildred's "nature was too passive and her love perhaps too strong" (p. 274). In light of nineteenth-century ideology about women, the suggestion that a woman could be too passive or her love too strong is unusual. Philip sacrifices happiness to honor and marries Mildred. She, in turn, sacrifices life to love and assumes the attitude of ultimate passivity: death. The tragedy in the poem stems from Mildred's inability to conceive of herself as a worthwhile human being independent of Philip's love and support. Procter states this point quite clearly in the poem.

> O poor heart! love, if thou willest; but, thine
>   own soul still possessing,
> Live thy life: not a reflection
>   or a shadow of his own:
> Lean as fondly, as completely, as thou willest,—
>   but confessing
> That thy strength is God's, and therefore can,
>   if need be, stand alone.
>
>   (p. 273)

Adelaide Procter was both a spinster and a feminist, a woman who not only wrote popular poetry but also helped to found the controversial *English Woman's Journal* and the Society for Promoting the Employment of Women. Perhaps because of her commitment to the cause of female independence, she was one of the few women poets who dared on occasion to proselytize against feminine self-denial. The traditional figure of the modest, self-sacrificing spinster provided an opportune focus for the expression of Procter's unconventional point of view.

Besides age, a broken heart, a self-sacrificing disposition, or lack of means, personal unattractiveness was another of the reasons women poets explored for a woman's not marrying. The ugly woman has traditionally been a convenient source of laughter, but women poets declined to ridicule her. The speaker in Eliza Cook's "Song of the Ugly Maiden" is the extreme opposite of the ideal English girl—almost, but not quite, to the point of parody.

> Oh! 'tis a saddening thing to be
>   A poor and Ugly one:
> In the sand Time puts in his glass for me,
>   Few sparkling atoms run.
> For my drawn lids bear no shadowing fringe,
>   My locks are thin and dry;
> My teeth wear not the rich pearl tinge,
>   Nor my lips the henna dye.[32]

The reader may be reminded of Shakespeare's sonnet 130, "My mistress' eyes are nothing like the sun," but Cook's ugly maiden does not merely fall short of the ideal; she stands in opposition to it, as a sort of anti-heroine. Potential suitors ignore her; ordinarily chivalrous men accord her neither courtesy nor respect. She feels herself an outcast: "Oh, Ugliness! thy desolate pain / Had served to set the stamp on Cain" (p. 304). She endures the "thoughtless jeers" and "laughing grin" of those who seem to imagine she is ugly by choice. So demoralized is she by scorn and neglect that she wishes she had never been born.

> For I stand in the blessed light of day
>   Like a weed among the corn,—
> The black rock in the wide, blue sea—
>   The snake in the jungle green. . . .
> Yet mine is the fate of lonelier state
>   Than that of the snake or rock;
> For those who behold me in their path
>   Not only shun, but mock.
>
>   (p. 305)

Eliza Cook herself was not a femininely attractive woman, as the frontispiece of her *Poetical Works* reveals; she flouted dress conventions,[33] and she never married. "Song of the Ugly Maiden" doubtless expressed a depth of bitterness and anger which was Eliza Cook's own. Certainly it straightforwardly accused (male) society of exhibiting a cruel and hypocritical attitude toward women.

An even stronger poem in this genre is Augusta Webster's "By the Look-ing-Glass" (1866). Webster's heroine is also a figure of pathos and pain, and a very sympathetic character. Standing by her mirror she soliloquizes about her fate:

> But the right of a woman is being fair,
> And her heart must starve if she miss that dower,
> For how should she purchase the look and the smile?
> And I have not had my part.[34]

As an amateur painter, she compensates by surrounding herself with beauty, feeding upon it "till beauty itself must seem / Me, my own, a part and essence of me, / My right and my being" (p. 151). But one look in the glass dissipates this hard-won sense of internal beauty. The psychological effect of her physical ugliness is a sensitivity to fancied mockery and scorn and a conse-quent withdrawal farther into the self. Yet she would most like "to forget me awhile, / Feeling myself but as one in the throng, / Losing myself in the joy of my youth!" (p. 151). Her self-consciousness is a burden she cannot shirk.

Once, when she was younger and still had hope, there was a man, but before he could declare the interest his eyes bespoke, he met her pretty sister. Soon the two had married and moved away, leaving the hopeless old maid alone with her "scatheless maidenly pride" (p. 155). Her only escape from the frustration and despair of her situation is the loss of consciousness afforded by sleep: "Let self and this sadness of self leave me free, / Lost in the peace of the night" (p. 160). When the failure to marry was presented as a catastrophe, when the ideal of womanhood presupposed youth and beauty, then the ugly spinster was a pathetic figure indeed. Both Eliza Cook and Augusta Webster treated the predicament of such a woman with a degree of solemnity appro-priate to the severity of her social disability.

In a truly rare exception to the customary depiction of spinsters as miserable or ridiculous women, George Eliot in 1870 composed "Agatha," a respectful, even idealized portrait of a saintly and contented old maid. According to Eliot's journal, the poem was written "after a visit to that St. Märgen de-scribed at the beginning of the poem. There was really an aged woman among those green hills who suggested the picture of Agatha."[35] The idyllic setting of the poem, in the Catholic, Old World countryside, complements the presen-tation of Agatha, a devoutly religious and well-beloved woman of St. Märgen. Agatha shares with her two unmarried cousins the one-room cottage which the elderly couple who employed her for thirty years left to her when they died. To earn their living, the three old maids work for the neighbors in house and field, "Patching and mending, turning o'er the hay, / Holding sick chil-dren. . . . "[36] In return, the villagers see to it that they are never in distress, for they think of her as "one who surely made a link / 'Twixt faulty folk and God by loving both" (p. 58).

Of course, it must be remembered that Agatha's life is not that of an urban Englishwoman. Such a woman as Agatha seems less uncommon in a simple, rural setting, where it seems altogether fitting that the local folk should adore her. Nevertheless, Eliot's idealized representation of the happy, useful old maid Agatha was truly extraordinary. The fact that it was based upon the life of a real woman may partially account for the poem's deviation from the nineteenth-century literary norm; the rest of the credit belongs to the decidedly unconventional imagination of George Eliot.

Mary Robinson's "The Wise-Woman" (1884) provides a sharp contrast with Eliot's "Agatha." The title of the poem is ironic, for the village old maid in this rural setting is a witch, who lives alone in a broken-down cottage with a leaky roof and a weedy garden and windows the village boys have shattered with stones.[37] The villagers blame her for everything that goes wrong and once even dunked her in the pond. For her part, she does not protest against their accusations, but encourages their awe and fear. The narrator of the poem, who is more sophisticated than the wise-woman's rural neighbors, does not believe in witchcraft but wonders why the old woman should accept the role in which the ignorant villagers have cast her.

> This is the house. Lift up the latch—
>   Faugh, the smoke and the smell!
> A broken bench, some rags that catch
> The drip of the rain from the broken thatch—
>   Are these the wages of Hell?
>
> Is it for this she earns the fear
>   And the shuddering hate of her kind?
> To moulder and ache in the hovel here,
> With the horror of death ever brooding near,
>   And the terror of what is behind?

The narrator resolves the question by recognizing the overwhelming loneliness of "a woman poor and old, / No longer like to be courted again," whose feelings of neglect and powerlessness might compel her to sacrifice her very soul.

> Who sooner would, than slip from sight,
>   Meet every eye askance;
> Whom threatened murder can scarce affright,
> Who sooner would live as a plague and a blight
>   Than just be forgotten; perchance.[38]

Like George Eliot's Agatha, Mary Robinson's wise-woman also commands
the respect of her neighbors, but at a terrible price. *The New Arcadia,* in which
this poem appeared, was a piece of social protest; in "The Wise-Woman,"
Mary Robinson depicted not only the misery of the poor and powerless but
also the cruelty of society toward single women. If English old maids occasionally were grotesque, the poem suggests, perhaps society itself was to blame.

A second poem in *The New Arcadia* which deals with the spinster is "The
Rothers," a tale of the rural aristocracy, rather than the rural poor. The old
maid in "The Rothers" is Miss May, a great-aunt, whose eccentricities are a
bit ridiculous but whose essential goodness and devotion to her nieces far
overshadow her foibles.

> —she would sigh,
>   And clasp her hands, and swear "by God";
> Her black wig ever slipped awry,
>   And quavered with a trembling nod;
> Her face was powdered very white,
> Her black eyes danced under brows of night.
>
> Such paint! Yet were I ever to feel
>   Utterly lost, no saint I'd pray,
> But, crooked of ringlets and high of heel,
>   I'd call to the rescue old Miss May;
> No haloed angel sweet and slender
> Were half so kind, so staunch, so tender.[39]

Miss May has renounced her single life in France in order to be a mother to
her two orphaned wards, Florence and Maud Rother. Some twenty years
later, both girls decide to marry, and Miss May is rewarded for her devotion
by being dismissed like a superfluous servant.

> Homeless, after so many years
>   Of sacrifice! Where could she go?
> But she, she smiled, choked back her tears,
>   "Of course," she said, "it must be so,—
> So kind, her girls, to let her come
> Three months to each in her married home!"

(p. 59)

The thoughtlessness and ingratitude of her adopted daughters are almost
beyond belief. After her first three-month stay with Maud, Miss May, seriously ill, is loaded into the back of a wagon and driven like a trussed calf to

Florence's house; she dies on the way. The narrator of the poem, a neighbor of the Rothers, seems to be the only one in the countryside who is sufficiently appalled that he refuses to socialize with the prestigious family of the Rothers. We the readers are to identify, of course, with him and to deplore the "murder" of poor old Miss May. *The New Arcadia* is melodramatic, and the story of "The Rothers" is almost too outlandish to be genuinely moving. However, as a comment upon the conventional expendability of maiden aunts, it deals with social reality, and in its depiction of Miss May herself, it represents a spinster who is comprehensible and deserving of our respect as a human being.

Generally, women poets in the nineteenth century did not portray the unmarried woman with the dignity her changing social status could have commanded, but instead either ignored her or treated her with the levity or sentimentality dictated by convention. Their conformity in this regard is particularly regrettable because it placed so many women writers in the uneasy position of directing ridicule or pity toward the group of English women to which they themselves belonged. Even so, these conservative poets frequently avoided endorsing in their poems the very stereotypes they were presenting there. And a few progressive writers—women like Adelaide Procter and Augusta Webster—succeeded in transcending the idea of the spinster as society's debris by publishing poems that exposed social injustice and expressed not only understanding but respect for their many unmarried sisters.

7

Representations of Women at Work

The history of women's work in nineteenth-century England is quite complex and has been traced in detail in a number of sociological, historical, and literary studies.[1] However, although fiction in the nineteenth century addressed the issue to an appreciable extent, poetry did so only rarely. Understandably, women poets expressed a great deal of interest in woman as artist, especially as poet, but they otherwise accorded the figure of the working woman rather slight attention, considering that the relationship between women and work was a major social issue of the century. Still, women poets' portrayals of women at work were generally more numerous, accurate, and sympathetic than men's were.

Basic to understanding the changing work situation for women is the recognition of England's complex class structure in the nineteenth century. The daily lives of upper-class women—whether nobility or gentry, town or "county"—were completely different from those of women in the lower, or laboring, classes; middle-class women were caught in the bind. In terms of wealth, privilege, and status, society was structured in a pyramid, with the aristocracy at the apex and the working poor at the base.[2]

THE ARISTOCRACY

Properly speaking, aristocratic ladies did not "work" at all, restrained as they were by "a spurious refinement, that cramps the energy and circumscribes the usefulness of women in the upper classes of society," as Margaretta Grey complained in 1853: "A lady, to be such, must be a mere lady, and nothing else. She must not work for profit, or engage in any occupation that money can command."[3] Coming from a less sympathetic position, J. W. Kaye intended to chide the "thousands of women who . . . lie softly, and live delicately, and fare sumptuously every day, without stretching forth a hand to attain for themselves the means of enjoyment. . . . Their only necessity is to be comely and amiable." Kaye, writing in the *North British Review* (1857), deplored the "false conventional notion . . . that to be useful is to be 'unfeminine,' " an idea which he felt inhibited women from indulging their "desires and faculties for better things, and for larger work."[4]

While it was certainly true that noblewomen and ladies were consumers, rather than producers, of goods and services, it was not the case that they were actually idle. In addition to the practice of feminine "accomplishments"—music, drawing, conversation, letter writing, etc.—aristocratic women would occupy their time with household instructions, morning calls, light reading, fashion, entertaining, or the demanding whirl of the social "Season." It was held to be their social duty to set a civilized example for the classes beneath their own. Maintaining a large household with from five to twenty-five servants, including a nanny or governess for the children, and observing the intricate etiquette of proper social behavior were elements in achieving that social purpose.[5]

Certainly, middle-class women often tried to imitate this leisured ideal, since personally undertaking household drudgery, or—even worse—accepting paid employment, meant certain loss of prestige, and sometimes presaged a decline into the ranks of the lower classes. In her study of the material culture of the Victorian middle class, Patricia Branca concluded that "no matter what her aspirations were," the *average* middle-class woman "could not afford the life of the 'perfect lady.' Most middle-class women were probably far too absorbed in the affairs of the house and caring for their husbands and children to worry about an image they could not attain."[6] Nevertheless, the high-status appellation of "lady" must have tantalized many socially ambitious women of the *upper* middle class.

This situation was ironic, for women writers who were themselves aristocrats often found occasion to protest against the essential emptiness of "what could be looked at as an intensely selfish way of life based on leisure, sport, dining, and entertainment."[7] For example, in her 1845 poem, "Soliloquy of a Modern Fine Lady," the Countess of Blessington described the characteristic malaise of a life composed exclusively of trivial entertainments. The poem is a catalog of complaints from a lady of leisure who takes no pleasure even in expensive clothes, fine dinners, and champagne, much less in the monotonous round of social activities she pursues every day:

> How dull it is to sit all day,
>   With nought on earth to do,

But think of concerts, balls, or routes,
  At evening to go to.
Perplex'd between a robe of pink,
  Or blue celeste, or white,
Or visits one is forced to pay,
  Or little notes to write.

How tedious in the Park to drive,
  Each day the same dull round,
And see the stupid visages
  That there are always found. . . .

How wearying at night to drive
  To op'ra, route, or ball,
And find the last is sure to be
  The dullest scene of all;
Then tired and cross, at last return
  To home, with aching head,
And quarrel with one's yawning maid,
  Before one gets to bed.

The import of this poem is ambiguous: does it mean to attack the social system which condemned upper-class women to dull and tedious lives? Or does it mean to expose the personal vacuity of women who accepted such lives for themselves? Perhaps the speaker of the poem is a newly made "fine lady" bragging about her status by asserting how unimpressed she is, while actually savoring her leisure to be bored. But the concluding lines seem rather to suggest a straightforward reading of the poem, by the genuine sense of hopelessness they convey:

Then wake next morn at half-past twelve,
  All languid and deprest,
And know that each succeeding day
  Will dull be as the rest.[8]

"Soliloquy of a Modern Fine Lady" represents the potential impact upon women of lives without active interest or useful work: boredom and depression.

For herself, Lady Blessington rejected this empty existence in favor of somewhat scandalous relationships with important men (Lord Byron, Count D'Orsay, Walter Savage Landor, and others); the maintenance of a drawing-room salon, of which Charles Greville reported in 1839, "There is no end to the men of consequence who go there occasionally. . . . All the *minor* poets, *lite-*

rati, and journalists without exception . . . ";[9] and, of course, her writing and editing activities, by which she supported herself and her household for about fifteen years. William Jerdan estimated that Lady Blessington made between £2,000 and £3,000 a year from her various novels, travelogues, poems, editorships, etc. Thus, "she must certainly have been the most highly paid woman in the country, apart from eminent courtesans."[10]

Aside from creating a more stimulating intellectual environment for herself, as Lady Blessington did, an upper-class woman might also engage in church activities, politics, "poor-peopling" (as Florence Nightingale called it), or writing. These last two activities—philanthropy and letters—upper-class ladies traditionally adopted as their own special province. More often than not, however, being under no necessity and without real training or power, they pursued "benevolence" in a dilettantish and ineffectual manner. At least that was the perception of such diverse social critics as Coventry Patmore and Frances Cobbe.[11] Many upper-class women may have never engaged in any "useful" activity at all, though they were constantly being urged to do so by the clergy and by the press. Into the acceptable category of "good works" fell such activities as personal financial patronage in the manner of "Lady Bountiful," donation of time or money to organized charities, workhouse visiting, distribution of religious tracts among the poor, provision of adequate and sanitary housing for the working classes, establishment and supervision of "ragged schools" or reform institutions, and even practical participation in the Christian Socialist activities of Charles Kingsley and F. D. Maurice. Later, activities such as these, practiced diligently by middle-class women, created the respectable profession of social work.

The consolation of philanthropy earnestly pursued is the theme of *The Lady of La Garaye* (1861) by Caroline Norton. The heroine, a young county gentlewoman and a recent joyful bride, is, apparently, overly "bold," for she is "pleased to share the manlier sports," such as horseback riding, with her husband. Consequently, she suffers a terrible accident one day, while jumping her horse across a dangerous canyon in imitation of her husband. The accident cripples her and renders her a pain-ridden invalid for life; even motherhood is no longer possible. Her previously ideal relationship with her husband falters, and he blames himself for encouraging the unfeminine behavior which precipitated the accident. Near despair, the couple turn first to religion and then to philanthropy. As they direct their attention and energies away from their own suffering and toward the succor of the poor, sick, and ignorant of La Garaye, they begin to recover their belief in life's value.

The wife develops the strength to perform the duties of nurse and teacher, and the pair earn the love and esteem of the entire region for their generous, outer-directed lives. Looking back, the heroine recognizes that her past life of leisure had been "thoughtless and thankless,"[12] leaving her no inner resources and wasting all her boldness and vitality in mere sport. Despite her invalidism, she is now happier and more useful in her pursuit of good works than she ever was in her self-centered enjoyment of leisure. Poems like *The Lady of La Garaye* clearly aimed to impress upper-class women with both the responsibility and the rewards of philanthropy.

As for humane letters, despite a certain amount of ridicule, intellectual women in the eighteenth century had won toleration among the upper classes. Writing for money became an exception to the upper-class "ban on paid employment," although, of course, "many who wrote for publication . . . did so under pseudonyms, or signed their work simply 'By a Lady,' " in order to avoid embarrassment.[13] Also, because the prevailing double standard of literary criticism condemned women's poetry and prose to less serious intellectual consideration than men's, nineteenth-century women writers (both upper and middle class) frequently published anonymously or under male pseudonyms.[14]

Aside from literary endeavors and "good works," which were by no means engaged in by all, the life of a nineteenth-century lady was chiefly characterized by social obligations and leisure until very late in the century, when the class structure of England began to lose some of its rigidity. In those relatively few poems which focused upon the daily activities of aristocratic women's lives, women poets generally praised pursuing rewarding activities such as authorship and philanthropy and deplored limiting one's life to a tiresome and trivial social round.

THE MIDDLE CLASSES

Meanwhile, without the rank appropriate for participation in the London social scene or the wealth necessary for the effective pursuit of philanthropy or the influence requisite for a voice in national politics, many middle- and upper-middle-class girls doubtless found the prescribed life of prestigious idleness either frustrating or stultifying. Edward Carpenter reported that in the mid-Victorian period "The life, and with it the character, of the ordinary 'young lady' . . . was tragic in its emptiness." Why?

> Girls were growing up with but one idea in life, that of taking their "proper place in society." A few meager accomplishments—plentiful balls and dinner-parties, theatres and concerts—and to loaf up and down the parade, criticizing each other, were the means to bring about this desirable result. . . . My six sisters had absolutely nothing to do except dabble in paints and music as aforesaid, and wander aim-

lessly from room to room to see if by any chance "anything was going on." . . . More than once girls of whom I least expected it told me that their lives were miserable "with nothing on earth to do." Multiply this picture by thousands and hundreds of thousands all over the country, and it is easy to see how, when the causes of the misery were understood, it led to the powerful growth of the modern "Women's Movement."[15]

Barbara Bodichon, one of the leaders of that movement, urged young women to refuse this empty life: "Arouse yourselves! Awake! Be the best that God has made you. Do not be contented to be charming and fascinating; be noble, be useful, be wise."[16] But it would have been extremely difficult for powerless and passive young women to make such a major social change all on their own.

One woman poet who recognized the tenacious grip of boredom and triviality on middle-class women's lives was Augusta Webster. In "Tired" (1870), an unusually perceptive husband of the "better classes" reflects upon the vacuity of his wife's existence:

> . . . that round
> of treadmill ceremonies, mimic tasks,
> we make our women's lives—Good heavens what work
> to set the creatures to, whom we declare
> God purposed for companions to us men. . . .
> So much to do among us, and we spend
> so many human souls on only this![17]

"Tired" is a poem on the Pygmalion theme: the husband has married somewhat beneath himself, hoping to educate a rough country girl to become something better than a woman of "society." He has failed, because, as he now realizes, he is himself so conscious of etiquette and status that he never allowed his wife the latitude to become otherwise than his peers. In other words, even those who deplored women's laziness and frivolity did not often choose to rend the social fabric in order to alter the situation that perpetuated these failings.

For the middle-class woman who was compelled to work for her living—whether a spinster, a widow, or perhaps a victim of her father's financial ruin—only a few occupations were within the bounds of respectability. Three which were acceptable because they had upper-class counterparts were lady's companion, social worker, and artist. Of these three, only the profession of artist appears in women's poetry, where it is in fact a favorite, frequently recurring theme.

The successful woman artist in the nineteenth century was most frequently a writer. Though of course women also made valuable contributions in the fields of music and the visual arts, female genius in those areas generally went unrecognized.[18] In 1841 the *Edinburgh Review* pointed out that music and drawing were part of nearly every educated girl's curriculum, and that these vocations were pursued as professions by many English women. "Yet where are the great names?" asked the *Edinburgh Review*. "There have been many men whose names will live as painters and composers of music. . . . We cannot name one [woman] whose title to such distinction would be ratified by the public voice."[19] This state of affairs with regard to women's achievements in the arts and their appreciation by the public did not change very much before the twentieth century; reasons for its persistence are still being clarified by feminist historians,[20] but women's poetry does offer some explanation.

Two poems about woman as singer will illuminate a few of the factors contributing to women artists' general obscurity. In "The Singer," Dora Greenwell states that the sources of true art, whether musical, visual, or poetical, are anguish, conflict, and strife—experiences which most middle-class women set out to avoid. Her heroine is a gifted vocalist whose musical inspiration is a failed love affair. The particular conflict Greenwell defines is between marriage and career, the ambitious artist and the womanly woman. The singer's triumph is bittersweet, for she has it only by renunciation of marriage and motherhood, a sacrifice many nineteenth-century women were understandably reluctant to make. As for poetry, the melancholy strain of women's verse could be explained, Greenwell theorized, by the unhappiness of the composers' personal lives: "These are not only Songs they sing, / They are the Singer's life!"[21] The woman artist's power and virtuosity generally flourished only in the absence of marital success; thus, the competing demands and attractions of the domestic ideal undoubtedly inhibited many talented young women in the nineteenth century from pursuing true artistic excellence.

George Eliot's dramatic poem *Armgart* (1870) examines the clash of personal, social, and career values which sorely troubled the artistic woman of nineteenth-century England.[22] Eliot had read and greatly admired Elizabeth Barrett Browning's important verse novel *Aurora Leigh* (1856), which dealt with the same issues from the perspective of the woman poet.[23] However, Eliot's heroine is not a writer, but, like Greenwell's, a gifted musician: a singer. Armgart is motivated by pride, ambition, passion, even rage. Her self-concept is inflated, her identity as an artist unshakeable, and her ego strength supreme. Armgart when we first meet her completely contradicts the meek and self-effacing ideal of Victorian womanhood. She and her suitor Graf Dornberg quarrel at length about her goals and achievements, with the Graf expressing sentiments akin to Ruskin's in *Of Queens' Gardens* or Tennyson's in *The Princess*.

GRAF: A woman's rank
    Lies in the fulness of her womanhood:
    Therein alone she is royal.
ARMGART: Yes, I know
    The oft-taught Gospel: "Woman, thy desire
    Shall be that all superlatives on earth
    Belong to men, save the one highest kind—
    To be a mother. Thou shalt not desire
    To do aught best save pure subservience:
    Nature has willed it so!" O blessed Nature!
    Let her be arbitress; she gave me voice
    Such as she only gives a woman child,
    Best of its kind, gave me ambition too. . . .
GRAF: Pain had been saved,
    Nay, purer glory reached, had you been throned
    As woman only, holding all your art
    As tribute to that dear sovereignty—
    Concentering your power in home delights
    Which penetrate and purify the world.
ARMGART: What! leave the opera with my part ill-sung
    While I was warbling in a drawing-room?
    . . . I am an artist by my birth—
    By the same warrant that I am a woman:
    Nay, in the added rarer gift I see
    Supreme vocation: if a conflict comes,
    Perish—no, not the woman, but the joys
    Which men make narrow by their narrowness.
    Oh, I am happy! . . . I have room
    To breathe and grow unstunted.[24]

Armgart rejects Graf Dornberg's suit, unwilling to compromise and confident in her ability to live without love but not to live without her singing.

Though she may be admirable for her defiance of conventional limits, her musical genius, and her certainty of self, Armgart is also revealed in succeeding scenes as a terrible egotist: arrogant, selfish, and exploitative of her family and friends. When an illness permanently damages her voice, she threatens suicide, disdaining to live " 'The Woman's Lot: A Tale of Everyday' " (p. 111).

ARMGART: I can do nought
    Better than what a million women do—
    Must drudge among the crowd and feel my life
    Beating upon the world without response,
    Beating with passion through an insect's horn

    That moves a millet-seed laboriously.
    If I *would* do it!
WALPURGA (coldly):   And why should you not?

(p. 113)

Walpurga's interruption is the turning point in the poem and in Armgart's understanding of life. A spinster cousin, a plain, lame girl with no prospects, Walpurga has for years devoted herself to Armgart's happiness and career, a sacrifice the singer has accepted without gratitude and almost without notice. Now Walpurga at last confronts Armgart with the selfishness of her relationships with others and the arrogance of her individual rebellion against the feminine condition.

WALPURGA: Are you no longer chartered, privileged,
    But sunk to simple woman's penury,
    To ruthless Nature's chary average—
    Where is the rebel's right for you alone?
    Noble rebellion lifts a common load;
    But what is he who flings his own load off
    And leaves his fellows toiling? Rebel's right?
    Say rather, the deserter's. . . .
                    Now, then, you are lame—
    Maimed, as you said, and levelled with the crowd:
    Call it new birth—birth from the monstrous Self
    Which, smiling down upon a race oppressed,
    Says, "All is good, for I am throned at ease."

(pp. 116, 119)

Armgart finally recognizes the loveless quality of her life of pure striving. Whereas the singer triumphant could not respond to the pleas of a lover, the woman humbled can absorb the criticism of a "sister." Henceforth, she vows to take up that dreaded burden of "woman's lot" and to repay Walpurga in kind for her years of devotion and service. George Eliot humbled the prideful Armgart not for her striving, but for her lovelessness and conceit. As Patricia Meyer Spacks has noted, "The puzzle of how power relates to love in a woman's experience is central to the dilemma of the woman as artist."[25] For George Eliot, the reconciliation of love with power (in the form of ambition and fame) is difficult and tenuous, but it is necessary to an ethical life.

    Besides the classic problem of marriage and career, *Armgart* takes up a number of other complex issues in the life of the woman of genius. How far do her rights as an artist extend? What does she owe to her friends and family and to other women? When do the "masculine" characteristics essential to success impinge too much upon her "feminine" self? To be a woman artist in the nineteenth century was to walk a tightrope between the demands of society and the demands of the self. Few women achieved the satisfying compromise which George Eliot both recommended in her art and approximated in her life. *Armgart* is the tragic story of a woman who perceived the necessity of doing so only after the opportunity had passed.

The career of a woman singer was less hampered by critical reluctance to acknowledge female achievement than that of a woman writer, as the adulation of the great opera star Jenny Lind clearly demonstrates.[26] Armgart explains, "The great masters write / For women's voices, and great Music wants me! . . . / Men did not say, when I had sung last night, / ' 'Twas good, nay, wonderful, considering / She is a woman' " (pp. 89, 87). The female authorship of Eliot's own highly acclaimed *Adam Bede* came as a shock to male critics, who were accustomed to condescend to "lady novelists" and "female poets."[27]

However, even despite the patronizing double standard of literary criticism, it was impossible in the nineteenth century to overlook the obvious competence, popularity, and talent of the many professional women writers in England. In the publication of history, biography, stories, novels, essays, journalism, and poetry, women were prolific and successful. Some who took up writing because of a financial crisis soon found they were able to support themselves and their entire families through their earnings.

Despite her growing visibility in society, the literary woman appeared as a character only occasionally in nineteenth-century poetry and fiction. While the male Romantic poets, for instance, were interested in the poet as visionary, they showed little or no literary interest in either the "poetess" or the writer (of either gender) as journeyman. When the figure of the poet or other artist appears in Victorian poetry written by men, it generally continues in the Romantic tradition of sublimity, as in Tennyson's "The Poet," or, if represented somewhat more realistically, as in Robert Browning's "Fra Lippo Lippi," resides in a male consciousness.

Women poets generally refrained from depicting the woman writer as the working professional she usually was and emphasized instead the nobility and responsibility of her calling. In doing so, they probably hoped to enhance public respect for their work by affiliating themselves with elevated nineteenth-century ideas about the function of poetry. They may also have hoped to deflect public criticism of themselves for being engaged in hard work and interested in earning money for it, since, as we have seen, this was barely acceptable behavior for women.

Of course, there were some exceptions to the general neglect or evasion of the subject of writing as an occupation. For example, Eliza Cook noted with

envy the difference between the natural mellifluousness of the nightingale and
the constraints and aggravations of the human songbird.

> I'll wish he had to *write* his song
>   Beneath a midnight taper;
> On pittance that would scarcely pay
>   for goose quill, ink, and paper;
> And then, to crown his misery,
>   and break his heart in splinters,
> I'll wish he had to see his proofs,
>   his publishers and printers.[28]

And Frances Havergal in 1873 acknowledged the hard work and the renunciation of leisure involved in composition: "I sat alone in my shadowy
room, / And worked away in its quiet gloom, / And the Robins flew
away."[29] However, women poets more often used the figure of the female
poet to express their ideas about art and the artist than to complain about the
social conditions and prejudices that hampered women writers in general.

Letitia Landon was the nineteenth-century woman poet who was most prolific on the subject of the poetess. As a very young woman, Landon received
so much praise for her juvenile poetry that she never fully exchanged her early
facility with verse making and make-believe for mature artistic discipline and
conversance with real life. As Ellen Moers says, young women poets are particularly vulnerable to "early spoiling," because "their verses lead them into
recitation, a performance which brings them the sort of praise that tends to
flatter their charms rather than refine their compositions."[30] In Landon's case,
"the pernicious action of spurious praise"[31] was to encourage her to conceive
of poetry as a spontaneous, improvisatory act rather than as a conscious discipline. Consequently, she produced in rapid succession a number of Romantic
verse narratives depicting the woman poet as *The Improvisatrice* (1824) or *The
Troubadour* (1825).

Each of her woman poets, inevitably associated with the lute or the lyre, is
the same "sensitive soul," as Lionel Stevenson puts it, "blasted by the rude
touch of the common world . . . with Byron's violence and 'Satanism' toned
down to a sweet ladylike pathos."[32] A characteristic example, from *The
Troubadour*, is the "pale maid, who, mute, / Dreaming of song leant o'er her
lute," then began singing in Landon's own voice:

> It was a low and silver tone,
> And very sad, like sorrow's own;
> She sang of love as it will be,
> And has been in reality,—

Of fond hearts broken and betray'd,
Of roses opening but to fade,
Of wither'd hope, and wasted bloom,
Of the young warrior's early tomb,
And the while her dark mournful eye
Held with her words deep sympathy.[33]

In "The History of the Lyre," Landon asserted that these "mournful notes" served an important social purpose:

To purify, refine, exalt, subdue,
To touch the selfish and to shame the vain
Out of themselves, by gentle mournfulness,
Or chords that rouse some aim of enterprise
Lofty and pure, and meant for general good.[34]

Unfortunately, in much of her verse, the sublime effect she intended was undermined by triteness, sentimentality, and posturing.

Lady Blessington undoubtedly had Landon in mind when she published, in 1833, "Stock in Trade of Modern Poetesses."

Lonely shades, and murm'ring founts;
Limpid streams, and azure mounts. . . .
Wither'd hopes, and faded flowers;
Broken harps, and untuned lyres;
Lutes neglected, unquenched fires . . .
Bursting tear and endless sigh—
Query, can she tell us why?[35]

Indeed, the bulk of Landon's work betrayed, even to her contemporaries, a serious lack of authenticity. In 1841, three years after her death, Laman Blanchard brought out The Life and Literary Remains of L.E.L., containing this revealing, previously unpublished fragment:

Oh! what a waste of feeling and of thought
Have been the imprints on my roll of life!
What worthless hours! To what use have I turned
The golden gifts which are my hope and pride?
My power of song, unto how base a use
Has it been put!

The concluding lines represent Landon's own belated recognition of her mediocrity as a poet and of the ironic reason for it: "Alas! that ever / Praise should have been what praise has been to me— / The opiate of the mind."[36]

Other women poets—especially those of later generations—were less naive than Landon was about the requisites of good poetry. Frances Havergal linked the criterion of authenticity with the recognition of writing as a difficult, demanding process. Making poetry is both "agony and bliss":

> Poetry is not a trifle,
>   Lightly thought and lightly made;
> Not a fair and scentless flower,
> Gaily cultured for an hour,
>   Then as gaily left to fade.
>
> . . . .
>
> 'Tis the essence of existence,
>   Rarely rising to the light;
> And the songs that echo longest,
> Deepest, fullest, truest, strongest,
>   With your life-blood you will write.[37]

Furthermore, Havergal believed, even at its best poetry will not be truly autobiographical, truly revelatory. It is art, not life, and writers can only hope to "cut little pieces out of their lives / And join them together. . . . / Though little enough of the life survives."[38]

> You will only give a transcript
>   Of a life-line here and there . . .
> Still, if you but copy truly,
>   'Twill be poetry indeed.[39]

Mary Coleridge also insisted on the necessity of poetic integrity, which she opposed against the forces of conventionality. Yet she, too, expressed misgivings:

> Narrow not thy walk to keep
> Pace with those who, half asleep,
>   Judge thee now . . .
> Only this one thing fulfil,
> Thine own heart's tremendous will.
>   Ay, but how?[40]

Katherine Bradley and Edith Cooper thought they had found their answer in a shared dedication to their art and to one another. Sometime around 1880, before the publication of their first volume, *Poems by Arran and Isla Leigh*, they made a mutual commitment to love and poetry.

It was deep April, and the morn
   Shakespeare was born.
My love and I took hands and swore
   Against the world, to be
Poets and lovers evermore.[41]

Subsequently, as "Michael Field," they blended their talents and energies almost beyond the possibility of separate critical analysis.

    . . . our souls so knit,
I leave a page half-writ—
The work begun
Will be to heaven's conception done,
If she come to it.[42]

Katherine Bradley and Edith Cooper considered themselves "closer married" than even Elizabeth and Robert Browning, whom they knew.[43] Bradley and Cooper's personal and professional relationship was unhampered by nineteenth-century role expectations for masculine and feminine behavior in courtship and marriage. But their choice was not available to most women writers. Even though some, like Charlotte Brontë for instance, considered or even yearned for such an arrangement, the power of social norms and sanctions prevented most women from making a primary commitment to another woman.[44]

For, of course, the middle-class woman was expected to marry and, once married, to subordinate her talents and interests to those of her husband. Here is Sarah Stickney Ellis' pronouncement on the subject: "In the case of a highly-gifted woman, even where there is an equal or superior degree of talent possessed by her husband, nothing can be more injudicious, or more fatal to her happiness, than an exhibition even of the least disposition to presume upon such gifts."[45] "*My* idea of a perfect woman," one man wrote in the *Leader* in 1850, "is one who can write, but won't."[46]

Perhaps in response to attitudes like these, nineteenth-century women poets wrote prolifically on the conflict between love and fame, especially early in the century. Jane Taylor's "Love and Fame," for example, depicts a young woman weighing the advantages and disadvantages of both. Love offers "pains and sighs" but promises a secure old age, while Fame talks of "glory" and "sway" and warns that Love may "laugh and leave her."

The maiden, wearied with debate,
   Arrests the fierce contention;
One anxious moment does but wait,
   In agonized suspension—

> Then urged by doubt, by pride, by shame,
> She sighed, and gave her hand to Fame.[47]

Jane Taylor was one of the few women poets to opt for fame in her poetry on this theme. Most agreed with the opinion Felicia Hemans expressed in "Woman and Fame":

> Happy—happier far than thou,
> With the laurel on thy brow;
> She that makes the humblest hearth
> Lovely but to one on earth.
>
> . . . .
>
> Fame, Fame! thou canst not be the stay
>   Unto the drooping reed,
> The cool fresh fountain in the day
>   Of the soul's feverish need:
> Where must the lone one turn or flee?—
> Not unto thee, oh! not to thee![48]

Nearly identical sentiments can be found throughout the poetry of Letitia Landon and Caroline Norton. In "The Poet's Choice," Norton even depicts a woman cheerfully abandoning a promising career as a poet for the contentment of a happy marriage, implying that had her own marriage been satisfying to her, she might never have become a writer.[49]

The most complex of the century's short poems focusing on this theme was probably Felicia Hemans' "Properzia Rossi," which contains a fuller statement of the sentiments she expressed in "Woman and Fame." Properzia Rossi is not a writer, but rather a celebrated female sculptor. Dying of unrequited love, she soliloquizes at length while carving one last sculpture to present to the object of her affections. The poem may be regarded as somewhat autobiographical: Felicia Hemans' husband abandoned her and his five sons after six years of marriage and settled alone in Italy, ostensibly "for the sake of his health."[50]

> —Tell me no more, no more
> Of my soul's lofty gifts! Are they not vain
> To quench its haunting thirst for happiness?
> Have I not loved, and striven, and fail'd to bind
> One true heart unto me, whereon my own
> Might find a resting place, a home for all
> Its burden of affections? I depart,
> Unknown, tho' Fame goes with me. . . .

The difference between the poet and her heroine is the difference between reality and romance: Properzia Rossi dies, and Felicia Hemans establishes a comfortable literary career.

The chief interest in "Properzia Rossi" lies less in its treatment of love and fame than in its consideration of the woman artist's relation to her work. The sculptor complains that her artistic power is fruitless since it cannot win love. Yet it also provides a "sudden joy" in all her loneliness and a sense of her own immortality. With exhilaration she watches the bas-relief of Ariadne take shape beneath her hand, investing it with her own anguish and carving it in her own form. The passage which describes this act of artistic creation seems also to express Hemans' theory of poetic creation.

> The bright work grows
> Beneath my hand, unfolding, as a rose,
> Leaf after leaf, to beauty; line by line,
> I fix my thought, heart, soul, to burn, to shine,
> Thro' the pale marble's veins. It grows—and now
> I give my own life's history to thy brow,
> Forsaken Ariadne! Thou shalt wear
> My form, my lineaments; but oh! more fair,
> Touch'd into lovelier being by the glow
> Which in me dwells, as by the summer-light
> All things are glorified.

Here are the organicism and spontaneity of Romantic art, as well as the self-revelation and the transmutation of experience into beauty.

From this movement, the poem recedes into plaintiveness. Properzia laments, "Oh! I might have given / Birth to creations of far nobler thought / . . . But I have been / Too much alone."[51] On the occasion of Felicia Hemans' death, Letitia Landon eulogized her vision and her verse, but emphasized the pathos of her broken marriage.

> Was not this purchased all too dearly?—never
>   Can fame atone for all that fame hath cost. . . .
> What do we know of the unquiet pillow,
>   By the worn cheek and tearful eyelid prest. . . .
> Alas! the kingdom of the lute is lonely—
>   Cold is the worship coming from afar.[52]

The conventional belief was that women must choose between love and fame, between success in marriage and success in career, and that the greater happiness lay in the womanly destiny of home and hearth. Fortunately, such opinions were not prohibitive in their effect upon women writers, partly because of the exigencies of finance and the continuing popular demand for the productions of women's pens.

Still, the idea of woman's proper sphere was pervasive and strong. It profoundly influenced the directions which women's employment was to take in the nineteenth century. Starting around 1750, the work alternatives for middle-class women became fewer and fewer, as the province of women gradually narrowed from the "world" to the "home."[53] Only if it became financially necessary might a middle-class woman respectably accept paid employment, and then only if that employment was in some way an expansion of her domestic duties.

For instance, from her womanly aptitude for teaching children and supervising their activities, it was reasoned that she might honorably serve as a governess. The feminine accomplishment of needlework might be turned to a profit, especially if she could arrange to perform the job in her own home. As the natural comforter and nurse of her loved ones when they were sick, she might also become a professional nurse, especially later in the century after Florence Nightingale had made that occupation not only respectable, but very nearly sanctified. Attempts to invade the province of men, however, were seen as a violation of the natural order, a threat to the home and the family, and a challenge to the superiority, authority, and dignity of husbands and fathers. Unfortunately, the few acceptable fields of occupation soon became seriously overcrowded, underpaid, and exploited through overwork. Eventual amelioration of the resulting social problems came about slowly, through the reform of existing conditions and through the eventual opening of new professional and white-collar fields to women.

The most genteel of the three "womanly" occupations was that of governess. The psychological and practical discomfort of the distressed gentlewoman turned governess has been chronicled in fiction and in fact so thoroughly that little need be said about it here.[54] The poor education which most women received hardly prepared them to function adequately as teachers, and prospective employers had no reliable way to discriminate among the many applicants for every existing job. Before long, families in the upper middle classes were acquiring, for a relatively small sum, the status symbol of an impoverished young "lady" to tutor their children.[55]

One obvious remedy was to educate and certify qualified governesses, for which purpose Queen's College was originally established (in 1852). Eventually, many graduates of women's secondary schools and colleges became not mere governesses, but, like Dorothea Beale of the North London Collegiate School and Frances Mary Buss of Cheltenham College, teachers and schoolmistresses. Thus, those women who were intellectually capable of teaching could earn an adequate income from it, and be freed from the "status incongruence" and other indignities of governessing.[56] Meanwhile, the Governesses' Benevolent Institution, founded in 1843, provided relief for destitute, aging women who had been unable to accumulate any savings on their meager salaries,[57] and who might otherwise end their lives in the workhouse or the lunatic asylum.[58]

Despite the social realities, the governess of fiction, who was customarily young, intelligent, and attractive, ordinarily remained employed just long enough to find a husband and embark on her real career: marriage. Women poets were not so enthralled with this heroine as women novelists were. Caroline Southey complained in "The Birthday" (1836) about the ineptitude of most governesses:

> —if folks at least
> Pretended to teach only what they know,
> Young ladies! how especially for you
> 'Twould simplify the training! No she-Crichtons,
> No petticoat professors would engage
> To teach all 'OLOGIES and 'OGRAPHIES,
> And everything in all the world (of course
> Accomplishments included), all complete
> In all their branches. What a load of rubbish. . . .[59]

The sentimental governess heroine is noticeably absent from women's poetry.

The related figure of the woman schoolteacher also received scant attention. One of the few poems which did feature a teacher heroine was "Gladys and Her Island" (1867) by Jean Ingelow, a delightful little poem which recounts the Carrollian holiday adventures of a dreamy young woman. Gladys, herself the product of an orphan school, daily suffers the indignities of her low rank and strains against the teaching duties for which she is remarkably ill suited, being "poetical" and exuberant by temperament. Her one-day vacation becomes a fantasy journey through history, nature, and poetry, made real through the magic of Gladys' imagination. The idyllic imaginary island and its inhabitants satisfy her yearnings for affection, companionship, adventure, and encouragement. During the course of the day, she explores the shimmering natural beauty of the island, stumbles in and out of the Garden of Eden, and speaks with such diverse personages as Isis, Evangeline, Miranda, and a fairy mother and her two daughters. Most of the figures she meets are female—projections of herself or of her unknown mother and sisters—and they "murmur certain thoughts / Which seemed to be like echoes of her own."[60] In one passage, voices from Parnassus offer this bracing advice about the rewards of human work:

> . . . who care
> Only to quit a calling, will not make
> The calling what it might be: who despise
> Their work, fate laughs at, and doth let the work
> Dull and degrade them.

(p. 323)

As the day draws to a close, Gladys bids farewell to the kingdom of her imagination and returns to school, fortified for her tasks by her one-day respite:

> . . . and her dames
> Were weary and right hard to please; but she
> Felt like a beggar suddenly endowed
> With a warm cloak to 'fend her from the cold.
> "For, come what will," she said, "I had *to-day*.
> There is an island."

(p. 326)

Immediately follows "The Moral," a hundred lines or so of discourse upon the advantages of a poetical temperament, even to women like Gladys, trapped in inappropriate jobs by poverty and by the scarcity of other opportunities. The poem concludes "with a word to the nobler sex":

> . . . we pray you set your pride
> In its proper place, and never be ashamed
> Of any honest calling—let us add,
> And end; for all the rest, hold up your heads
> And mind your English.

(p. 328)

A second over-filled and unappealing "honest calling" for nineteenth-century Englishwomen was that of seamstress. The needlewoman (a generic term including piece-workers, plain sewers, milliners, laceworkers, and dressmakers) was in even worse circumstances than the governess. Since the garment industry was seasonal, she sometimes worked twenty-hour days under appalling conditions for wages so low that she could not sustain herself and her dependents.[61] By 1843, the report of the Children's Employment Commission had brought the distressing situation of the seamstresses of England fully before the public. Sickness, blindness, and early death were often the rewards of this employment. According to *Eliza Cook's Journal*, many of the large millinery and dress-making establishments were said "to kill a girl a year."[62]

Thomas Hood's famous poem "The Song of the Shirt," which appeared in *Punch* in December of 1843, vividly depicted the plight of the thousands of women "Sewing at once, with a double thread, / A Shroud as well as a Shirt" (31–32). A few months later, Hood published "The Lady's Dream," placing the blame for the seamstresses' misery on upper-class ladies whose caprice and thoughtlessness in ordering dresses often forced their impoverished sisters to labor all night.

Caroline Norton made the same point in *The Child of the Islands* (1845), contrasting the joyless life and early death of the seamstress with the self-indulgence and unconcern of the fashion plate. The seamstress:

> Earning scant bread, that finds no appetite,
> The sapless life she toils for, lingers on;
> And when at length it sinks in dreary night,
> A shallow, careless grave is dug,—where none
> Come round to bless her rest, whose ceaseless tasks are done.

The fashion plate:

> Onward she moves, in Fashion's magic glass,
> Half-strut, half-swim, she slowly saunters by:
> A self-delighting, delicate, pampered mass
> Of flesh indulged in every luxury
> Folly can crave, or riches can supply. . . .
> Careless of all conditions but her own,
> She sweeps that stuff along, to curtsey to the throne.[63]

Of course, the real responsibility for the seamstresses' plight lay with the readiness of English society to countenance employers' exploitation of their women workers. Despite the establishment of a relief association in 1843, and despite continuing exposés by government investigators, the sweated conditions of needlework prevailed to the end of the century—forcing numerous women out of the middle class altogether.

E. Nesbit's "In Praise of Work," published in 1888, depicts an overworked, lower-class laborer and his seamstress wife on one of their four annual holidays: Whit-Monday. The title of the poem is ironic, for the man is well aware of their exploited condition.

> Work, work, still work! It's always the cry,
> Work if you'd live, and work till you die;
> Work for your masters, they who sit
> And idly taste the sweet fruits of it;

> Work when they bid you—and thank them, too,
> If they'll only give you the work to do.

The wife's health is rapidly deteriorating from the unreasonable demands of her job. Her husband sadly assures her, "You have not much longer to work, my sweet"; death will free her before long. Of course, neither the careful diction and grammar of the speaker nor the romantic nature of his relationship with his wife was a particularly accurate reflection of lower-class reality; rather, they must be understood as poetical strategies that enabled Nesbit's middle-class readers to identify with their fellow human beings in distress.

The husband/speaker concludes with a threat born of frustration and rage: "God—hold our hand on the reckoning day, / Lest all we owe them we should repay!"[64] Such poems of social protest, along with numerous popular novels about milliners faced with the awful choice between starvation and "vice," became an established literary tradition during the nineteenth-century's long exploitation of seamstresses. Although they succeeded in keeping the deplorable conditions of needleworkers before the public consciousness, these sympathetic representations of women workers nevertheless failed to effect any concrete social or economic reforms. It has even been suggested that too frequent repetition of the plight of the poor seamstress in popular literature and art served to "deaden the impact" of the message—to allow Victorians to exorcise through a sentimental response the pity that might otherwise have moved them to ameliorative action.[65]

Women engaged in nursing were more fortunate than either governesses or seamstresses. Thanks to Florence Nightingale, whose work during the Crimean War was greatly admired by the public, nursing underwent professionalization the most easily and rapidly of all middle-class occupations for women. The nurse began to appear in fiction as a ministering angel, reflecting the public image of "The Lady with the Lamp." Somewhat surprisingly, women poets showed virtually no interest in the professional nurse as a poetical figure. Neither did they write about woman as medical doctor, although by the mid-1870s it had become possible for a few English women to study and practice medicine. Indeed, the female physician, having invaded a masculine profession, was seldom featured in fiction or poetry, by men or by women, even toward the end of the century.

Because so few acceptable employment opportunities existed for middle-class women, there was much agitation for the opening of appropriate male occupations such as clerk, typist, telegraphist, printer, shop assistant, watchmaker, and hairdresser. Some feminists wanted to see *all* occupations thrown open to women, asserting that there was little danger of women succeeding in any field for which they really were unsuited. Opposition was based on the "natural division of labor" and the doctrine of "woman's sphere," both of which relegated women exclusively to work associated with domesticity. It was feared that working would cause middle-class women to lose their femininity and neglect their families, and would threaten men's jobs or wage levels.

An important and influential group of feminists, the "Ladies of Langham Place,"[66] contended that allowing women to work outside the home would improve, not subvert, both the family and society at large, and appealed to traditional British compassion and sense of fair play and to the doctrine of *laissez faire*. They established the *English Woman's Journal* to address women's employment problems and seek solutions, organized the Society for Promoting the Employment of Women, and lobbied for women's rights in the Association for the Promotion of Social Science. By the turn of the century middle-class women had made inroads in gaining respectable employment in the various fields just mentioned and in others besides, although of course their wages and working conditions were (and are) still unsatisfactory.

Patricia Thomson found in her study of the Victorian heroine that the image of the working woman underwent a significant change during the second half of the century. "It was only a matter of time before the democratic doctrines regarding women and work, which from 1857 onwards were so sturdily upheld and widely circulated, made their full impact upon fiction. So that . . . we find . . . some twenty years later, in Grant Allen's novel—A Typewriter Girl composedly filling the role of novel-heroine."[67] In nineteenth-century poetry, on the other hand, the middle-class working woman was depicted less often, perhaps because her occupation, as opposed to her relationships or her personal qualities, was not considered a particularly poetical—or sentimental—subject.

THE LABORING CLASSES

Whether employed in agriculture, industry, or domestic service, nineteenth-century English workers, who were often women and children, led especially harsh lives. Although the Industrial Revolution may ultimately have improved the material quality of working-class women's lives, the period of transition from an agrarian to an industrial society was very difficult for them.

Of this period in English history, Alice Meynell later wrote, "The Lady Poverty was fair; / But she has lost her looks of late, / With change of times and change of air." The woman who used to live a pure and simple life, in stony fields under cloudless skies, has now turned "slattern," or else she "scolds in parlours, dusts and trims."[68] The once-wholesome toil of the rural poor had turned into near slavery in the modern cities. Displaced from the cottages wherein their contributions to the family income had traditionally been made, lower-class women now found themselves either out of work altogether or forced into agricultural gangs, the mills, the factories, the mines, or domestic service in town.

As for the dwindling work opportunities in agriculture, women had always worked in the fields. Suddenly, instead of working alongside their husbands for shares of the produce, they found themselves employed as day laborers or gang members. In this occupation, they might have to trudge long distances from their cottages daily just to get to work. Their wages were low and their continuous employment uncertain, so that often they failed to contribute enough to the family earnings even to ensure subsistence. By the middle of the nineteenth century, mechanization, unionization, and the conversion of much arable land to pasture were forcing women out of the rural areas and into the industrial workplace: the city. "By the end of the century, women had almost ceased to be employed as wage earners in agriculture."[69]

"Tibbie Inglis" by Mary Howitt, "Reflections" by Jean Ingelow, and "Reapers" by Mathilde Blind all contain nostalgic, idealized representations of women as agricultural workers: shepherdess, milkmaid, and field worker, respectively. "Tibbie Inglis" is a pastoral variation on the ideal-maiden theme, not an attempt to depict a working sheeptender. Tibbie's praises are sung by the swain who courts her.

> Sixteen summers had she seen,
>   A rose-bud just unsealing,
> Without sorrow, without fear,
>   In her mountain shieling.
>
> . . . .
>
> Crimson was her sunny cheek,
>   And her lips seemed moving
> With the beatings of her heart—
>   How could I help loving!

By the end of the poem, the suitor has won his bride, and the two are "happy ever after,"[70] quite a different future from the one which most rural workers were facing in the nineteenth century.

Ingelow's poem is reminiscent of Howitt's. The male speaker stands by a gate observing a milkmaid at her work and is so charmed that he falls in love.

> I saw reflected yesterday
>   A maiden with a milking-pail.

There, neither slowly nor in haste,
One hand upon her slender waist,
   The other lifted to her pail,
She, rosy in the morning light,
Among the water-daisies white,
   Like some fair sloop appeared to sail.

Against her ankles as she trod,
The lucky buttercups did nod.
   I leaned upon the gate to see:
The sweet thing looked, but did not speak;
A dimple came in either cheek,
   And all my heart was gone from me.

By the end of this poem, the speaker has won a kiss from the "rosebud lips" of the graceful milkmaid.[71] Like "Tibbie Inglis," "Reflections" is an idyllic, pastoral treatment of the ideal English girl.

By contrast, in Mathilde Blind's "Reapers" the speaker is more objective, the tone less romantic; yet "Reapers," too, is picturesque rather than realistic.

Sun-tanned men and women, toiling there together;
   Seven I count in all, in yon field of wheat,
Where the rich ripe ears in the harvest weather
   Glow an orange gold through the sweltering heat.[72]

These sun-bronzed field workers most resemble the women whose displacement Meynell lamented in "The Lady Poverty." Toiling rhythmically alongside the men—probably their husbands—they are anachronistic figures. For a truly realistic depiction of the hardships endured by female agricultural workers in the nineteenth century, one must look to fiction, where Thomas Hardy's Tess Durbeyfield is one of the last such figures in English literature.

Conditions in the various branches of industry which women entered were little better. Women (and children) often worked more than eighty hours a week in conditions which were unsanitary, unsafe, and unhealthy. In the cotton mills they might inhale fluff all day, which precipitated early respiratory disease. In the factories, their clothing or hair would sometimes catch in the unfenced machinery, and they would be mangled or scalped. Overseers sometimes insisted that the women have sexual relations with them or lose their jobs. In the mining industry, women who were pregnant continued as drawers in the coal-pits until they miscarried or gave birth in the damp, dark mines. The wages women received for this kind of risk and toil were inadequate even to provide for elementary dietary needs or child care.

After government investigations in 1833 and 1842 brought these facts to light, reformers concentrated either on relieving the terrible working conditions and bolstering the low wages or on forcing the women out of employment. To this end, numerous poems presented in the most graphic terms the squalor and misery of English factory workers' lives. Women poets were in the vanguard of this assault on poverty and industrial exploitation; they were especially distressed by the plight of very young children banished to the factories as soon as they were physically able to go. Caroline Norton's *A Voice from the Factories* (1836) emphasized the pathos of "the pale children of the Poor, . . . / Debarred of summer-light and cheerful play," and forced to go instead "To that receptacle for dreary woe, / The Factory Mill."[73] Mary Howitt's "The Rich and the Poor" (1838) described an encounter between a rich woman and a ten-year-old factory girl. The child is of "sunken eye and thin pale face, / And body dry and lean," and when the factory bell rings, she starts and runs away, "A frightened, toiling thing of care, / Into the toiling swarm."[74] The condition of adult women in the factories was also represented in women's poems, though with less emphasis than given to the children.

The combined force of government investigations and of the public outrage expressed in poems such as these produced a series of reforms that succeeded with women factory workers where they had failed with needlewomen. After 1843, women were prohibited entirely from working underground in the mines. The Factory Acts of 1833, 1842, 1847, and 1850 reduced the working day and provided for inspection of health and safety conditions. Factory women's wages rose, though not to the same levels as men's. In providing for these and other reforms, Victorians were motivated not only by the distress of the women workers themselves, but by the breakdown of the family which was attributed to the employment of married women. By allowing these women more time for housekeeping and more money for child care, it was hoped that, if they would not be persuaded to go home, at least they would be enabled to perform more successfully in their two roles, as worker and as wife and mother. In *The Child of the Islands* Norton mentions poor women's problems with housekeeping as one of the matters to which the Prince should one day turn his attention.[75]

Although the numbers of women employed in industry were great, the numbers in domestic service—an extension of traditionally female household work—were greater, swelled by the increasing supply of young women migrating from the countryside to the city. According to the 1841 census, one of every ten English women was a domestic servant.[76] By 1851 there were 905,000 female domestics, over 100,000 in London alone.[77] Ten years later, one-third of all women in London between the ages of fifteen and twenty-four were servants.[78] Nevertheless, the woman servant in women's poetry is just as much a phantom as the nurse. Jane Taylor, when she died, left the fragmentary verse narrative *Philip*, which contained a representation of a domestic servant, Peggy, as a sensible woman and a faithful friend to her male employer; but the poem was never completed.[79] Aside from *Philip*, it is difficult to locate a single poem in which a female domestic is even a recognizably human character, let alone a heroine.

Both the rapid turnover rate of domestics and the obvious class barriers between them and their employers doubtless contributed to the apparent detachment of women writers from women servants. And as Marion Glastonbury says, "Writers of all classes have a vested interest in ignoring or disguising their own dependence upon the female poor, . . . and denying the validity of [their] perceptions."[80] Deborah Gorham suggests also that middle-class writers showed more interest in "essentially marginal groups" like seamstresses (and prostitutes) because "the reformation of their condition did not imply an uncompromising challenge to the social system."[81] Women—especially writers—were not eager to sacrifice the time, energy, and money that upgrading or curtailing domestic service would have cost them.

Nevertheless, by the turn of the century, as other occupations opened up for women, middle-class households found it increasingly difficult to get and hold competent help; domestic service was a declining occupation. Furthermore, the class balance of England was shifting, so that the base of the pyramid was no longer so wide, nor were its inhabitants so thoroughly exploited. Many employed women began to resemble the middle-class career woman or homemaker of the modern day more than the downtrodden wage-slave—"mastered for life"[82]—of the past.

Nineteenth-century poets continued to depict the working-class woman (if at all) either in the social protest mode of the early Victorian age or in the pastoral mode of days gone by. Otherwise, her life seems not to have offered a particularly inviting subject for verse-making. Poetry representing the upper-class woman at work was even more rare, probably because society really didn't expect her to be working in the first place. And poetry about the middle-class woman engaged in paid work generally reflected certain conventional beliefs: that she could not perform competently except in work associated with woman's domestic vocation; that if she chose to work, she faced inevitable conflicts between work and love; and that she probably would not be in the work force at all if she could have avoided it. Some women poets accepted this paradigm and some did not; however, none ignored it entirely. Like class distinctions, it was an inescapable aspect of the culture. In depicting women at work, women writers necessarily looked to contemporary life and to their own experiences for inspiration. The ongoing social changes which were progressively widening women's "sphere" of acceptable activity and bridging the gulf of class prejudice did not pass unnoticed in women's poetry, but neither did they constitute, just yet, a new understanding of the world and woman's place in it.

8
The New Woman

The progress we have surveyed—social, political, and economic—in the lives of middle-class women, along with significant additional changes in English life in the nineteenth century, created the social and literary phenomenon popularly known as the "New Woman." Originally modelled after the 1860s generation of feminist crusaders, the New Woman herself surpassed them in many ways. Whereas her predecessors had remained cautious in their challenges to such cherished traditions as chastity, marriage, and motherhood, the so-called New Woman had, by the 1890s, become thoroughly unconventional, inside and out. As such, she represented, of course, a composite figure, a type rather than a person; she was the embodiment of ideological extremes, and she came across as sometimes a positive and sometimes a negative figure, depending upon the bias of the person describing her. Surprisingly, popular women poets by and large avoided dealing with the New Woman, for reasons we can best understand after a brief survey of the social and literary context.

The attack on marriage, which began with the Free-Love advocates (William Godwin, Mary Wollstonecraft, Percy Shelley, Charles Fourier, Robert Owen, and the Saint-Simonians) and gained momentum from John Stuart Mill and his circle, finally developed in the 1880s and 1890s into a heated public debate. Articles questioning "The Morality of Marriage" appeared and were countered by denunciations of "The Anti-Marriage League."[1] During the 1870s a spate of sensational novels by women capitalized on the new freedom of discussion about marriage and women's economic oppression and presented women characters in rebellion against these institutions, albeit still in the framework of "feminine" conventions that demanded the erring heroine's destruction.[2] Soon, even very conservative women's magazines began to take the marriage issue seriously.[3]

Finally, in 1884 and 1896, the divorce laws were twice amended in women's favor. Even so, the New Woman, believing marriage to be a kind of social prison, usually remained unmarried on principle. Sometimes she preserved her chastity, but perhaps more frequently she entered into short- or long-term liaisons, even purposely bearing children out of wedlock.[4] At the very least, her behavior and opinions with regard to sexuality and the dynamics and form of male/female relationships were unorthodox.

The New Woman's insistence on her right to sexual freedom was sustained by a combination of factors: the increasing availability of contraception, the growing social recognition of female sexuality, the gradual relaxation of strict middle-class sexual morality, and the widening influence of popular French fiction. Some of the older feminists were quite alarmed at the turn things were taking. Frances Cobbe, for one, spoke out in an effort to curb what she saw as a dangerous new tendency toward immorality among her followers:

> There are women who call themselves "emancipated" now, who are leading lives if not absolutely vicious, yet loose, unseemly, trespassing always on the borders of vice; women who treat lightly, and as if of small account, the heinous and abominable sins of unchastity and adultery.[5]

Women who thus flirted with vice were considered "fast." They might sometimes be seen wearing men's clothing, smoking, gambling, drinking, and keeping very late hours, unchaperoned and in the company of men. The scandalous reputation of George Sand was based on this kind of behavior as much as on her sexual indiscretions.

It must be remembered, however, that not all "emancipated women" chose to behave in this way. On the contrary, many were engaged in paid employment and spent their leisure in healthy physical exercise. As we have seen, it had become much easier in the last quarter of the century for middle-class women to obtain respectable jobs and thus to support themselves and to become responsible for their own lives. As the twentieth century approached, the effect of advancing technology, modernity, and mobility was to further open the job market to women. Accordingly, the education of women for economic self-dependence also continued to expand.

In recognition of women's increasingly active lives and in order to help them develop stamina and physical coordination, most schools for young women began to include in the curriculum polite forms of such games as hockey, tennis, and golf. Other kinds of hearty exercise in which women began to engage were horseback riding (side-saddle at first, of course), hiking, skating, swimming, and, most significant of all, cycling. After their appropriation of the bicycle, women "were no longer prisoners in their own houses; they could spin off, if they chose, as far as six or seven miles away; they could visit their friends, and be no longer dependent for these joys upon the convenience of the rest of the family, but only upon their own muscles."[6]

Besides fostering independence, the bicycle (and other forms of exercise) necessitated loosening and lightening the heavy, cumbersome clothing which severely restricted women's freedom of movement. A gradual change in women's fashions began. The "bloomer," a pair of Turkish trousers gathered at the ankle, which was introduced (though not designed) by Amelia Bloomer in 1851, had been a colossal failure; the public simply would not accept it.[7] However, in 1887, the "Rational Dress Society" began its crusade against stays, crinoline, high-heeled shoes, and other restrictive or unhealthy apparel. By the turn of the century, their campaign had achieved partial success in improving the average woman's wardrobe.[8] The New Woman, always ahead of the general public, could frequently be found in attire which was more sensible (and less stylish) than that recommended by fashion.

Of more importance, though, than the New Woman's spurning of the mores and morals of her day was the rationale for her refusal to acquiesce to the demands of her traditional role. As a social and literary phenomenon, the New Woman was of more than passing significance because she rejected deep-seated nineteenth-century beliefs about woman's place and woman's nature. Most fundamentally, she regarded self-fulfillment, rather than self-renunciation, as both her right and her duty. No more a "relative creature," the New Woman vowed to be self-reliant, not dependent; active, not passive; assertive, not submissive. At the risk of ridicule, she would be, in a word, "strong-minded."

This repudiation of some of the most basic tenets of nineteenth-century thought about women provoked a reaction in the press which was extreme in its rancor. Journalists reviled the New Woman as shrill and improper, immoral and irreligious, ugly and masculine. In 1883 Eliza Lynn Linton renewed her objections to the "modern girl," accusing her of sexual abnormality, and denouncing "The Epicene Sex":

> Hard, unblushing, unloving women whose ideal of happiness lies in swagger and notoriety; who hate home life and despise home virtues; who have no tender regard for men and no instinctive love for children; who despise the modesty of sex as they deny its natural fitness—these women have worse than no charm for men, and their place in the human family seems altogether a mistake.[9]

The Westminster Review countered in 1884 with a summary of the health and vigor of the "new order of women":

> The mental life of a single woman is free and untrammelled by any limits except such as are to her own advantage. Her difficulties in the way of development are only such as are common to all human beings. Her physical life is healthy and active, she retains her buoyancy and increases her nervous power if she knows how to take care of herself, and this lesson she is rapidly learning. The unmarried woman of today is a new, sturdy, and vigorous type. We find her neither the exalted ascetic nor the nerveless inactive creature of former days. She is intellectually trained and socially successful, her physique is as sound and vigorous as her mind. The world is before her. . . . [10]

By the nineties, even the *Saturday Review*, which had been hostile to women all throughout the nineteenth century,[11] began to relent, with a series of more positive articles on the New Woman, titled "Dies Dominae" (1895). Still, in periodical literature if not in fiction, the New Woman's detractors outnumbered and outshouted her supporters.

It is not difficult to understand why social critics were so intolerant. For one thing, the depiction of "fast" women in literature appeared to many to be contributing to a lamentable decadence and impurity in contemporary literature.[12] Even more important, the New Woman challenged numerous assumptions upon which the existing social order had been based for many years. Linda Dowling has shown how the figure of the New Woman seemed to raise a profound challenge to the established class structure of English society and even to threaten the perpetuation of "the race"—that is, the British people and their culture—by refusing traditional motherhood.[13] Furthermore, to assail, as she did, the prevailing definitions of womanhood, marriage, love, morality, and propriety was to threaten the security of those who had built their lives upon the conventional ideology of earlier times. Victorian men in particular had for decades cherished their ideal woman as if she really could save the nation from moral decay and religious despair. They found it much harder even than women did to exchange the "angel in the house" for the "New Woman."

As a literary figure, the New Woman appeared mainly in fiction, and mostly between 1883 and World War I. Her appearance was anticipated by a few unconventional women characters in Tennyson, Trollope, the minor novelists of the seventies, and others. However, she first emerged in her fully developed form in Olive Schreiner's *The Story of an African Farm* (1883), published by Chapman and Hall on the recommendation of George Meredith.[14] Lyndall, the heroine of this book, grows from a rebellious young girl on a desolate African farm into a mature, intelligent woman with strong views on women's rights and a vocation for acting. This impressive transformation is accomplished by the unusually liberal and self-directed education she acquires for herself in an English boarding school. Full of small failings, frustrated in her goals, she nevertheless inspires love and devotion in virtually every other character in the book, through her intelligence, loyalty, beauty, and strength of character. Although Lyndall's life ends with the punishment usually meted out to fallen women (she dies after giving birth to an illegitimate child, who also dies), there is an important difference. Rather than our pity and forgiveness, Lyndall earns our admiration and respect.

The many subsequent treatments of the New Woman in nineteenth-century fiction took their cue either from Schreiner's novel or from the denunciations of the New Woman in the press. Certain characteristics remained fairly constant: the New Woman was usually "dark-haired and healthy in appearance, independent and active in spirit, sexual as well as intellectual."[15] She was never merely conventionally pretty. In the more favorable representations, she was attractive, but in her own unique way. In the unfavorable treatments, she might be hard and masculine looking or pale and neurotic.

In *The Victorians and Their Reading*, Amy Cruse contrasts the negative and positive versions of the New Woman in the minds of the Victorian public. For some, the New Woman was "a blatant female who made herself conspicuous and at the same time absurd by going about loudly demanding her 'rights,' denouncing man as her natural enemy, affecting an uncouth singularity in dress and manners, and generally transforming herself into as unlovely and unfeminine an object as nature would permit."[16] The suffragette, in particular, was typically regarded as "a pinched, sexless, fanatic, usually androphobic" old maid.[17] Others, however, saw the New Woman as a perceptive social critic "who, courageously and hopefully, stepped off the beaten, easy track and forced a way through the thick growth of prejudice and established custom to the open regions where free development was possible." In this version, she gratefully accepted all offers of assistance, from male or female, and did not regard herself as superior either to men or to other women.[18] Although feminists complained that Grant Allen, George Gissing, Thomas Hardy, and other male fiction writers were presenting the New Woman as both more radical and less successful than she really was,[19] most of those attempting to deal seriously with the theme of modern womanhood rejected the extremes in favor of a more realistic portrait of the New Woman's goals and struggles in nineteenth-century society.[20]

As for poetry, one piece by John Davidson, "To the New Woman" (1894), illustrates that the old, sentimental ideal of woman's vocation still had its devotees. The poem begins with a characterization of the New Woman:

> Free to look at fact,
> Free to come and go,
> Free to think and act,
>
> . . . .
>
> Abler than man to vex,
> Less able to be good,
> Fiercer in your sex,
> Wilder in your mood,
> Seeking—who knows what?

To that time-honored and perplexing question "What do women want?" Davidson offers the old, unsatisfactory answer:

> Love and love alone,
> As simple as can be,
> Can make this life atone.

For regardless of how "free" and "new" they might think they are, these are yet "women, from whose bright womb / The radiant future springs."[21] According to this poem, love, marriage, and motherhood remain the sole female *raison d'être*.

Despite their own history of conservatism, it is still somewhat surprising to find in the work of nineteenth-century women poets a real scarcity of poetry representing the New Woman, since traditional sanctions against the depiction of unconventional female figures were clearly lighter in the last two decades of the century than they had been for the eighty years preceding. Elaine Showalter suggests several reasons that the battles for sexual freedom and for woman suffrage were not fought primarily in women's literature. As for sexuality, women preferred, as we have seen, to require self-control from men, rather than to seize sexual freedom for themselves. And women authors' public opposition to woman suffrage stemmed "partly from women writers' reluctance to take on the extra burden of this huge battle and partly from their own sense of being superior and exceptional." What "revolutionary energies" they did possess were most frequently "projected onto male figures," not embodied in the New Woman or any other female figure.[22]

Similarly, those few women poets depicting sexual passion were likely to put their words into the mouths of male speakers. For example, Margaret Veley's "A Japanese Fan," which appeared in *Cornhill Magazine* in September 1876, contains a strong if involuted acknowledgment of female passion, spoken as it is by a man:

"Oftentimes I met her, often
　　Saw her pass,
With her dusky raiment trailing
　　On the grass.
I would follow, would approach her,
　　Dare to speak,
Till at last the sudden colour
　　Flushed her cheek.
Through the sultry heat we lingered
　　In the shade,
And the fan of pictured paper
　　That she swayed
Seemed to mark the summer's pulses,
　　Soft and slow,
And to thrill me as it wavered
　　To and fro.
For I loved her, loved her, loved her,
　　And its beat
Set my passion to a music
　　Strangely sweet."[23]

A respectable nineteenth-century woman writer like Margaret Veley, seeking to express sexual passion, might well find herself stymied for want of appropriate vocabulary. As Carol Dyhouse remarks, "late-Victorian culture did not readily supply women with the language which would have facilitated an analysis of their own repression, particularly in this area where gender prescriptions govern the expression of sexuality."[24] B. Ifor Evans characterized "A Japanese Fan" as "a delicate study in irony and sentiment."[25] Veley, who frequently wrote poems of thwarted or muted passion, may have been struggling to express something stronger; yet without violating decorum, and thus risking the opprobrium attached to the New Woman, she could not. For female sexuality was still the one prohibited topic, even in "comparatively liberated and 'advanced' intellectual circles."[26]

Of course, Victorian writers had for years been creating occasional female characters with some, though not all, of the other traits and behaviors of the New Woman: Tennyson's Princess Ida is an outstanding example. Women poets mostly chose to continue in this less risky tradition, highlighting in a given poem one isolated aspect of the typical New Woman's life or personality, and almost always presenting her as being in some kind of dilemma.

For example, Mary Elizabeth Coleridge worried in 1883 about the fate of

"A Clever Woman," hearkening back to Charlotte Yonge's pessimistic novel, *The Clever Woman of the Family* (1865), in which the progressive feminist Rachel finally retreats from anti-feminist ridicule into marriage and motherhood. Although it was not easy for a clever woman to fulfill her potential, the New Woman characteristically strove to do so. In Mary Coleridge's poem she pays a high price for her efforts at self-improvement:

A CLEVER WOMAN

You thought I had the strength of men,
  Because with men I dared to speak,
And courted Science now and then,
  And studied Latin for a week;
But woman's woman, even when
  She reads her ethics in the Greek.

You thought me wiser than my kind;
  You thought me "more than common tall";
You thought because I had a mind,
  That I could have no heart at all;
But woman's woman you will find,
  Whether she be great or small.

And then you needs must die—ah, well!
  I knew you not, you loved not me.
'Twas not because that darkness fell,
  You saw not what there was to see.
But I that saw and could not tell—
  O evil Angel, set me free![27]

"A Clever Woman" is one of Mary Coleridge's many poems in which the speaker finds herself, frustratingly, trapped behind the surface of conservative nineteenth-century notions about womanhood.[28] In this case, the person addressed has lived and died unable to see "what there was to see"—the real woman and the potential for a love relationship between the two. Ironically, this missed opportunity is attributable both to the constraints of "feminine" behavior, which have blocked the woman speaker from initiating anything, and to the man's failure to recognize that a "clever" (intelligent, educated) woman can be "feminine" in the first place. Developing new patterns for male/female relationships was among the most challenging and difficult tasks the New Woman set for herself. Often, she did not succeed.

Finding someone to imitate, a woman whom we would today call a "role model," could be crucial. George Eliot, hardly a radical feminist, served as an early example to women of a woman living by the dictates of her own conscience. Her "marriage" to George Henry Lewes was, after all, extra-legal, a challenge to nineteenth-century marriage laws and customs. What's more, its unconventional role structure enabled her to combine love and career effectively. When she died in 1880, women writers especially felt that they had lost a guiding light. Emily Pfeiffer commemorated her death in "The Lost Light," representing George Eliot—despite her refusal to sign the 1866 petition for woman suffrage[29]—as guardian of "the banner of insurgent womanhood."[30]

In 1888, the would-be New Woman in "Under Convoy" by E. Nesbit is still experiencing the old, familiar female dilemma of love versus achievement. A "convoy," of course, is a protective escort, which is the role the female speaker of Nesbit's poem both appreciates and resents her husband for filling in her life. On the one hand, it means the end of her "chance of a life-work, / . . . of a soul's worthy fight!"

> And so you are left me—what matters
>   Of Freedom, or Duty, or Right? . . .
> End my chance to oppose—ah, how vainly!—
>   Vast wrong with its mass and its might!

On the other hand, his love offers "a haven, / . . . for the storm-blown and tossed"; and perhaps, " 'Tis better to be safe and ignoble, / Than be free, and be wretched, and true." The possibility that woman might be free and *contented* and true is discounted. As with love and fame, society will not allow a woman this kind of integration. Further, the speaker comes to doubt her own ability, strength, and dedication:

> Too many the questions, too subtle
>   The doubts that bewilder my brain!
> Too strong is the strength of old custom
>   For iron convention's cold reign;
> Too doubtful the issue of conflict,
>   Too leafless the crown and too vain!

The subsequent image is that of a swimmer in the sea, too weak, blind, imperfect, and irresolute to persevere against wave after crashing wave of opposition. If Mary Coleridge's "clever woman" paid the price of her personal self-fulfillment, Nesbit's woman has forfeited her self-determination in exchange for security:

> And you know not how under your kisses
>   The soul of me shrinks and is lost:

And you save me my ease as a woman,
   —And the life of a soul is the cost.[31]

Nesbit's premise in "Under Convoy," while reinforcing the conventional notion that career and marriage don't mix, nevertheless anticipates modern feminist rhetoric in its recognition of the inhibiting yet seductive qualities of masculine protection. In rare poems such as these, addressing particular facets of New Womanhood, popular women poets of the nineteenth century struck their most modern-sounding notes.

One last poet whose depiction of woman is startling in its modernity is Dollie Radford, who published from time to time in the *Savoy* and the *Yellow Book*. "From the Suburbs" and "A Novice" are housewives' laments which might have been written last year, but which appeared in 1895. In the latter, the housebound wife, waiting for the world to open its doors to women, wryly praises the consolations to be gained in the meanwhile from—of all things—a cigarette!

"What is it, in these latter days,
Transfigures my domestic ways,
And round me, as a halo, plays?
      My cigarette.

If I, in vain, must sit and wait,
To realize our future state,
I shall not be disconsolate,
      My cigarette!"[32]

In "From Our Emancipated Aunt in Town," Radford depicts an unmarried woman who, though not precisely a New Woman herself, is, by her very independence, helping that creature to develop. The aunt is aware of living in an age of transition for women; she finds herself "stranded, / With old ideals blown away, / And all opinions, in the fray, / Long since disbanded." Eagerly, she, who stands, "By evolution, in a band / Of poor pathetics / Who cannot go alone, / Who cling to many a worn out tottering thing / Of a convention," looks to her nieces "To beautify our history book / For coming readers, / . . . and take your place / As future leaders. . . . " Meanwhile, she asks them, when they think of their maiden aunt in town, to "Remember she prepares your way, / With many another Aunt today, / And send her greetings."[33] Published in 1895 also, this poem reflects a nineties consciousness of changing times and represents the "old" woman, like the old century, welcoming the new—attempting to "live beyond culture," as Dowling puts it.[34]

A small, separate vein of women's poetry, which was essentially political, arose also in the nineties. Showalter quotes "The New Woman" (1895) as a verse rendition of the "messianic fervor" of feminist writers:

> Saw the infants doomed to suffering,
> Saw the maidens slaves to lust,
> Saw the starving mothers barter
> Souls and bodies for a crust.
> Then she rose—with inward vision,
> Nerving all her powers for good;
> Feeling one with suffering sisters
> In perfected womanhood.[35]

Another futuristic feminist poem she discovered was *Woman Free* (1893) by "Ellis Ethelmer," which sought to document women's oppression and to celebrate the glorious day when the cessation of menstruation and the triumph of bachelor motherhood would free women to achieve utopia.[36]

"In its extreme form," Showalter explains, "feminist literature advocated the sexual separatism of Amazon utopias and suffragette sisterhoods"; however, most verse on those themes was highly polemical and hardly qualifies as poetry in any aesthetic sense of the word.[37] One exception, which can serve to conclude our discussion of women poets' responses to the New Woman controversies, is Mary Coleridge's "The White Women," composed in the year 1900. Although, as Showalter says, Coleridge's Amazonian figures "are creatures of an imagined golden age, not models for the future,"[38] they do personify the most radical of feminist ideals. They are strong, tall, beautiful, large-boned, and war-like—fully competent to engage the promise and threat of active life. They have "never bowed their necks beneath the yoke"; they have never dwelt with men, and thus have never sinned, though they are unabashedly sexual beings.

> . . . they never sinned,
> But when the rays of the eternal fire
> Kindle the West, their tresses they unbind
> And fling their girdles to the Western wind,
> Swept by desire.

Their love is lesbian, their reproduction parthenogenetic: "Lo, maidens to the maidens then are born, / Strong children of the maidens and the breeze. . . . "[39] They speak a language uniquely female and unintelligible to men, and simply to behold them is to die, for their utopian civilization is maintained by total isolation from the profoundly heterosexual human race. More than anything else, "The White Women" is a vision of a feminist paradise regained.[40]

Unlike the sentimental Victorian ideal, the buoyant, unconventional "New Woman" of the late nineteenth century never came to dominate either literature or society. But her spirited challenge to women's traditional roles made the slow evolution of the modern, independent woman more certain. The books and poems in which the New Woman was the heroine were not those most widely read, but they left their mark, for "even when she is not a New Woman, the young heroine of this period is capable of independent thought, of developing and using her mind, and even of arguing with man as his intellectual equal."[41] And though the average middle-class girl of the nineties still did not smoke or work or reject marriage, she had gained the right and the means to do so if she wished and if she was prepared to forfeit male protection. From this perspective, it becomes clear that women poets' relatively rare representations of the "New Woman" must not be seen as a failure, but, in their best efforts, as a contribution, however small, to constructive change.

9

Elizabeth Barrett Browning

The publication in 1856 of Elizabeth Barrett Browning's verse novel *Aurora Leigh* marked the climactic point in her poetical treatment of women's personal and social roles. Along with *Sonnets from the Portuguese* (1850) and *Casa Guidi Windows* (1851), *Aurora Leigh* revealed Barrett Browning at the height of her poetical powers. She herself staked her entire critical reputation on it: "I mean that when you have read my new book, you put away all my other poems or most of them, and know me only by the new."[1] Previously, Barrett Browning's poetical representations of women, though sometimes subtly critical, had remained well within conventional expectations and traditional forms. With *Aurora Leigh*, however, she departed from feminine tradition with sufficient force to impress many, alarm some, and startle nearly all of her readers. Before evaluating the innovativeness of *Aurora Leigh* and the achievement of the poems thereafter, we must first glance at some of Elizabeth Barrett Browning's earlier poetic renderings of women's roles.

In her early portrayals of women, Barrett Browning generally responded to the expectations of Victorian readers; even so, an imaginative difference, a creative twist of plot, or a particularly skillful manipulation of imagery frequently distinguished her poetry from that of contemporaries like Felicia Hemans and Letitia Landon. In *Aurora Leigh*, Aurora comments upon the difficulty of simultaneously observing and transcending conventionality:

> My critic Belfair wants another book
> Entirely different, which will sell (and live?),
> A striking book, yet not a startling book,
> The public blames originalities. . . .
> Good things, not subtle, new yet orthodox,
> As easy reading as the dog-eared page

That's fingered by said public fifty years,
Since first taught spelling by its grandmother,
And yet a revelation in some sort:
That's hard, my critic Belfair.[2]

Her own ability to achieve this difficult balance often lifted Elizabeth Barrett Browning's early poems above the level of most giftbook verse.

For example, "A Romance of the Ganges," which appeared in *Findens' Tableaux* for 1838,[3] is exotic, romantic, and reminiscent of "The Hindoo Girl's Song" by Letitia Landon. Both poems are based upon the same superstition and belong to the same wider tradition of pseudo-Oriental sentimentalism which was very popular among readers of the annuals. Landon's poem is slight, insignificant; William Bell Scott places it among her minor poems.[4] Barrett Browning's poem clearly belongs among *her* minor works also; yet reviewers of *Findens' Tableaux* for 1838 found "A Romance of the Ganges" to be "comparatively unhackneyed" and "incomparably the best poem" in the volume.[5] In it she had managed, at least, to differentiate among her characters and to avoid easy sentimentality—both unusual accomplishments in giftbook poetry. Nevertheless, "A Romance of the Ganges" ends quite conventionally, as the betrayed maiden flings herself into the river and her rival sheds tears of sorrow for her lost female friend and of disillusionment with her inconstant male lover (196–213).

After the success of "A Romance of the Ganges," the editor of *Findens'*, Barrett Browning's friend Mary Russell Mitford, featured "The Romaunt of the Page" and "The Lay of the Brown Rosary" in the 1839 and 1840 editions of the collection. The *Athenaeum* declared "The Romaunt of the Page" to be "one of the most beautiful things from a woman's hand which has appeared for many a day."[6] Despite the proviso, this was high praise for giftbook verse. What was extraordinary in this pseudo-medieval ballad was the accomplished versification and the contemporary theme. All three of the poems for *Findens'* were written to order, a custom whereby the editor first selected a book's illustrations and then commissioned poems to accompany them. Therefore, the sentimental situation in the poem—a new-made bride disguises herself as a page and accompanies her husband to the Crusades—was not of the author's devising. However, the indictment of the contemporary marriage ideal which the poem contains was hers alone.

In battle the faithful page-wife has proved her nobility, courage, and devotion to her lord; three times she has even saved him from death. When she tries to learn what his attitude will be after the deception is discovered, he replies, to her dismay, "My love, so please you, shall requite / No woman, whether dark or bright, / Unwomaned if she be" (194–196). The page demands, " 'But what if she mistook thy mind / And followed thee to strife?' " (223–224), to which the knight replies, " 'I would forgive, and evermore / Would love her as my servitor, / But little as my wife' " (227–229). A woman's honor, he explains condescendingly, lies in purity, restraint, and isolation; it is not won but forfeited by her participation in worldly strife.

While the knight rehearses conventional nineteenth-century views about woman's ideal qualities and her proper sphere of activity, the page, suddenly spying an approaching band of Saracens, makes a pretext to send the knight ahead. As she awaits her own certain death, which will procure her lord's (double) escape, she soliloquizes bitterly about his repudiation of her active and courageous love, even though it has saved his life several times over:

> "Yet God thee save, and mayst thou have
>   A lady to thy mind,
> More woman-proud and half as true
>   As one thou leav'st behind!
> And God me take with HIM to dwell—
> For HIM I cannot love too well,
>   As I have loved my kind."
>
> (280–286)

When her murderers arrive, she stands among them calmly, "False page, but truthful woman" (297), and consummates her marriage at last by dying:

> She felt the scimitar gleam down,
>   And met it from beneath
> With smile more bright in victory
>   Than any sword from sheath.
>
> (323–326)

The poet thus depicts the woman herself as incontestably noble and the man as arrogant and imperceptive. It is his inflexible beliefs about marriage, not the roving band of Saracens, which truly take her life. Thus, in "The Romaunt of the Page," Barrett Browning employs a sentimental tale of extreme wifely devotion and self-sacrifice in order to arraign the maleficence of current nineteenth-century notions about women and marriage.

This subtle manipulation of a traditional plot or poetic genre in order to subvert convention was not always present in Barrett Browning's poems. "The Lay of the Brown Rosary," for example, is an uninspired jumble of marriage and sin, nuns and angels, evil spirits and overwise little boys, succumbing to the demands of the picture it was written to accompany. Its Gothic appeal and some few similarities with "Christabel" do not redeem it from sheer preposterousness; the poet's intent was clearly to supply the commissioned poem to her friend Mary Russell Mitford and perhaps to earn a little extra money. It was the last of her contributions to *Findens' Tableaux*. "The Romaunt of Margret" (1836), which represents a woman drowning herself in despair over her lover's death, is perhaps unconventional in representing the act of suicide though certainly *not* in depicting a heroine who is unable to endure life after her beloved has died. The theme of the poem is the futility of reliance upon human love; the moral purpose, the author said, was to show "that the creature cannot be *sustained* by the creature."[7] Thus the implication of the ending is not that Margret should have mustered the strength to stand on her own, but that she ought to have relied upon the unfailing love of God. To convey this message, a hero would have been only slightly less appropriate than a heroine. At no point does the poem seriously challenge convention.

In a companion poem, "The Poet's Vow" (1836), the message is "that the creature cannot be *isolated* from the creature"[8] and that the artist in particular must not remove himself from the rest of humanity. Leaving aside the question of "the poet" (who in this poem, at least, is male) and his place in Elizabeth Barrett Browning's aesthetic theory, let us notice the character designed to represent humanity: Rosalind. When the poet hero announces his intent to divorce himself from his fellow men and suggests that Rosalind, his fiancée, marry his best friend instead of himself, she upbraids him for his heartlessness and, of course, refuses to wed Sir Roland. Like a conventional heroine, she pines and fades into death. But there the story, for once, does *not* end. Before her death, Rosalind commands that her funeral bier be carried to the poet's door, along with a scroll charging him to break his vow of isolation. The written accusations of the corpse are more effective than the pleas of the living woman, and the poet capitulates.

Thus Rosalind is powerful in death where she failed in life: the spectre of her suffering and death provokes the poet to an agony of guilt and regret, culminating finally in his own demise—of a broken heart and an excess of human pain. Though she has done so as a corpse, Rosalind has triumphed at last. Aside from the poem's stated moral about art and love, isolation and commitment, Barrett Browning's message for women seems to be that womanly love, truth, and constancy will prevail at last and thus contain their own justification. The two lovers are buried together and the spirit of the poet goes to join the soul of his betrothed in God's heaven. Despite its apparent advocacy of feminine self-sacrifice, "The Poet's Vow" represents the exertion of the author's intelligence and creativity upon a recognizable feminine poetic tradition: the potential fatality to women of romantic love.

It is unclear just how attentive Elizabeth Barrett Browning was to the existing feminine conventions and traditions. In her early work, she seems to be alternately in consonance and in struggle with them. She was certainly familiar with the poetry of Felicia Hemans and Letitia Landon; she wrote thoughtful poems upon the deaths of both of them.[9] And since she was publishing in various annuals and giftbooks, she probably followed the trade.[10] Gardner Taplin notes that she knew the writings of Mary Howitt and Caroline Norton and also records an instance of her satisfaction with a copy of *The Literary Souvenir* in 1826.[11] Given her voracious appetite for reading materials, it is undoubtedly safe to assume that she was well acquainted with women's poetry.

Yet she also felt keenly the lack of significant female predecessors: "I look everywhere for grandmothers and see none."[12] Helen Cooper has postulated that Barrett Browning was exploring "what it meant to be a woman poet writing out of a male tradition,"[13] instead of joining a consciously female one. Clearly, Cooper's assessment contains more than an element of truth. On the other hand, among Barrett Browning's poems prior to *Aurora Leigh* are many which reflect prevailing themes and forms of women's verse; more than a few of these poems manipulate feminine literary traditions so as to resist or at least undermine conventional Victorian beliefs regarding women.

Criticism of nineteenth-century marriage conventions and representation of pining, lovelorn maidens are only two of the feminine traditions which Barrett Browning explored—and, sometimes, exploited. One more example of each will suffice to illustrate her early interest in these genres. "The Rhyme of the Duchess May" (1844) was a popular success which, in its protest against financially motivated, arranged marriages, was not particularly original. However, the double suicide in the tale's conclusion reached a height of drama not attained in most women's poetry. Furthermore, in her numerous representations of female suicides, Barrett Browning was violating both a feminine literary convention and a Christian doctrine. She herself did not much like this particular poem, and Harriet Preston has suggested that her reservations may be traceable to the "signal glorification of suicide implied in the denouement."[14] Perhaps also she recognized some justice in William Aytoun's denunciation of the poem as "Spasmodic."[15]

"Bertha in the Lane" (1844) is a better executed though still thoroughly conventional representation of the pining maiden figure. In plot it is nearly identical with Landon's "The Secret Discovered," published in *Friendship's Offering* in 1837. In each, the heroine accidentally discovers that her fiancé and her younger sister are in love and heroically relinquishes her own claim in favor of the two young lovers. The chief difference is that Landon's Elinore accepts the difficult fate of spinsterhood, whereas Bertha instead pines away and dies. Both poems emphasize the self-sacrifice involved in renunciation of marriage: Elinore devotes the rest of her days to her aging father and Bertha forces herself to complete the needlework on her sister's wedding gown before she gratefully embraces her death. The implicit Christ identification of a martyrdom thus incurred becomes explicit in "Bertha in the Lane":

> Jesus, Victim, comprehending
>   Love's divine self-abnegation,
> Cleanse my love in its self-spending,
>   And absorb the poor libation!
> Wind my thread of life up higher,
> Up, through angels' hands of fire!
> I aspire while I expire.
>
> (232–238)

The poem was admired for the sentimentality of its tone, the pathos of its situation, and the religiosity of its conclusion.[16] It is thus a completely typical nineteenth-century woman's poem.

In the other poems which appeared before *Aurora Leigh*, Barrett Browning also pursued traditionally feminine themes such as the death of a child, the contrast between woman's love and man's, and the tension between love and fame. Of the poems about child mortality, "The Mourning Mother" (1844) is the most entirely conventional, in its glorification of mother-love and its promise of heavenly reunion. As Taplin has remarked, "it had precisely the qualities which appealed to many of her readers," although he suspects we may find it "mawkish" today.[17] "A Child's Grave at Florence" (1849), written to commemorate the death of sixteen-month-old Alice Cottrell, though also conventional, is more genuinely moving—perhaps because the grief it portrays was real rather than fancied, and because Barrett Browning was by this time a mother herself.[18]

The earlier poem, "Isobel's Child" (1838), however, violates convention (and common sense) by having a dying child suddenly open his eyes and discourse, at three months of age, about "celestial palaces" and "vistas of high palms / Making finites of delight / Through the heavenly infinite" (422–425). The infant begs his mother to revoke her selfish prayers for his life and to allow him to go to God.

> Mother, mother,
> I tremble in thy close embrace,
> I feel thy tears adown my face,
>   Thy prayers do keep me out of bliss—
> O dreary earthly love!
> Loose thy prayer and let me go. . . .
>
> (501–506)

Either a miracle has occurred, and the child's sudden powers of articulation and revelation are heaven-sent, or else the mother, who has cried and prayed (but not slept) for eight straight days, is hallucinating from grief and fatigue. The poem's conclusion would seem to support the former interpretation; after the mother's change of heart, the child dies and she herself feels calm and blessed, cherishing her own hope of heaven. Whereas Isobel at first epitomizes the conventional idea of the divinity of a mother's love (250–251), she ends by acknowledging instead the supremacy of God's.

Barrett Browning does not mean to deny the strength of maternal love and grief, of course, but only to remind the reader of the justice and beauty of God's will. She concludes the poem with a stated moral:

> Take courage to entrust your love
> To Him so named who guards above
>   Its ends and shall fulfil!
> Breaking the narrow prayers that may
> Befit your narrow hearts, away
>   In His broad, loving will.
>
>   (545–550)

Although "Isobel's Child" takes a fantastic turn in plot, the sentiments it expresses are conventionally religious ones after all. In this case, Barrett Browning's successful infusion of the familiar, traditional form with an originality of development won this poem great critical approbation. "Christopher North" (John Wilson), for one, wrote in *Blackwood's* that "Isobel's Child" was "beyond all dispute" the production of a genius.[19] The poem was as highly praised in its day as some of her more durable efforts, such as "The Sea-Mew" and "Cowper's Grave."

Two companion poems, "A Woman's Shortcomings" and "A Man's Requirements," published in *Blackwood's* in October 1846, strike the same note about woman's and man's love as numerous previous poems by popular women poets. The first reproves the fickleness in love of some young women of fashion and emphasizes the essential constancy of true woman's love:

> Unless you can feel, when left by One,
>   That all men else go with him. . . .
> Unless you can swear "For life, for death!"—
>   Oh, fear to call it loving!
>
>   (27–32)

The same sentiment occurs in Barrett Browning's "Loved Once" (1844) as well as in *Aurora Leigh*, where the idealistic Aurora tells her rival, Lady

Waldemar, "But I know, / A love that burns through veils will burn through masks / And shrivel up treachery. What, love and lie! / Nay—go to the opera! your love's curable" (III. 706–709).

In "A Man's Requirements," Barrett Browning delineates the masculine expectations raised by such conventional ideas regarding woman's love. A woman must love her man once and forever, with the entirety of her being, holding nothing in reserve:

> Love me, Sweet, with all thou art,
>   Feeling, thinking, seeing:
> Love me in the lightest part,
>   Love me in full being.
>
> .   .   .   .
>
> Through all hopes that keep us brave,
>   Farther off or nigher,
> Love me for the house and grave,
>   And for something higher.
>
> (1–4, 37–40)

Judging by *Sonnets from the Portuguese*, we might conclude that the poet herself agreed with this idea.[20] However, "A Man's Requirements" takes a cynical turn as the speaker of the poem reveals what the woman thus plighted may expect in return:

> Thus, if thou wilt prove me, Dear,
>   Woman's love no fable,
> *I* will love *thee*—half a year—
>   As a man is able.
>
> (41–44)

Were it not for the apparent humor in this concluding stanza, the forty lines which precede it would be a completely idealized portrayal of woman's love. The sudden change of tone casts a light of suspicion over both poems: don't they perhaps satirize not only masculine inconstancy but also feminine sentimentality? Yet "A Woman's Shortcomings" seems to be completely serious and straightforward. At any rate, in the ambiguity of tone, as in the choice of subject matter, both poems fall well within established traditions of women's poetry.

"Crowned and Wedded" (1840), which Barrett Browning wrote on the occasion of Queen Victoria's marriage, was an interesting opportunity for commenting upon a woman in whose life the tension between love and fame was unavoidable. After comparing the attractions of the bridal wreath with those of the royal crown, Barrett Browning writes, "Let none say, God preserve the queen! but rather, Bless the bride!"(46). To Prince Albert, she charges, "Esteem that wedded hand less dear for sceptre than for ring, / And hold her uncrowned womanhood to be the royal thing" (57–58). The sheer conventionality of this sentiment is disappointing, even in a public poem such as this one. However, most of the poems in which women depicted Queen Victoria were similarly uninspired. The queen herself was in such an unusual situation for a woman that, in the capacity of representing all of England, she became an inappropriate symbol for struggling nineteenth-century womanhood.[21] The theme of love versus fame, of course, receives its most thorough exposition from Barrett Browning in *Aurora Leigh*.

Before turning to that poem there is one additional and very important tradition of women's poetry in which Elizabeth Barrett Browning's contributions cannot be ignored: social protest. "The Cry of the Children" appeared in August 1843, in response to the infamous revelations of the Children's Employment Commission (written in part by her friend Richard Hengist Horne). In "The Soul's Travelling" (1838), Barrett Browning had written of the London poor, of the "flower-girl's prayer to buy roses and pinks / Held out in the smoke, like stars by day," of the "drop on the stones of the blind man's staff / As he trades in his own grief's sacredness," of the "brothel shriek, and the Newgate laugh" (27–28, 37–38, 39). She had joined the ranks of Caroline Norton, Mary Howitt, Thomas Hood, and others in direct protest over outrageous social conditions with "The Cry of the Human," published in the *Boston Miscellany of Literature and Fashion* in 1842 and reprinted in England in her *Poems* in 1844. "The Cry of the Children," which was probably the best known and most effective of her protest poems, was followed by "The Runaway Slave at Pilgrim's Point" (1848) and "A Song for the Ragged Schools of London" (1854).

Of these five poems, only "The Runaway Slave at Pilgrim's Point" focuses directly upon a woman. The heroine is a Black American slave, who has escaped and made her way to Plymouth Rock, where she dies rather than be recaptured. For a mid-nineteenth-century poem, "The Runaway Slave" is astonishingly frank about whippings, rape, and infanticide. The woman has been violently separated from the fellow slave whom she loved, and has been forced to conceive and bear her master's child. Crazed with grief and rage, she murders the newborn baby, whose light complexion seems to mock her blackness, and carries its body for a month before burying it in a hand-dug grave. The most horrifying representative in nineteenth-century poetry of "unnatural motherhood," this woman's motivation to child murder is also the most compelling. "The Runaway Slave at Pilgrim's Point" may be, as

Taplin believes, "too blunt and shocking to have any enduring artistic worth,"[22] and it may have played only a small part in the American abolitionist movement. But it stands virtually alone among nineteenth-century Englishwomen's poems in its unflinching relationship to a taboo subject and in its painfully raw emotionality.

Another important poem of Barrett Browning's, which is sometimes considered a poem of social protest for the democratic sentiments it expresses, is "Lady Geraldine's Courtship" (1844). It was the popular success of this poem, subtitled "A Romance of the Age," which encouraged Barrett Browning in her plans for the eleven-thousand-line *Aurora Leigh*. It was also, of course, her complimentary reference to Robert Browning in this poem which first prompted him to seek her acquaintance. Lady Geraldine is an aristocrat, a self-determining woman of great beauty, accomplishment, intelligence, and virtue—in short, a very paragon. Furthermore, whereas all her friends are snobbish and hypocritical, Lady Geraldine is wonderfully democratic. No wonder the peasant-born poet-hero Bertram worships her and falls into a swoon when he believes his suit is hopeless. All ends well, of course: Lady Geraldine defies her friends and agrees to marry the humbly born yet incontestably noble poet. Their romantic engagement in defiance of society, the poem's chief departure from convention, prefigures Romney's engagement to Marian Erle in *Aurora Leigh*. Lady Geraldine's comparative freedom from social pressures and family obligations in choosing her own match is, of course, explained by her personal wealth and by her aristocratic station. It was a luxury middle-class girls (and poetic heroines) did not ordinarily possess, but it was not really out of line with social reality.

The social protest made explicit in the overt feminism of *Aurora Leigh* was also anticipated in a few of Barrett Browning's previous works. At the age of twelve, the young Elizabeth Barrett had read Mary Wollstonecraft's *Vindication of the Rights of Woman*. She recalled in 1842 that it had impressed her so thoroughly that "through the whole course of my childhood, I had a steady indignation against Nature who made me a woman."[23] *A Drama of Exile* (1844) contains a lengthy prediction of the hardships and injustices which await Eve in the guise of woman's lot:

> Something thou hast to bear through womanhood,
> Peculiar suffering answering to the sin,—
> Some pang paid down for each new human life,
> Some weariness in guarding such a life,
> Some coldness from the guarded, some mistrust
> From those thou hast too well served, from those beloved
> Too loyally some treason; feebleness

Within thy heart, and cruelty without,
And pressures of an alien tyranny
With its dynastic reasons of larger bones
And stronger sinews.

(1857–1867)

In *Casa Guidi Windows* (1851), she demanded of England, "Have you . . . /
No help for women sobbing out of sight / Because men made the laws?" (II.
632–639). Feminist outbursts such as these demonstrate a continuity in her
opinions on women's condition which it might otherwise be hard to divine
from conventional poems like, for example, "My Kate," which appeared in
Keepsake for 1855, only a year before *Aurora Leigh*.[24]

Despite some few early warnings, the public, which had so liked "Bertha in
the Lane," "Isobel's Child," and "Lady Geraldine's Courtship," was stunned
by *Aurora Leigh*. Algernon Charles Swinburne remarked years later, "The
advent of 'Aurora Leigh' can never be forgotten by any lover of poetry who
was old enough at the time to read it. . . . They never had read, and never
would read anything in any way comparable with that unique work of
audaciously feminine and ambitiously impulsive genius."[25] *Aurora Leigh* was a
courageous, thorough-going exposition of feminist ideas about nineteenth-
century women. Yet Barrett Browning conveyed these socially advanced ideas
in a vehicle which—despite its claim to singularity as a verse novel—represented well-known female characters involved in specifically female predicaments,
all of which were quite familiar to the reading public. The audacity and the
achievement of *Aurora Leigh* resided in its confrontation all at once of so
many social and personal facts of nineteenth-century English life and in its
challenge to the validity of the conventions which customarily concealed those
facts.

The author realized, of course, just what she had dared to do; consequently,
she was astonished by the poem's sensational popular success. She had fully
expected, she said, "to be put in the stocks" for it "as a disorderly woman and
free-thinking poet." Yet she also believed it to be "nearer the mark . . . fuller,
stronger, more sustained" than any of her previous poems.[26] Apparently the
technique of presenting radical ideas within a familiar context ("new yet
orthodox") constituted a camouflage sufficient to get the poem past the reading public's barricades of self-defensive disapprobation.

Of course, there *were* objections from some quarters to the alleged immorality and impurity of the situations and to an unfeminine shamelessness and
coarseness of the language in the poem. Furthermore, despite its continuing
popularity, *Aurora Leigh* was not a critical success. In addition to their other
reservations, reviewers were nearly unanimous in finding the poem's charac-

terizations weak and its major figures unattractive. Since, with the exceptions of Romney Leigh and Aurora's father, all the major characters are female, it is most illuminating to approach the poem's relationship to its social and literary context by examining Barrett Browning's various representations of English womanhood within it.

In *Aurora Leigh*, Barrett Browning emphasizes one female character from each of the three social classes in England. Lady Waldemar represents the upper class. She is an idle aristocratic lady, who dabbles somewhat carelessly in philanthropy and affairs of the heart. Aurora Leigh, despite the aristocratic heritage from her father, is essentially a middle-class professional woman, who depends upon her own earnings as a writer for support. Marian Erle comes from the lower class. The daughter of a "tramp," she has become (with the help of Romney Leigh) a seamstress, in order to avoid a life of prostitution. Until she and her illegitimate child are rescued by Aurora, she lives a life of abject poverty which constantly borders upon outright destitution.

From the poem's glorification of Marian Erle and vilification of Lady Waldemar, we might conclude that all of Barrett Browning's sympathies lay with the oppressed lower classes of England. However, that would be an over-simplification. Marian's father is an unsavory character who drinks, beats his wife, and evades employment; in turn, her mother abuses Marian and tries to barter her daughter's virginity for favors from a neighboring squire. Lady Waldemar's servant later succeeds where Marian's mother failed, by selling Marian into sexual slavery. Furthermore, the throngs of angry poor people who threaten and finally maim the generous if misguided aristocrat Romney Leigh are a nasty, brutish, and ungrateful mob. Romney himself is a gentleman in the best sense of the word, and though his social peers are sometimes snobbish and hypocritical, they also include admirable men like Vincent Carrington, the painter, and Lord Howe, Aurora's faithful friend and correspondent. Despite the novelistic way in which characters of diverse social classes are made to rub elbows throughout the poem, class consciousness does not supply its unity of perspective. Feminist consciousness does.[27]

In *Aurora Leigh*, Elizabeth Barrett Browning explored virtually all the women's roles with which the public was familiar in mid-nineteenth-century England. By considering the poem's female characters in terms of their social roles and in light of the accompanying feminist commentary upon women in general which Aurora provides, we discover the full force of the poem: *Aurora Leigh* rejects the conventional wisdom about women at virtually every point.

The interaction between Aurora and the three women who were significant figures in her childhood immediately illustrates some of the poem's departures from tradition. To begin with, Aurora's mother was not an Englishwoman at all, but a foreigner, a Florentine, whose southern charms won the heart of

Aurora's austere English father "after a dry lifetime spent at home / In college-learning, law, and parish talk" (I. 66–67). Through love of her, he "had suddenly / Thrown off the old conventions, broken loose / From chin-bands of the soul . . . " (I. 176–178). Unfortunately, this woman was so weakened by the birth of Aurora that she died when the child was only four years old. Aurora's recollection of her sense of loss owes something, perhaps, to many popular women poets' descriptions of maternal death as well as to Barrett Browning's own bereavement at age twenty-two.

> I felt a mother-want about the world,
> And still went seeking, like a bleating lamb
> Left out at night in shutting up the fold,—
> As restless as a nest-deserted bird. . . .
>
> (I. 40–43)

Yet her dead mother's portrait on the wall stirs the child not simply to adoration but also to terror.

> And as I grew
> In years, I mixed, confused, unconsciously,
> Whatever I last read or heard or dreamed,
> Abhorrent, admirable, beautiful,
> Pathetical, or ghastly, or grotesque,
> With that still face. . . .
>
> (I. 146–151)

The mother figure becomes for Aurora a kind of "Lamia," alternately benign and malignant, according to the child's own fantasies and fears. This unsentimental depiction of childhood bereavement is much more psychologically sound than the treatment of the subject in most women's poetry.[28]

In her natural mother's stead, Aurora has Assunta, an Italian servant whose devotion to the child is quite touching. Assunta cares for Aurora until she is thirteen, when her father suddenly dies and his relatives send for Aurora to come to England. Once again, Aurora is separated from maternal love; both she and the faithful servant are devastated with grief.

> I do remember clearly how there came
> A stranger with authority, not right
> (I thought not), who commanded, caught me up
> From old Assunta's neck; how, with a shriek,
> She let me go,—while I, with ears too full
> Of my father's silence to shriek back a word,

> In all a child's astonishment at grief
> Stared at the wharf-edge where she stood and moaned. . . .
>
> (I. 223–230)

The demands of English laws and customs separate the child from her surrogate mother—who is, after all, only a servant and thus beyond consideration; we feel both the injustice and the inevitability of this outcome. By the time Aurora, as a grown woman, returns to Italy, her beloved Assunta is dead. The long-lasting affection between Barrett Browning and her maidservant Elizabeth Wilson may have contributed to the representation of this woman servant in *Aurora Leigh*. In any case, the sympathetic depiction of Assunta is extraordinary, considering that women's poetry in the nineteenth century generally failed to characterize female domestics at all; and the recognition of a genuine love between mistress and servant shows unusual sensitivity on Barrett Browning's part to the humanity of the serving class.

Reaching England, Aurora is turned over to the care and tutelage of her maiden aunt, whom Barrett Browning depicts neither with ridicule nor with sentimentality, but with a degree of individuality which distinguishes this particular spinster from current poetical stereotypes.

> She stood straight and calm,
> Her somewhat narrow forehead braided tight
> As if for taming accidental thoughts
> From possible pulses; brown hair pricked with grey
> By frigid use of life. . . .
> Eyes of no colour,—once they might have smiled,
> But never, never have forgot themselves
> In smiling; cheeks, in which was yet a rose
> Of perished summers, like a rose in a book,
> Kept more for ruth than pleasure,—if past bloom,
> Past fading also.
>
> (I. 272–276, 282–287)

This physical description of Aunt Leigh emphasizes the repression and rigidity of a single woman who found herself consigned to "A harmless life, she called a virtuous life, / A quiet life, which was not life at all" (I. 288–289). She fills her days with the poor club, the book club, obligatory calls from the neighbors—and hatred for her brother's wife, Aurora's mother. When she dies, some seven years after Aurora's arrival in England, she is found sitting "Bolt upright in the chair beside her bed" (II. 925) with blank open eyes and an unbudging posture that aptly reflect her living personality.

Looking back, Aurora recognizes the conflict of temperament between her aunt and herself, and expresses it through a classic image in women's poetry—that of the caged bird.

> She had lived
> A sort of caged-bird life, born in a cage,
> Accounting that to leap from perch to perch
> Was act and joy enough for any bird.
>   . . . I, alas
> A wild bird scarcely fledged, was brought to her cage,
> And she was there to meet me. Very kind.
> Bring the clean water, give out the fresh seed.
>
> (I. 304–307, 309–312)

Aurora was not an ideal English girl when she came to Aunt Leigh, but a natural, undisciplined Italian child. The spinster determined to take her in hand and mold her into the courtesy-book ideal of English maidenhood. Consequently, Aurora, who had been tutored by her father from his own store of genuine knowledge, was now set to the task of absorbing the English girl's customary mix of trivial information, accomplishment, and conventionality. Only her communing with nature and her clandestine reading from her father's library enable her spirit to survive. The long passage in which Aurora describes the struggle (I. 372–481) is classic in its denunciation of both the process and the product of women's education. Aunt Leigh fails in her attempts to extinguish the spark of independence and intellectuality which Aurora brought within herself from her Italian girlhood. "Certain of your feebler souls," Aurora concedes, "Go out in such a process; many pine / To a sick inodorous light" of English womanhood. "My own," she thanks God, "endured" (I. 470–472).

The character of Aurora is the most fully delineated in the poem, which traces her growth and maturation, the cultivation of her talents, and the education of her heart. After her successful defiance of the conventional demands of English girlhood, Aurora continues to reject current social ideas which pertain to her own situation and to the condition of women in general. She refuses to marry her cousin Romney and subordinate or abandon her artistic pursuits in order to participate in his own vocation of social work. "You want a helpmate, not a mistress, sir," she accuses, "A wife to help your ends,—in her no end" (II. 402–403). Mistakenly, she believes their match would be loveless and utilitarian, and she chooses instead to award her devotion to her art. "You'll grant that even a woman may love art, / Seeing that to waste true love on anything / Is womanly, past question" (II. 495–497). Aurora's objections to marriage are undeniably feminist and, in light of English law and custom, justifiable. Yet she misunderstands her own emotional needs, and we the readers, though sympathetic to her needs for self-assertion and achievement, also recognize from the beginning what it takes Aurora many lonely years to perceive: her need for intimacy and her love for her cousin Romney.

So deep are these emotions that Aurora, in absence of any other opportunity, acts them out by playing husband and father to Romney's affianced Marian Erle and her illegitimate child. All through Book VII of the poem, Aurora takes on an androgyny of character,[29] dismissing her tears and fears and letting the masculine in her personality (VII. 212, 230) predominate over the feminine. "It is very good for strength," she learns, "To know that someone needs you to be strong" (VII. 414–415). She takes full responsibility for Marian and her baby, conveying them to Italy and safety in her own dead father's house, where the three form a family group. Aurora soon discovers, through assuming the male role, that male/female personality differences are artificial, and that there is no magic in masculinity after all.

> Note men!—They are but women after all,
> As women are but Auroras!—there are men
> Born tender, apt to pale at a trodden worm. . . .
>
> (VII. 1017–1019)

This new-found recognition of men as human beings like herself is part of what softens Aurora toward Romney and enables her in the poem's conclusion to recognize and declare her love for him. Of course, the fact of his blindness is significant also. His handicap finally equalizes them, in a way, and allows Aurora to exercise both her sympathy and her strength.[30]

The marriage they now contemplate will be passionate, mystical, mature—a union of separate souls each bringing its own capacities to the joint endeavor humbly to do God's work:

> The world waits
> For help. Beloved, let us love so well,
> Our work shall still be better for our love,
> And still our love be sweeter for our work,
> And both, commended, for the sake of each,
> By all true workers and true lovers, born.
>
> (IX. 923–928)

If this is an idealized version of marriage, it is at least more egalitarian than the conventional structure of complementary male/female roles (as set forth, for example, in the conclusion of *The Princess*). In a letter to Robert Browning in 1846, shortly before their (now legendary) elopement, Barrett Browning rejected the Ruskinian idea of marriage:

> Men like to come & find a blazing fire & a smiling face & an hour of relaxation. Their serious thoughts, & earnest aims in life, they like to keep on one side. And this is the carrying out of love & marriage almost everywhere in the world—& this, the degrading of women by both.[31]

In a recent reevaluation of *Aurora Leigh,* Taplin compares Aurora to the New Woman heroine of the 1880s, pointing out how the resolution of the poem allows Aurora "both love and freedom of action."[32] Certainly, Barrett Browning has managed here to do something that even the most critical of contemporary women poets failed to do: not only to reject the existing structure of marriage, but boldly to envision a joyful alternative to it.

In thus viewing Aurora in relationship to her future husband, we must not neglect her other great passion: her art. Ellen Moers has rightly called *Aurora Leigh* the "epic of the literary woman."[33] Despite Swinburne's protest that Aurora's life as a professional writer on her own in the city was "too eccentric" to be believed, it is quite convincingly presented.[34] We see her struggling with the double standard of literary criticism (II. 232–243), opening her fan mail (III. 210–232), and experiencing doubts about the quality of her work (I. 881–895). Aurora is constantly aware of financial pressures, writing for cyclopedias, magazines, and weekly papers, just to buy a little time to pursue her poetry (III. 306–328). She is her own most severe critic, always unsatisfied with her completed work and striving to make the next poem better than the last. Barrett Browning does not shrink from admitting the diligent work and punishing schedule Aurora's artist life requires:

> I worked on, on.
> Through all the bristling fence of nights and days
> Which hedges time in from the eternities,
> I struggled,—never stopped to note the stakes
> Which hurt me in my course. The midnight oil
> Would stink sometimes; there came some vulgar needs:
> I had to live that therefore I might work,
> And, being but poor, I was constrained, for life,
> To work with one hand for the booksellers
> While working with the other for myself
> And art.
>
> (III. 295–305)

Aurora has a high conception of her calling and a determination to maintain her integrity as a poet. When, in her story's conclusion, she tells Romney, "Art is much, but Love is more" (IX. 656), it is not as a repudiation of art but as a greater testimony to the joy of love. "O Art, my Art, thou'rt much," she continues, "but Love is more! / Art symbolises heaven, but Love is God / And makes heaven" (IX. 657–659). Thus, Barrett Browning's final verdict on the dispute between love and fame is similar to the position George Eliot expressed in *Armgart* fourteen years later: the pursuit of artistic excellence and public fame is not wrong in itself, but only insofar as it necessitates the sacrifice of human love. Both Elizabeth Barrett Browning and George Eliot were living proof that this sacrifice was avoidable, even for nineteenth-century Englishwomen.

Lady Waldemar, the villain of the poem, confronts Aurora on their first meeting with the contemporary stereotype of the literary woman:

> You stand outside,
> You artist women, of the common sex;
> You share not with us, and exceed us so
> Perhaps by what you're mulcted in, your hearts
> Being starved to make your heads: so run the old
> Traditions of you.
>
> (III. 406–411)

Yet in her arrogance, she reveals not a truth about women artists, but rather a hint of her own potential for cruelty. Some critics have felt that Lady Waldemar is made to appear worse than she actually is by being presented only through the eyes of the jealous Aurora, and that judged impartially, she would become a more sympathetic character.[35] Others have dismissed her as a mere adventuress or as a stereotypical "Wicked Lady of Quality."[36] But she can perhaps be judged most accurately by observing in her the dilemma of the post-Regency aristocrat, the bored lady of leisure. Both her coarseness of language and her sophistication of manner can be seen as attributes of Regency society. Now that a different era is upon her, she attempts to take on the colors of the "modest women" (III. 580) of the present day, but succeeds only in achieving hypocrisy. She is the "charming woman" (IV. 527) of Lady Dufferin's 1835 satire, a "woman of the world" (III. 629; IV. 513).

Lady Waldemar's chief crime is that she does not take life as seriously as a proper Victorian woman ought to do. She unintentionally mocks Romney's attempts to do good by playing at philanthropy as a sort of lovers' game, and she offends Aurora by the frankness and physicality of her feelings for Romney.

> Am I coarse?
> Well, love's coarse, nature's coarse—ah, there's the rub.
> We fair fine ladies, who park out our lives,
> From common sheep-paths, cannot help the crows
> From flying over,—we're as natural still
> As Blowsalinda.

                                          (III. 454–459)

Outrageous though she may be, Lady Waldemar's earthiness and cynicism are attractive in their own colorful way—to the modern reader, at least, if not to the likes of Romney, Aurora, and their peers. The callous way in which she dispatches Marian Erle to the colonies is reprehensible, of course. But the blame for Marian's abduction and rape lies with the unscrupulous servant, not with Lady Waldemar directly. Probably she is sincere when she expresses her regrets about the incident and writes to "thank" Aurora Leigh "For proving to myself that there are things / I would not do—not for my life, nor him" (IX. 19–20). She is not merely a conventional villainess, nor yet simply a careless aristocrat. She seems rather to be an anachronism, a vital, energetic woman vexed by the century's continuing encroachments upon her freedom to express those qualities. Her attachment to Romney Leigh, invested though it is with pride, represents a genuine attempt to find a niche. "I cannot choose but think," she writes Aurora, "That, with him, I were virtuouser than you / Without him" (IX. 167–169), and the statement has a ring of truth.

The well-known case of Marian Erle must be considered in light of both existing social conditions and the mid-century literary tradition of the fallen woman. As we have seen, the primitive living conditions among the lowest classes of England were indeed conducive to the type of casual immorality epitomized in Marian's mother's attempt to sell her daughter to a local squire. Marian's frantic flight into the city, the hopelessness of her life as a seamstress (like Lucy Gresham), and the squalor of her living quarters are accurately presented. Furthermore, the horrifying circumstances of her abduction, rape, and imprisonment in a Paris brothel were not unrealistic, as W. T. Stead's series of articles on the white slave trade would later attest. Neither is Marian's reintegration into society unlikely; had she married a respectable man and settled into a bland domesticity, it would not have violated probability, but only literary and social convention.

In "A Year's Spinning" (1846), Barrett Browning had depicted the fallen woman's fate in an entirely conventional sequence: seduction, abandonment, illegitimate motherhood, infant death, and the grave. In *Aurora Leigh,* Marian's childhood friend Rose Bell, who apparently has become a prostitute of the sort later interviewed by Bracebridge Hemyng, seems to be irrevocably lost to sin.[37] Even Marian pities Rose: "I heard her laugh last night in Oxford Street, / I'd pour out half my blood to stop that laugh, / Poor Rose, poor Rose!" (III. 927–929). Barrett Browning, of course, knew, and on occasion adhered to, this literary tradition of the harlot's inevitable progress to the grave or to perdition.

In depicting Marian Erle, however, she rejected those familiar patterns entirely. Marian's story is in consonance with the reality, not the myth, of the "great social evil" of England. She is not seduced, but raped; she is not abandoned by a faithless lover, but flees from sexual captivity. Her devotion to her illegitimate son is rewarded by smiles and affection, not by bereavement. The child cannot even be properly said to "redeem" his mother, for, though despoiled, she has never sinned. When Marian is offered the option of honorable marriage, she refuses; nor does she then sink into the grave, but lives peacefully on for the sake of her son.

It is only as a mother, and not as a ruined woman, that Marian approaches conventionality. In declining Romney's offer of marriage, she replies, "Here's a hand shall keep / For ever clean without a marriage-ring, / To tend my boy . . . " (IX. 431–433). No doubt the story of Marian Erle owed something to Elizabeth Gaskell's groundbreaking novel *Ruth* (1853), whose fallen heroine regains a position of social and self-respect by serving as a sick-nurse during a typhoid epidemic. Ruth is not allowed to resume a "normal" life, however; she dies of the disease, which she contracts, appropriately enough, from her former lover. Thus, Marian Erle's destiny far exceeds Ruth's for social realism and sheer audacity.[38] Furthermore, the astonishing facts are that *Aurora Leigh* appeared one year before William Acton's earliest study on *Prostitution*, six years before *London Labour and the London Poor*, and almost thirty years before "The Maiden Tribute of Modern Babylon." Her literary representation of Marian Erle was far ahead of its time.

Contemporary critics who disliked the characters of Aurora Leigh and Lady Waldemar adored Marian Erle, although they found her idealistic beliefs and elegant language to be out of synchrony with her lower-class background.[39] The sentimental appeal of the guiltless sexual victim was perhaps irresistible. However, the unrelenting realism with which Barrett Browning articulated Marian's wrongs and alluded to the extent and horrors of English prostitution raised eyebrows among conservative readers. In describing these taboo subjects in the most explicit language, Barrett Browning purposely defied both literary and social conventions. In defense of her frankness on the subject, she proclaimed, "If a woman ignores these wrongs, then may women as a sex continue to suffer them; there is no help for any of us—let us be dumb and die."[40]

Aurora Leigh believed in performance, rather than argument, as the way to prove the validity of women's God-given abilities and prerogatives (VIII. 813–846). Elizabeth Barrett Browning obviously shared the opinion, for *Aurora Leigh* was an incredibly wide-ranging and intense poetical production, for any poet. This magnificent effort was doubtless exhausting; "afterward," Taplin feels, "she had almost nothing new to say, and for the remaining four and one-half years of her life she produced only a few short poems, most of which were written to express her sympathy with the Italian cause. . . . "[41] Among these poems are "The Dance" and "A Court Lady" (1860), "Parting Lovers" and "Mother and Poet" (1862), all of which depict women as Italian patriots.

"Little Mattie" (1861) and "Only a Curl" (1862) are both poems in the child mortality tradition. The former acknowledges the maternal feelings of anger at the dead child which accompany the grief and pain of bereavement, and the latter contains an unusually realistic description of childbirth and mother-love (31–40). Otherwise, they are both quite conventional poems. "Amy's Cruelty" (1857) is a sentimental treatment of romantic courtship, which nonetheless recognizes the risks women take in awarding their love: "Unless he gives me all in change, / I forfeit all things by him" (33–34). Amy is "cruel" to her suitor, because she fears the consequences of commitment. In its theme and in its cuteness, "Amy's Cruelty" hearkens back to "A Man's Requirements." These verses and the poems upon noble Italian womanhood are neither much better nor much worse than many of Barrett Browning's earlier efforts.

However, four remaining poems, all published in *Last Poems* (1862), deserve notice as being different in their themes and in their representations of women from the poetry Barrett Browning published before *Aurora Leigh*. The first of these, "Lord Walter's Wife," deals with adultery. It was submitted to *Cornhill Magazine* in 1861, but William Thackeray declined it as being unsuitable for some of his more "squeamish" readers.[42] The celebrated adultery in the poem never actually takes place, for Lord Walter's wife, by appearing suddenly to give her consent, exposes the inauthenticity of the would-be seducer's suit. "Lord Walter's Wife" is a highly sophisticated poem —quite daring for its day—and an early example of the tendency to cross the imagery of the virtuous wife and mother with that of the fallen woman. Barrett Browning withdrew the poem and sent Thackeray "Little Mattie" in its place.

"Void in Law" also concerns a type of marital offense—in this case, annulment. The poem exposes the immorality of a man's legal right to abandon his wife and disinherit his child on the basis of a technical error in the marriage ceremony. However, the speaker of the poem, the disowned wife, is not bitter or angry, but only vows, "Let him learn we are waiting before / The grave's mouth, the heaven's gate, God's face, / With implacable love evermore" (46–48). Although "Void in Law" is certainly a poem of social protest, it is extremely gentle in tone.

"Where's Agnes?" can be read as an unusual poem on the subject of the fallen woman. The model for Agnes is generally held to be Mrs. Sophia Eckley, an American woman who in 1857 had "fallen in love" with her, Barrett Browning reported to a friend, and who worshipped her friend Elizabeth "with a blind passion in all sorts of ways."[43] Elizabeth also had strong feelings for Sophia, according to Robert, and regarded her as a "perfection of purity."[44] Their friendship of several years' duration broke off in 1860 when Elizabeth discovered that, in an attempt to intensify their relationship, Sophia had been pretending greater interest and experience in Elizabeth's new-found passion—spiritualism—than was strictly accurate.[45] Robert says that Elizabeth "disguised . . . the circumstances" when she poured her anger and disappointment with Sophia into "Where's Agnes?"[46] But of course art is not merely disguised life, and in the artistic use Barrett Browning made of her own disillusionment, she engaged Victorian tensions about womanhood in a larger context, as a close analysis of the diction and imagery of the poem will reveal.

To begin with, as is evident from lines 71–80, the speaker of this dramatic monologue is not a woman, but a man. He is clearly an angry suitor reacting to the news of his beloved Agnes' "corruption." He had worshipped her as the ideal Victorian woman—angelic, saintly: "Her very gown, her cloak / Fell chastely" (26–27). Now he wonders, how could such a paragon have been seduced? The remainder of the poem is devoted to answering that extremely pertinent question. First of all, Agnes' feminine virtue was, perhaps, too exaggerated to be sustainable:

> Had she any fault at all
>   'Twas having none; I thought too—
> There seemed a sort of thrall;
>   As she felt her shadow ought to
> Fall straight upon the wall.
>
> Her sweetness strained the sense
>   Of common life and duty;
> And every day's expense
>   Of moving in such beauty
> Required, almost, defence.
>
>   (41–50)

Further, he wonders, of what use is a woman so obviously unfit for the common work of humanity, or even for plain speaking? Previously, he had thought her very "Being" was sufficient justification. Perhaps God had sent her "Just to show what beauty may, / Just to prove what music can" (71-72), in order to lead a man toward prayer. Now his concept of woman's divine mission has proved delusionary:

> What! She fell
>   Like a woman, who was sent
> Like an angel, by a spell?
> She, who scarcely trod the earth,
>   Turned mere dirt? My Agnes,—mine!
> Called so! felt of too much worth
>   To be used so! Too divine
> To be breathed near, and so forth!
>
> (83-90)

The speaker's disillusionment with Agnes is proportionate to his previous idealization of her. Her defection threatens his faith in God and in the beauty of Nature; her ruination somehow entails his own.

If we consider the speaker as the representative Victorian male he seems to be, then this poem sheds some light on the severity of social sanctions for unchastity in women. As objects of worship, emblems of God's presence, receptacles of virtue and beauty, etc., Victorian women were not meant to be of practical utility, but to preserve the human race from sin and degradation. Thus when the ideal woman suddenly fell, it could seem to man as though "Sin blots out the universe" (109). Now that the "white rose" has fallen from its branch, and only *because* it was a rose, the speaker decides to prefer women more substantial, if less appealing to him, than the lovely but fragile Agnes:

> Then henceforth may earth grow trees,
>   No more roses!—hard straight lines
> To score lies out! none of these
>   Fluctuant curves, but firs and pines,
> Poplars, cedars, cypresses!
>
> (116-120)

In other words, he is now prepared to abandon the delicate ideal of the Victorian lady in exchange for the hardier reality of the New Woman.

This reading of the poem is not meant to deny its genesis in Barrett Browning's pain and sense of betrayal over losing Sophia Eckley. Indeed, using a male speaker to convey strong emotions toward a woman is not uncommon in women's poetry, and the parallels here between the actual "circumstances" and the poetic vehicle are clear. Possibly the relationship between the two women was one of those "romantic friendships" so common between women in the nineteenth century.[47] Even though they expressed "nothing but what it is natural Ba should feel for 'Agnes,' " Robert Browning was concerned that Sophia might try to publish the letters Elizabeth had sent her; she was known to be "making a show" of them seven years after Elizabeth's death. Here is Robert's response:

> Well, when she [Sophia] called on me in London . . . bathed in tears and so on—I could not, for the life of me, feel angry—any more than the poor fellow, in "Madame Bovary," with the man whom, after his wife's suicide, he finds, by a bundle of love letters, had seduced his wife. I rather thought—"After all, you thought she was worth damning your soul for, and I agree with you!"[48]

It is a measure of the depth of Elizabeth Barrett Browning's involvement with her friend—and therefore of the bitterness of her anger—that she should choose the sexually resonant figure of the fallen woman to convey the enormity of Sophia's sin against her.

One final poem, "Bianca Among the Nightingales," will serve to illustrate Barrett Browning's late-found capacity for depicting sexual passion. Alethea Hayter feels that it was not until this particular poem, "when she was a dying woman in her fifties, [that Barrett Browning] was able to convey the passionate intensity and excitement of young lovers."[49] Yet in *Aurora Leigh* she had made a few tentative attempts to do so, as, for instance, when Aurora defends true love to the fickle Lady Waldemar:

> I comprehend a love so fiery hot
> It burns its natural veil of August shame,
> And stands sublimely in the nude, as chaste
> As Medicean Venus.
>
> (III. 703–706)

The embrace of Romney and Aurora in the poem's final scene is passionate, though elliptically described:

> There were words
> That broke in utterance . . . melted, in the fire,—
> Embrace, that was convulsion, . . . then a kiss
> As long and silent as the ecstatic night,
> And deep, deep, shuddering breaths, which meant beyond
> Whatever could be told by word or kiss.
>
> (IX. 719–724)

But even in the audacious *Aurora Leigh*, the passion is not as sustained as it is in "Bianca Among the Nightingales."

The poem belongs to the tradition of the pining maiden. Bianca's true love Giulio has been beguiled away from her by an English *femme fatale*, who came to "intrude / 'Twixt two affianced souls, and hunt / Like spiders, in the altar's wood" for Giulio (114–116). Bianca has followed the pair from Italy to England, and she now stands in the English moonlight, surrounded by nightingales whose singing tortures her with regret and frustrated love. She recalls the days of their courtship, when heaven and earth seemed to respond to the heat of their mutual passion:

> The cypress stood up like a church
>   That night we felt our love would hold,
> And saintly moonlight seemed to search
>   And wash the whole world clean as gold;
> The olives crystallized the vales'
>   Broad slopes until the hills grew strong:
> The fireflies and the nightingales
>   Throbbed each to either, flame and song.
> The nightingales, the nightingales.
>
>   (1–9)

The sexual imagery of the upright cypress tree and swelling hills and of the fire and throbbing of the creatures thronging the air symbolizes, of course, the physical nature of the lovers' passion:

>   Such leaps of blood, so blindly driven,
> We scarce knew if our nature meant
>   Most passionate earth or intense heaven,
> The nightingales, the nightingales!
>
> We paled with love, we shook with love,
>   We kissed so close we could not vow;
> Till Giulio whispered, "Sweet, above
>   God's Ever guaranties this Now."
>
>   (15–22)

Against this Edenic experience of youthful passion suddenly arises the specter of the Englishwoman: "What a head, / What leaping eyeballs!—beauty dashed / To splendour by a sudden dread" (78–80). Bianca sees what Giulio cannot: the falsity of the woman's unscrupulous nature.

A worthless woman; mere cold clay
   As all false things are: but so fair,
She takes the breath of men away
   Who gaze upon her unaware.

                                              (100–104)

The English intruder is the serpent in the garden. Says Bianca, "She . . . reached him at my heart / With her fine tongue, as snakes indeed / Kill flies" (91–93). In the last stanza Bianca anticipates her own doom: "They'll sing through death who sing through night, / They'll sing and stun me in the tomb— / The nightingales, the nightingales!" (142–144). The sexual excitement of the lovers and the frenzied frustration of Bianca secure for this poem an important place in the small but significant canon of nineteenth-century women's poetry about sex.

After *Aurora Leigh*, no subsequent poem by Elizabeth Barrett Browning ever "caught the crowd" in quite the same way.[50] The poetry she published between 1856 and her death in 1861 reached a certain level of sophistication appropriate to her age and experience, but by and large it also lapsed into tradition and conventionality in its characterization of women. With the achievement of *Aurora Leigh*, however, the continuing significance of her contribution to the literature of women was assured. The risk she had dared to take in defense of nineteenth-century womanhood was justified by the popular impact, if not by the critical reception, of her longest poem. Today, without a hint of condescension, we may pronounce *Aurora Leigh* the nineteenth-century masterpiece among English poems written by and about women.

10
Christina Rossetti

Unlike Elizabeth Barrett Browning, Christina Rossetti seldom engaged explicitly social themes in her poetry. "It is not in me," she wrote to her brother Dante Gabriel, "and therefore it will never come out of me to turn to politics and philanthropy with Mrs. Browning: such many-sidedness I leave to a greater than I, and, having said my say, may well sit silent."[1] Rossetti was primarily a poet of the internal self; she wrote beautifully personal lyric poems on love, death, religion, and nature.[2] In addition, she composed verses for children (*Sing-Song*, 1872) and short stories for young adults (*Maude*, 1850, and *Speaking Likenesses*, 1874). Her canon is much larger than many people realize, filling five separate volumes, including one (*New Poems*, 1896) published after her death by her brother William Michael. However, in all this, as Walter de la Mare remarked in 1926, "We shall search almost in vain for reference to the sesames and shibboleths, to the public events and crises of her own day."[3]

Our search will indeed be "almost in vain"—almost, but not quite. For example, Christina Rossetti's strong sympathy with animals, which led her to participate in the anti-vivisectionist movement, and her equally strong antipathy for war educed several poems of protest upon those particular issues. More relevant to our purposes here is her concern for the plight of the English lower classes, manifest in "A Royal Princess" (1851),[4] whose heroine defies the feudal patriarchy (in the person of her father, the king) by flinging her gold and jewels to a starving, angry mob. The tale is told entirely from the point of view of the princess, who is a virtual prisoner of rank and of self:

> All my walls are lost in mirrors, whereupon I trace
> Self to right hand, self to left hand, self in every place,
> Self-same solitary figure, self-same seeking face.

> Then I have an ivory chair high to sit upon,
> Almost like my father's chair, which is an ivory throne;
> There I sit uplift and upright, there I sit alone.[5]

This resplendent isolation is monotonous to her, though envied by her father's impoverished subjects. Suddenly she seizes her right, "in the name of God" (108), to act the Lady Bountiful with her father's goods. It is a heroic gesture, of course, but probably a futile one, for the crowd is already preparing to fire the castle.

Dante Gabriel scoffed at this poem because it ended with the princess' exit from her room, rather than her confrontation with the threatening crowd. Christina's rejoinder shows that the ambiguity of the conclusion was deliberate: "I do not fight for the R. P.'s heroism, though it seems to me that the royal soldiers might yet have succeeded in averting *roasting*. A yell is *one* thing and a *fait accompli* quite another."[6] The courageous, if over-protected, princess is a symbol of Victorian womanhood, emerging from isolation, coming down from her ivory pedestal, in order to pursue philanthropy. However, her efforts, though admirably motivated, may well prove both tardy and ineffectual, and the lower classes of England may churn into justifiable revolt against their oppressors; the outcome remains in doubt. The medieval setting and the Pre-Raphaelite beauty of the decor do not obscure the meaning of "A Royal Princess" when one takes into account the rising social involvement of women and the turbulence of England in the mid-nineteenth century. Rossetti contributed the poem to Emily Faithfull's 1863 anthology *Poems: An Offering to Lancashire, Printed and Published for the Relief of Distress in the Cotton Districts.*[7]

Mackenzie Bell believed "A Royal Princess" to be "the single instance where Christina Rossetti frankly avows democratic sentiments."[8] However, in "Maggie a Lady" (1865), she depicts a woman from the rural working class whose extraordinary beauty has won the heart of the lord of the manor and the approval of his family for their wedding. Marriage across lines of class distinction was, of course, a dominant theme in Victorian fiction and drama. In poetry, Barrett Browning had employed it upon several occasions to express democratic beliefs, most notably in "Lady Geraldine's Courtship" (1844) and *Aurora Leigh* (1856). In Rossetti's poem, the new lady of the manor finds she was happier as plain Maggie. For though she is now "a great lady in a sheltered bower, / With hands grown white thro' having nought to do" (45–46), she has sacrificed the more appropriate love she bore for her sailor cousin Phil. (To be fair, Maggie had been told that Phil was lost at sea; she accepted the proposal of "my lord" almost immediately thereafter.) The message here seems somewhat similar to that in *Aurora Leigh*: upper and lower classes *may* merge if they choose, but the result is not likely to be altogether satisfactory, even for the "inferior" of the two parties.

In several other poems, Rossetti depicted rural working women as, on the whole, happy and contented with their lot. One of the four women reapers in "Songs in a Cornfield" (1864) is indeed sad, but it is not that her work is tedious or displeasing, but only that her sweetheart is away. The others sing merrily as they work, and at noon enjoy their midday repast with some enthusiasm. The female figures are more fully delineated in this poem than in Mathilde Blind's "Reapers," but they are equally picturesque. "A Farm Walk" (1864) is comparable with Jean Ingelow's "Reflections" upon the subject of a lovely idealized milkmaid. (Christina Rossetti admired Elizabeth Browning, was a friend of Jean Ingelow, and had met Mathilde Blind.) Rossetti's representation of working women seems derivative and traditional enough. However, the very situation in "Maggie a Lady" was unconventionally democratic, and the poetic treatment of reapers and milkmaids, however idealized, was, as we have seen, quite unusual among nineteenth-century women poets generally. In "A Royal Princess," Rossetti's meaning, as well as her choice of subject, reveals a concern for lower-class women which, though genuine, was not a theme she often pursued in poetry.

Concerning feminism: Rossetti was not only reluctant to proselytize for women in her poetry; she was unalterably opposed to the methods and aims of the burgeoning new women's movement. Despite her personal admiration of ardent feminists like Augusta Webster, Emily Faithfull, Barbara Leigh Smith Bodichon, and Mathilde Blind, Christina Rossetti never assented that women were equal with men. Nor did she agree that women could or should try to intrude themselves into traditional provinces of masculinity. She even declined to endorse women's right to vote. In 1885, she wrote Augusta Webster, "Does it not appear as if the Bible was based upon an understood unalterable distinction between men and women, their position, duties, privileges? . . . I do not think that the present social movements tend on the whole to uphold Xtianity, or that the influence of some of our most prominent and gifted women is exerted in that direction; and thus thinking, I cannot aim at 'women's rights.' "[9]

Cora Kaplan finds the "conservative implications" of poetry such as Rossetti's to be "embarrassing" for feminist critics. In a recent essay she outlines in the work of Rossetti (and Emily Dickinson) an "unresolved contradiction . . . between progressive social struggle and the recalcitrant female psyche," in order to explain what, to modern eyes, seem to be puzzling discrepancies.[10] Jerome J. McGann, on the other hand, speculates that Rossetti's refusal to endorse contemporary women's movement activities did not signify conservatism on her part, but rather a radical rejection of middle-class feminist reformism, in favor of an altogether new social order: "The principal factor which enabled her to overleap [contemporary feminism] was her severe Christianity."[11]

While McGann's thesis may be appealing in some ways, it fails to account for the numerous poems in which, throughout her career, Rossetti echoed the conventional wisdom of the early nineteenth century on the subject of women. For example, included in her earliest publication (in 1847) was "Eleanor," which depicted an ideal English girl: sweet, pretty, cheerful, accomplished, noble, angelic, etc. (p. 105). In 1854, Rossetti wrote, revealingly, "It's a weary life, it is . . . / Doubly blank in a woman's lot; / I wish and I wish I were a man" ("From the Antique," p. 312). However, the very next line, "Or, better than any being, were not," reveals the true movement of this poem—not toward social emancipation, but toward death. Life, which is perhaps doubly blank for women, is pronounced sufficiently blank and tiresome to weary anyone. Being male would not really alter the speaker's situation, but being dead *would*. The urge is not toward increased activity (conventionally masculine), but toward final passivity (conventionally feminine).

"The Lowest Room," written in 1856, only a few months before the appearance of *Aurora Leigh*, comes the closest of any of Rossetti's poems to Barrett Browning's manner and mode. Dante Gabriel complained that "The Lowest Room" suffered from "a real taint . . . of modern vicious style . . . a falsetto muscularity," derived from Barrett Browning. "Everything in which this tone appears is utterly foreign to your primary impulses," he reproached his sister.[12] William Michael's opinion was that "if anything of that kind shows in the earlier part of the poem, it shows only to be waved aside."[13] Both men are correct in their observations, but perhaps mistaken in their value judgments.

On the most obvious level, the poem is an argument between two sisters about the relative merits of antiquity and the modern age. The "muscularity" which Dante Gabriel deplored appears most forcefully in the older sister's early outbursts against contemporary life.

> "A shame it is, our aimless life:
>   I rather from my heart would feed
> From silver dish in gilded stall
>   With wheat and wine the steed—
> The faithful steed that bore my lord
>   In safety thro' the hostile land,
> The faithful steed that arched his neck
>   To fondle with my hand."
>
> (81–88)

This sister is a spinster and a poet. She laments over her book that, unlike Homer, *she* "cannot melt the sons of men," and "cannot fire and tempest-toss" (33–34) with her writing. The younger sister is domestic, "feminine" (37). An ideal Victorian woman, she does needlework and floral arrangements while waiting for her fiancé, and, of course, she defends the present day: "To me our days seem pleasant days, / Our home a haven of pure content" (149–150). Unspoken in their conversation, but clear enough in the older sister's mind, is the rivalry between the two and the relegation of the unmarried older sister, with all her wisdom and spirit, to the "lowest place" (271) in society. It is possible to read the older sister's complaints as an enunciation of the common problem of all gifted, fiery women artists of the age. She resolves the dilemma by commending her burdensome life to the Lord and, interestingly, by anticipating that apocalyptic day when "all deep secrets shall be shown, / And many last be first" (279–280).

In this interpretation, the two sisters symbolize the lonely woman artist and the loving wife and mother of the Victorian period. By regarding these two roles as irreconcilable alternatives, the speaker (and perhaps Rossetti herself) finds, it is "My lot in life, to live alone / In mine own world of interests, / Much felt but little shown" (262–264). Unlike George Eliot or Elizabeth Barrett Browning, Christina Rossetti does not suggest the possibility of acceptable compromise between the two roles. Her vision of nineteenth-century womanhood is thus far more constrictive than theirs. She appears to recognize but not to resolve the gifted woman's dilemma, except by a reversion to religious consolation—both in this poem and, perhaps, in her own life as well.

In "Enrica, 1865," Rossetti rose to the defense of Englishwomen, who might seem "trim, correct, / All minted in the selfsame mould" (9–10), by contrast with Italian womanhood, in the person of one Enrica Barile Filipanto, a banished wife who tried, briefly, to earn a living in England by giving lessons in Italian.[14] Whereas Enrica, with her more natural grace and open cordiality, might regard Englishwomen as "like our sea, / Of aspect colourless and chill, / Rock-girt," nevertheless, Rossetti (who was herself three-quarters Italian) insisted, "she found us still / Deep at our deepest, strong and free" (21–24). This assertion that the conventionally correct Englishwoman was more ardent and self-respecting than she might appear cannot be read as a sudden conversion to feminist ideas about womankind. For in the same year Rossetti also wrote, "Men work and think, but women feel" ("An 'Immurata' Sister," p. 380); and sometime during the last years before her death she wrote "A Helpmeet for Him," expressing the most conventional notions possible about woman's "sphere."

A HELPMEET FOR HIM

Woman was made for man's delight;
    Charm, O woman, be not afraid!
His shadow by day, his moon by night,
    Woman was made.

Her strength with weakness is overlaid;
  Meek compliances veil her might;
Him she stays by whom she is stayed.

World-wide champion of truth and right,
  Hope in gloom and in danger aid,
Tender and faithful, ruddy and white,
  Woman was made.[15]

It is true that the speaker of "An 'Immurata' Sister" reacts with despair to the traditional role assignments of men and women: "And so (for I'm a woman, I) / And so I should be glad to die / And cease from impotence of zeal." But she concludes by offering her soul to God as a "burnt-offering" (p. 380), and the sincerity of that resolution is not undercut by what we may perceive as its tragedy. Because Rossetti's poems so frequently exhibit this movement from earthly discontentment to spiritual consolation, critics must be careful not to remove early stanzas from their full poetic context and set them forth as representing Rossetti's final position. Similarly, we must not infer irony in poems like "A Helpmeet for Him" where none is implied, no matter how "embarrassing" such conventionality may be.

In fact, looking at "A Helpmeet for Him" as a genuine statement by Christina Rossetti of what she perceived marriage to require from women can help us to answer the question that has perplexed her various biographers for so long: Why did she never marry?[16] Perhaps from believing that she could not be at once the dedicated artist which her talent demanded and the devoted helpmeet which her husband would have expected, she quite simply preferred the artist's vocation to that of the wife and mother.

Returning to the issue of Rossetti's involvement with contemporary social questions, there is one additional area where she evinced a definite interest, both in a practical way and in her poetry: the recognition and reclamation of the fallen woman. During the 1850s and 1860s, Christina Rossetti was a frequent visitor—and finally an "associate"—of the St. Mary Magdalen Home for fallen women at Highgate.[17] In fact, it was there that she corrected the proofs for *Goblin Market and Other Poems*, issued in 1862. Numerous poems in this volume and several in *The Prince's Progress and Other Poems* (1866) represent the plight of the fallen woman. Clearly, Rossetti's activities at the Magdalen home prompted her to compose these poems. "A Triad," "Cousin Kate," and "Sister Maude" from *Goblin Market* and "Light Love" from *The Prince's Progress* were dropped from editions of her poetry subsequent to 1866, a decision which William Michael later attributed to his sister's "overstrained scrupulosity."[18] After her death, he restored the poems to her collected works. "Under the Rose" (1865), later retitled "The Iniquity of the Fathers

Upon the Children," was never suppressed, but appeared in numerous successive editions of her poetry from 1862 to 1904.

In these and other poems about fallen women, Rossetti consistently presents
her fallen heroine in contrast with some other, purer female figure—often a
sister or a rival.[19] In "Sister Maude" (1860?), for instance, one self-righteous
and meddling sister has snitched upon the other. The fallen woman heroine
accuses and curses the sister whose betrayal has brought about the death of her
lover:

> Who told my mother of my shame,
>   Who told my father of my dear?
> Oh who but Maude, my sister Maude,
>   Who lurked to spy and peer.
>
> . . . .
>
> If my dear and I knocked at Heaven-gate
>   Perhaps they'd let us in:
> But sister Maude, O sister Maude,
>   Bide *you* with death and sin.
>
> (1–4, 19–22)

If William Michael's assessment can be trusted, then it seems obvious why
"Sister Maude" was cancelled: the self-righteous spy and not the fallen
woman receives the curse.

In the case of "Under the Rose," the new title "The Iniquity of the Fathers
Upon the Children" points the moral, that sexual sin has inevitable and far-
reaching consequences. An aristocratic young woman, the last of a noble line,
secretly gives birth to an illegitimate daughter and commends the child into
the care of a faithful nurse. Years later, when the nurse dies, the mother—
still unmarried—invites the child to the great hall "To be my Lady's maid: /
'Her little friend,' she said to me, / 'Almost her child' " (301–303). The
pathos and irony of the situation are not lost upon the young girl who, with
more acumen than such characters usually possess, comes to understand that
the Lady of the Hall is indeed her mother.

> Now I have eyes and ears,
> And just some little wit:
> "Almost my Lady's child";
> I recollect she smiled,
> Sighed and blushed together. . . .
> I guess not who he was
> Flawed honour like a glass

And made my life forlorn,
But my Mother, Mother, Mother,
Oh, I know her from all other.

(364–382)

One sad consequence of that mother's fall is the early separation of mother
and daughter, an alienation which can never be overcome, even were the
Lady suddenly to acknowledge her motherhood. Bitterly, the daughter
decides to hold her peace, nor does the mother herself choose to drop the
mask and reveal a secret which "Would set her in the dust, / Lorn with no
comforter, / Her glorious hair defiled / And ashes on her cheek" (403–406).
An even sadder effect of the mother's hypocrisy can be observed in the personality of the child. Deprived, rejected, and sneered at from infancy to adulthood, she yearns for a home and family like everyone else has, but she aban-
dons that "dream," determined instead never to marry but to go nameless to
her grave.

In "Under the Rose," the guilt lies with the father, the mother, and the
unforgiving attitude of society—but the chief punishment falls upon the innocent child. While the poem's moral indictment of the two sinners is in consonance with conventionality, its sympathetic attitude toward the child conveys
a plea for greater social tolerance. As Lona Packer has observed, "Although
the work ['Under the Rose'] is not outstanding, Christina's treatment of the
subject, which is frank, realistic, unsentimental, and psychologically convinc-
ing, seems decades ahead of the mid-century Victorian novelists on the same
subject."[20] In 1898, Mackenzie Bell speculated that the inspiration for
"Under the Rose" might have come from Lady Dedlock in Dickens' *Bleak
House*, which was published in 1853.[21] At any rate, it is clear that with
"Under the Rose" Rossetti was ahead of her time. The poem was likely
retained throughout various editions of her poetry, despite its daring subject,
because its indictment of society's callousness was tempered by its strong
moral position against seduction and hypocrisy.

In "Light Love" (1856) and "Cousin Kate" (1859), the fallen woman,
abandoned in favor of a rival of unquestioned chastity, not only acknowledges
but cherishes her illegitimate child as compensation for her blighted love and
lost reputation.

She strained his baby in her arms,
    His baby to her heart:
"Even let it go, the love that harms:
    We twain will never part;
Mine own, his own, how dear thou art."

("Light Love," 36–40)

Yet I've a gift you have not got,
    And seem not like to get:
For all your clothes and wedding-ring
    I've little doubt you fret.
My fair-haired son, my shame, my pride. . . .

("Cousin Kate," 41–45)

The spunky heroine of "Cousin Kate" challenges her pure, chaste cousin—
who has married the heroine's seducer—to recognize her own complicity in
her cousin's ruination.

If he had fooled not me but you,
    If you stood where I stand,
He had not won me with his love
    Nor bought me with his land;
I would have spit into his face
    And not have taken his hand.

(35–40)

Sentiments like these tend toward rehabilitation of the literary figure of the
fallen woman. Rossetti's fallen heroines were stronger willed and more durable
than convention allowed; her activities at the Magdalen home doubtless led
her to form this general opinion of their character. All in all, she is not particularly condemnatory in her poetic representations of the figure, but expresses
greater anger with seductive men, unfeeling rivals, and unforgiving society
than with women whose passion, vulnerability, or utter need had drawn them
into an untenable situation. It is unfortunate that second thoughts moved her
to withdraw these poems from public consideration.

"A Triad" (1856) was probably withdrawn not so much for its depiction of
the fallen woman—"one with lips / Crimson, with cheeks and bosom in a
glow, / Flushed to the yellow hair and finger tips" (1–3) who "shamed herself
in love" (9)—as for the unsympathetic representations of the wife and of the
pining spinster. The wife is portrayed as "sluggish" (10) and self-satisfied:
"One droned in sweetness like a fattened bee" (13). The spinster is sexually
frustrated: "blue with famine after love" (6). The poem equally condemns all
three of these conventional figures, for they are "All on the threshold, yet all
short of life" (14). If Christina became uneasy about the "moral tones" of this
poem, as William Michael suggested,[22] it was probably the poem's expressed
opinion about married women, not about fallen women, which most dis-
turbed her. Yet who is to say that "A Triad" did not, after all, reflect her true
point of view, at least in 1856? Once again, women are seen in contrast to
other women, and once again all available roles are unsatisfactory. Rossetti

was more likely to find faults in conventionally admirable figures and redeeming qualities in conventionally deprecable ones than were most women poets of her day.

Two of Christina Rossetti's most popular poems were "An Apple Gathering" (1857) and "Goblin Market" (1859), both published in the 1862 volume of verse. Each of these quasi-allegorical poems can be interpreted as a characteristic treatment by Rossetti of the figure of the fallen woman in contrast with other female figures of greater or more secure virtue (i.e., chastity). The first stanza of "An Apple Gathering" places it within the tradition of women's symbolic poems of defloration and of lost virginity.[23]

> I plucked pink blossoms from mine apple-tree
> And wore them all that evening in my hair:
> Then in due season when I went to see
> I found no apples there.
>
> (1–4)

Because her maidenhood has been precipitately lost, this heroine comes up empty-handed when the other girls (Lilian, Lilias, Gertrude) reap the harvests of girlish innocence and romantic love.

> Ah Willie, Willie, was my love less worth
> Than apples with their green leaves piled above?
> I counted rosiest apples on the earth
> Of far less worth than love.
>
> (17–20)

In other words, prompted by love, she chose to surrender her virginity to Willie, heedless of the probable forfeit of life's more lasting rewards. Now Willie has gone, and the neighbors mock her, and the fallen heroine is, literally, left out in the cold:

> I let my neighbors pass me, ones and twos
> And groups; the latest said the night grew chill,
> And hastened: but I loitered, while the dews
> Fell fast I loitered still.
>
> (25–28)

Of course this situation is emblematic also of any careless waste of life's promising resources. However, considering Rossetti's position at the Magdalen home and her other poetical treatments of the fallen women theme in the 1850s and 1860s, it seems safe to presume she realized the sexual implications of "An Apple Gathering."

Similarly, "Goblin Market" is, on one level at least, a story of three different women's responses to sexual temptation: one is hopelessly lost, one fallen
but redeemed, and the third heroically chaste and therefore capable of saving
others. The erotic associations of the goblins' fruits are established both by
their traditional symbolic value and by the human-like qualities which
Rossetti assigns to them.

> Plump unpecked cherries . . .
> Bloom-down-cheeked peaches,
> Swart-headed mulberries,
> Wild free-born cranberries . . .
>
> (7–11)

Even the virtuous Lizzie recognizes the sexual excitement in the proffered
fruits; it causes her cheeks and fingertips to tingle, and she blushes (35–39).
Laura warns, "We must not look at goblin men, / We must not buy their
fruits" (42–43). Both girls are aware of the prohibition: the goblins' wares are
forbidden fruit. The goblins themselves are all masculine and all grotesque,
animalistic—perhaps not an inaccurate rendition of adolescent girls' first reactions to male sexuality. Yet how tempting are their sensuous wares and how
seductive their attentions.

> The whisk-tailed merchant bade her taste
> In tones as smooth as honey,
> The cat-faced purr'd
> The rat-paced spoke a word
> Of welcome, and the snail-paced even was heard;
> One parrot-voiced and jolly
> Cried "Pretty Goblin" still for "Pretty Polly";—
> One whistled like a bird.
>
> (107–114)

Laura falls; and the scene in which she first tastes the fruits of sexual passion
is among the most explicit passages in Victorian literature. It is comparable
with the poetry of Swinburne at its most consciously erotic moments.

> She clipped a precious golden lock,
> She dropped a tear more rare than pearl,
> Then sucked their fruit globes fair or red:
> Sweeter than honey from the rock,
> Stronger than man-rejoicing wine,

> Clearer than water flowed that juice;
> She never tasted such before,
> How should it cloy with length of use?
> She sucked and sucked and sucked the more
> Fruits which that unknown orchard bore;
> She sucked until her lips were sore;
> Then flung the emptied rinds away
> But gathered up one kernel-stone,
> And knew not was it night or day
> As she turned home alone.
>
> (126–140)

The snipped hair and the irreplaceable tear symbolize defloration and, perhaps, the attendant bleeding. The sucking symbolizes the sensual enjoyment of sexual activity and the female experience of absorbing the masculine fluid. Dazed with ecstasy, Laura returns home to her sister.

At this point in the tale, the third character is introduced—Jeanie, who indulged herself just as Laura did and then "pined away" to death. That Laura's experience with the goblin men was sexual in nature becomes even more clear from the example of Jeanie, "Who should have been a bride; / But who for joys brides hope to have / Fell sick and died" (313–315). The trouble with both these girls seems to be that sexual initiation can occur only once: the first fall from virtue is the only significant one. Consequently, Laura cannot partake of the goblins' fruits again. The price she paid for them—her virginity—cannot be paid twice. Like Jeanie, Laura begins to pine. During the day she dwindles like any melancholy spinster, and at night she tosses and turns with "baulked desire" (267). At one point, she attempts to coax the kernel-stone into growth—perhaps a symbol of a hoped-for pregnancy—but to no avail. She sinks into despair.

> She set it by a wall that faced the south;
> Dewed it with tears, hoped for a root,
> Watched for a waxing shoot,
> But there came none.
>
> (281–284)

Finally Lizzie can tolerate her sister's misery no longer, but determines in one way or another to reclaim her. For although it is too late for Jeanie, it may not be too late for Laura to be saved. She first tries to purchase her sister's salvation with money, but that is not the answer. The goblins refuse to sell their wares so cheaply. What ensues when Lizzie not only resists the temptation of the fruits, but also demands a refund can best be described as an attempted rape. The goblins

> Tore her gown and soiled her stocking,
> Twitched her hair out by the roots,
> Stamped upon her tender feet.
> Held her hands and squeezed their fruits
> Against her mouth to make her eat.
>
> (403–407)

Lizzie offers a passive resistance,

> Like a royal virgin town
> Topped with gilded dome and spire
> Close beleaguered by a fleet
> Mad to tug her standard down.
>
> (418–421)

Through it all she does not "open lip from lip / Lest they should cram a mouthful in" (431–432). Finally, "Worn out by her resistance," they leave her bespattered with their juice; it "syrupped all her face, / And lodged in dimples of her chin, / And streaked her neck" (434–438). Bruised and dazed, but nevertheless intact, Lizzie runs home to Laura with the goblin juice, the symbol of her triumph and the means of Laura's restoration.

Laura's initial reaction is terror that her devoted sister may have sacrificed too much:

> "Lizzie, Lizzie, have you tasted
> For my sake the fruit forbidden?
> Must your light like mine be hidden
> Your young life like mine be wasted,
> Undone in mine undoing
> And ruined in my ruin,
> Thirsty, cankered, goblin-ridden?"—
>
> (478–484)

However, all is well. Lizzie has not been "ruined," and Laura, overcome with love and remorse, undergoes a kind of exorcism, during which the purity and devotion of Lizzie's love overwhelm the sensuality and bitterness of Laura's soul. "Swift fire spread thro' her veins, knocked at her heart, / Met the fire smouldering there / And overbore its lesser flame" (507–509). Laura swoons, and when she reawakens, she is completely and miraculously restored to virginity.

> Laura awoke as from a dream,
> Laughed in the innocent old way,
> Hugged Lizzie but not twice or thrice;
> Her gleaming locks showed not one thread of grey,
> Her breath was sweet as May,
> And light danced in her eyes.
>
> (537–542)

Through love and suffering, the fallen woman has been raised up by her courageous and devoted sister and returned to a healthful life.

Just so, perhaps, did serious young women like Christina Rossetti descend into the "depths" of society in hopes of reclaiming "lost" women from death and despair. Laura's redemption is so absolute that, just like Lizzie, she is able to become a happy wife and mother. This interpretation of the poem makes the final six lines seem less incidental:

> "For there is no friend like a sister
> In calm or stormy weather;
> To cheer one on the tedious way,
> To fetch one if one goes astray,
> To lift one if one totters down,
> To strengthen whilst one stands."
>
> (562–567)

What else was the avowed undertaking of the "sisters" and "associates" of the St. Mary Magdalen Home for fallen women, where Christina donated so much of her time and energies to her fellow women? Unlike many conventional Victorian women, Rossetti was able both to sympathize and to identify with her fallen sisters. As Packer puts it, "she did not consider the gap between herself and the Highgate penitents so wide as to appear incomprehensible."[24] "Goblin Market" and Rossetti's other poems of the fifties and sixties on the subject of fallen womanhood reveal a social dimension to her work which has gone largely unnoticed heretofore.

To turn from Christina Rossetti's masterpiece "Goblin Market" to her poems about infant mortality, her verse tributes to her mother, and her wistful lyrics about thwarted love seems anti-climactic. Yet Rossetti did indeed participate in these and several other feminine traditions in poetry as well, including such familiar figures as the pining maiden and the fading spinster. Like Barrett Browning, she even, as a mature woman, wrote compellingly of sexual passion. In the later years of her life, she turned her attention as a poet increasingly from representing human interaction to writing on another traditionally feminine poetic theme—but one which does not concern us directly— religion and spirituality. Focusing on her contributions to identifiable female traditions of verse will remind us how much and in what ways Christina Rossetti was indeed a part of nineteenth-century women's culture.

For example, her several tributes to dead children—including one on the Duke of Clarence (1892) and one on her nephew, little Michael Rossetti (c. 1883)—invite comparison with Jean Ingelow's poems on the same theme.[25] In "Three Moments" (1850), Rossetti depicted a bereaved mother's grief with a degree of violence and a depth of psychological realism not commonly found in women's teary-eyed poetry on this subject.

> The Woman knelt, but did not pray
> Nor weep nor cry; she only said,
> "Not this, not this!" and clasped her hands
> Against her heart, and bowed her head,
> While the great struggle shook the bed.
> "Not this, not this!"
>
> (pp. 300–1)

For the most part, however, she wrote nothing very remarkable on the theme of child mortality, but reserved her finest musings upon death for poetry of a more general nature.

The poems she composed for and about her beloved mother, most notably "Wishes" (1847), a series of valentines (1876–1886), and the dedicatory sonnet in *A Pageant and Other Poems* (1881), are not extraordinary either, although several are quite lovely specimens of lyric verse. Rossetti would not have appreciated a comparison with Eliza Cook, whose work she held in very low esteem,[26] but the two poets were alike in the sincerity of their devotion to their mothers and in the frequency with which they commemorated them in verse. A characteristic example from Rossetti's canon is the 1882 valentine, which begins, "My blessed Mother dozing in her chair / On Christmas Day seemed an embodied Love, / A comfortable Love with soft brown hair / Softened and silvered to a tint of dove . . . " (p. 392). Nothing to be found in Rossetti's poetry denies the sterling quality of mother-love; the unacknowledging mother in "Under the Rose" is as close to unnatural motherhood as Rossetti's representation of women ever comes.

Unlike most women poets, Christina Rossetti does not employ marriage as an important motif in her poetry, except by its impossibility or its frustration through death or separation. An occasional poem such as "Child's Talk in

April" (1855) or "A Ring Posy" (1863) appears to celebrate the domestic ideal, or a pseudo-Gothic ballad like "Love from the North" (1856) to reject it, but on the whole, her most characteristic poetic attitude toward marriage is that represented in the sonnet "An Echo from Willow-Wood."

> AN ECHO FROM WILLOW-WOOD
> O ye, all ye that walk in willow-wood
> *D. G. Rossetti*
>
> Two gazed into a pool, he gazed and she,
>   Not hand in hand, yet heart in heart, I think,
>   Pale and reluctant on the water's brink,
> As on the brink of parting which must be,
>   Each eyed the other's aspect, she and he,
>   Each felt one hungering heart leap up and sink,
>   Each tasted bitterness which both must drink,
>   There on the brink of life's dividing sea.
> Lilies upon the surface, deep below
>   Two wistful faces craving each for each,
>   Resolute and reluctant without speech:—
> A sudden ripple made the faces flow,
>   One moment joined, to vanish out of reach:
>   So those hearts joined, and ah were parted so.
>
>   (pp. 385-386)

William Michael Rossetti thought this poem referred to the stormy marriage of Dante Gabriel and the tragic death in 1862 of his wife Elizabeth Siddal; he assigned it a "conjectural" date of 1870.[27] However, it seems more closely connected to Jean Ingelow's lovely lyric "Divided," which appeared in her *Poems* in 1863. Theo Dombrowski notes, "The theme of split love is explored with such tenacity, with such interest in countless variations, that it seems in carrying out such an exploration Christina Rossetti was attempting to exorcise the specter of her own isolation."[28] At any rate, "An Echo from Willow-Wood" illustrates two of Rossetti's recurrent themes: the sadness of inevitable separation and the ephemerality of human love.

Those poems by Rossetti in which woman's love fails of completion by marriage are many and various. However, they all tend to represent the heroine as a passive, pining maiden—sometimes even as a corpse[29] or a phantom.[30] In "The Prince's Progress" (1861–1865), she is a Sleeping Beauty whose prince arrives too late. In *Monna Innominata* (1882) she is an imaginary woman poet of the Italian Renaissance whose honor prevents the consummation of her love in marriage. To characterize the recurrent heroine of these and dozens of other poems as passive and unfulfilled is not to denigrate, in this case, the quality of the verse.[31] *Monna Innominata* challenges Elizabeth Barrett Browning's *Sonnets from the Portuguese* and Dante Gabriel's *The House of Life* for recognition as the loveliest sonnet sequence in the language since Shakespeare's. However, the female figure in no wise represents a departure from current conceptions of woman (and her proper relation to man). One could pick any sonnet at random from *Monna Innominata* and find in it a sentiment such as "With separate 'I' and 'thou' free love has done, / For one is both and both are one in love" (Sonnet 4, p. 60), or "O love, my world is you" (Sonnet 1, p. 59), or "Since woman is the helpmeet made for man" (Sonnet 5, p. 60). Yet all these sonnets are incontestably beautiful. In this and countless others of her poems, Christina Rossetti succeeded in presenting a conventional female figure at a level of artistry seldom achieved in women's poetry.[32]

Her spinsters, for instance, are occasionally sprightly and self-possessed, although more often they fit the stereotype of the lonely, fading, pathetic old maid. In "No, Thank You, John" (1860) and "Promises Like Pie-Crust" (1861), the unmarried woman refuses her suitor's proposal of marriage and recommends that they resume their friendship as before. In the first poem, her explanation is that she never loved the man; in the second, that "promises" can only mar a good relationship.

> Promise me no promises,
>   So will I not promise you:
> Keep we both our liberties,
>   Never false and never true:
>
> . . . .
>
> If you promised, you might grieve
>   For lost liberty again:
> If I promised, I believe
>   I should fret to break the chain.
>
>   (pp. 350-351)

The characterization of marriage as bondage and the suspicion attached to promise giving seem quite a modern rationale for refusing marriage. Packer identifies the rejected suitor of both poems as Christina's friend Charles Cayley, who was at that time trying to win her hand.[33] The heroine in these two poems is completely sure of her own mind, and, by virtue of the offer, is in no way pitiable.

By contrast, Millie, the heroine of "Brandons Both" (before 1882) is pining away for secret love of her cousin Walter. Millie is doubly forlorn, because she not only loses Walter to a rival—she also lacks a mother. Her fate is described as comparable to that of a plucked rose: "the petals drop from the drooping perished flower, / And only the graceless thorns are left of it" (p. 404). Though Millie resolves to maintain her self-respect anyway, it is difficult for the reader to see how she can succeed in doing so, given the metaphor of the ruined rose.

In "Last Night" (1863) the unmarried heroine has also lost her suitor to a rival, the coquettish Kate. She accepts this turn of events quite reasonably and with only a hint of self-pity. "I'm not one to grow downhearted and thin," she assures the young man. "Some girls might cry and scold you a bit, / And say they couldn't bear it; but I can" (p. 361). She does not even appear to resent the victorious rival. "I wish her a husband steady and true," she says. The poem concludes, however, with a self-revealing bit of advice which the spinster tells her fickle suitor to pass along to Kate:

> Not to let time slip if she means to mate;
> For even such a thing has been known
> As to miss the chance while we weigh and wait.
>
> (p. 362)

Perhaps this is what has already happened to *her*. Despite her air of self-possession, she cannot help being disappointed to find once again that "all things begin and all have an end" (p. 362), even love.

The specter of the aging beauty or coquette was conventional in women's poetry; both "Helen Grey" (1863) and "Beauty Is Vain" (1864) fit squarely into that tradition. In the former poem, an unidentified speaker cautions the handsome and haughty Helen Grey against the danger of her prideful hesitations:

> Stoop from your cold height, Helen Grey. . . .
> For years cannot be kept at bay,
>   And fading years will make you old;
>   Then in their turn will men seem cold,
> When you yourself are nipped and grey.
>
> (p. 355)

By attempting to play at the enjoyable game of courtship for too long, a woman runs the risk of entirely losing at love. The consequence—miserable spinsterhood—is, literally, chilling to contemplate.

References like these to fading, coldness, and greyness and to the curtailment and loneliness of aging and death abound in Christina Rossetti's poetry generally. Thus, it is not surprising to find them in her poetic treatments of woman as spinster, where the weight of literary convention would seem especially to require them. Typical poems in this vein are "May" (1855) and "Three Seasons" (1853), which ends its brief survey of a spinster's life cycle with "memory for the evening grey / And solitary dove" (15–16). The emphasis on seasonality in so many of these poems reflects the contemporary notion that normal women's lives followed a single appropriate sequence and that unmarried women were somehow out of synchrony: they were unnaturally barren and prematurely old. Hence, the spinster is most characteristically associated, in Rossetti's poetry, with autumn. "Autumn Violets," for example, recommends:

> Keep love for youth, and violets for the spring:
>   Or if these bloom when worn-out autumn grieves,
>   Let them lie hid in double shade of leaves,
> Their own, and others' dropped down withering. . . .
>   Or if a later sadder love be born,
>   Let this not look for grace beyond its scope,
> But give itself, nor plead for answering truth—
>   A grateful Ruth tho' gleaning scanty corn.
>
> (1–4, 11–14)

The excessive humility inherent in this view of unmarried women did not prevent Rossetti from regarding "Autumn Violets" as one of her favorite poems. Sometime before 1869 she wrote this poem and sent it as a gift to another spinster poet, her friend Dora Greenwell. Greenwell appreciated it so much that she sent back a lovely poem, "To Christina Rossetti," in praise of Christina's personal and poetical genius.[34]

A somewhat more positive reconciliation to spinsterhood can be found in a later poem, "Passing and Glassing" (before 1882), which moves from a classic vision of the aging woman to a philosophical (and implicitly religious) resignation.

>   All things that pass
>   Are woman's looking-glass;
> They show her how her bloom must fade,
> And she herself be laid
> With withered roses in the shade;
>   With withered roses and the fallen peach,
>   Unlovely, out of reach
>   Of summer joy that was.
>
>   . . . .
>
>   All things that pass
>   Are wisdom's looking-glass;

> Being full of hope and fear, and still
> Brimful of good or ill,
> According to our work and will:
>   For there is nothing new beneath the sun;
>   Our doings have been done,
>   And that which shall be was.
>
>   (p. 411)

Besides the general conventions regarding the depiction of the unmarried woman, Christina Rossetti was probably influenced by Tennyson's treatments of the subject. In 1848 she wrote "A Pause of Thought," and between 1875 and 1882 her own "Mariana," both likely inspired by Tennyson's "Mariana" (1830). In 1858, she composed "From House to Home," reminiscent of "The Palace of Art" (1832), and "Autumn," which resembles "The Lady of Shalott" as well as "Mariana." In "Autumn," Rossetti's most distinctive representation of single womanhood, the heroine dwells alone on a river strand, observing life and love passing her by like the gold-laden boats that sail past her shores.

> Fair fall the freighted boats which gold and stone
>   And spices bear to sea:
> Slim, gleaming maidens swell their mellow notes,
>   Love-promising, entreating—. . . .
> Their songs wake singing echoes in my land—
>   They cannot hear me moan.
>
>   (7–10, 16–17)

She herself is like the "One latest solitary swallow" that flies across the "rough autumn-tempest tost" waters. "Poor bird," she queries, "shall it be lost?" (19–20).

A rainbow spider web, recalling the magical web of the Lady of Shalott, symbolizes her entrapment in this isolated life:

> A spider's web blocks all mine avenue. . . .
>   So fair, few creatures guess it is a trap;
>   I will not mar the web,
>   Tho' sad I am to see the small lives ebb.
>
>   (33, 38–40)

As a fleet of becalmed sailing ships suddenly catches the wind and begins to move out of sight, she speculates on the passengers' private opinions about her. "Perhaps they say: 'She grieves, / Uplifted, like a beacon, on her tower' " (52–53). In other words, perhaps they project upon her the conventional idea of the unmarried woman's secret sorrow. But the truth is, she has become a captive of her own self-containment. Although it has been her own choice, apparently, to dwell alone, to retain the fragile web of isolation, the decision is not without its regrets:

> My trees are not in flower,
> I have no bower,
> And gusty creaks my tower,
> And lonesome, very lonesome, is my strand.

> (60–64)

Even though "Autumn" reiterates the unpleasant stereotype of the lonely old maid, it also transcends the limitations of that subject, just as Tennyson's comparable poems do, and portrays the very real pain inherent in alienation of the self from humankind. Probably it represents, like "The Lowest Room," Christina Rossetti's perception of her own difficult situation as a woman and an artist in nineteenth-century England.

Tennyson's Lady of Shalott is drawn away from her isolated yet protective tower by the sensual beauty of Lancelot. The speaker in "Autumn" is likewise attracted by human beauty and sensuous pleasures, though no man is mentioned as the source of these temptations. Rather, she seems to be hearing a siren song of "slim gleaming maidens" whose songs "wake singing echoes in my land." Indeed, Rossetti frequently represented the perilous or sinful lure of the flesh as erotically female. Consider that in "Goblin Market" Laura's recovered innocence is shown by her hugging Lizzie "but not twice or thrice" (539). Likewise, the erotic implications of "Hug me, kiss me, suck my juices" (468), "Eat me, drink me, love me" (471), and "she kissed and kissed her with a hungry mouth" (492) seem very clear. The lesbian overtones in Rossetti's work are frequently ignored or dismissed, on grounds of presumed innocence of sexuality and therefore lack of authorial intent, or perhaps out of a misguided respect for her womanly purity. We pay her more genuine respect, however, by acknowledging what she has written and crediting her with some awareness of her own sensitivities. To do so is *not* to assert that Christina Rossetti was actively and consciously homosexual. No biographical evidence (except possibly her reluctance to marry) supports such a view, and poems like "The World" (1854) express attraction to such eroticism cancelled by rejection of it (as, indeed, does "Goblin Market").

The temptress in "The World" is in the tradition of John Keats and of Rossetti's contemporaries and friends, the Pre-Raphaelites. However, the soul she tempts is not specified as to gender. Earthly joy is represented as a Lamia—by day, "soft, exceeding fair" (1), but by night, "Loathsome and foul with . . . subtle serpents gliding in her hair" (3–4). In the classic mode of the *femme fatale*, she "wooes" [*sic*] the speaker's soul with "Ripe fruits, sweet flowers, and full satiety" (6). (The sexual connotations are clear.) At night, she stands revealed, "In all the naked horror of the truth" (10), as a creature damned, deformed, and clutching. Appalled, the soul rejects earthly satisfactions and turns its face toward heaven, for

> Is this a friend indeed; that I should sell
>   My soul to her, give her my life and youth?
> Till my feet, cloven too, take hold on hell?
>
> (12–14)

The personal tone of "The World" and the fact that Rossetti included it among her devotional poems suggest that we read it as a personal acknowledgment of and resistance to the attractions of worldly (read "sexual") pleasure.

Nor is "The World" her only religious poem to fully recognize but also reject the lure of earthly passion. "The Convent Threshold" (1858) and "Soeur Louise de la Miséricorde, 1674" (before 1882) both depict sexual passion as a compelling force not lightly to be defeated.

> For all night long I dreamed of you:
> I woke and prayed against my will,
> Then slept to dream of you again.
> At length I rose and knelt and prayed:
> I cannot write the words I said,
> My words were slow, my tears were few;
> But thro' the dark my silence spoke
> Like thunder. When this morning broke,
> My face was pinched, my hair was grey,
> And frozen blood was on the sill
> Where stifling in my struggle I lay.
>
> (126–136)

Having thus exorcised her sexuality, the woman in "The Convent Threshold" is able to take the veil at last. Similarly in the later poem, Soeur Louise (the ex-mistress of Louis XIV) renounces sexual passion in order to enter a Carmelite convent, exclaiming against the "vanity" of the "disenkindled fire" of desire (p. 411). Though the ascetic impulse in Christina Rossetti may have been strong, it seems obvious from her poetry that the sexual impulse was powerful as well.

Before leaving the poetry of Christina Rossetti, it is germane to emphasize the frequency with which she depicted women in relationship not only to men, but to other women—sisters, rivals, co-workers, friends, etc. In addition to those already discussed, there are such poems as "Maiden Song" (1863), a kind of benign counterpart to "Goblin Market"; "The Queen of Hearts" (1863), a drawing room scenario of gentle feminine rivalry; and "Maud Clare" (1858), a jaunty ballad of female confrontation. "Look on This Picture and on This" (1856) depicts in its two female characters such a daring contrast of pure and sinful love that an embarrassed William Michael was tempted to drop it out of her collected works.[35] The list could tolerate much extension, but the point is that, as we have seen, no matter how conventional her representations of female figures may sometimes have been, Christina Rossetti clearly broke with tradition by the energy and attention she devoted to the portrayal of women and by the emphasis she placed upon their relationships with one another, rather than always upon their relationships with men.

Afterword

In an episode in her whimsical novel *Orlando* (1928), Virginia Woolf describes what she thought had happened to women's poetry in the nineteenth century. It is early in Queen Victoria's reign, and the androgynous and centuries-old Orlando has just taken up her pen with the intention "to indite some reflection upon the eternity of all things," when, "to her astonishment and alarm, the pen began to curve and caracole with the smoothest possible fluency." What follows is a tongue-in-cheek commentary upon nineteenth-century women's verse.

> Her page was written in the neatest sloping Italian hand with the most insipid verse she had ever read in her life. . . . She wrote without a stop as Bartholomew [the housekeeper] and Basket [the butler] grunted and groaned about the room, mending the fire, picking up the muffins.
>
> Again she dipped her pen and off it went. . .
>
> > Bright burning blushes, torches of the tomb,
>
> but here, by an abrupt movement she spilt the ink over the page and blotted it from human sight she hoped for ever. She was all of a quiver, all of a stew. Nothing more repulsive could be imagined than to feel the ink flowing thus in cascades of involuntary inspiration. What had happened to her?[1]

Woolf appears to mean by this question something like: Why was the profuse women's poetry of the nineteenth century so facile, sentimental, conservative, and trite? The question thus posed admits of several answers. First, I hope we can agree by now that not all of women's poetry was like this—

Woolf is clearly exaggerating for humorous effect. Second, the many literary and social restraints upon women, stemming from the idea of woman's proper sphere and the definition of femininity as sweetness and subordination, often inhibited them from more imaginative and authentic renditions of female experience. The miracle is that, despite an overall tendency toward a safe and sometimes even "insipid" conservatism, the landscape of women's poetry in nineteenth-century England is nowhere near as bleak as Woolf makes it out to be. Certainly it has its dull and monotonous areas, but it also contains mountain peaks like Elizabeth Barrett Browning's *Aurora Leigh*, hidden and mysterious coves like Christina Rossetti's "Goblin Market," and small oases of great beauty like Jean Ingelow's "Divided" and Alice Meynell's "A Study." What's more, the rest of the vast and previously uncharted expanse is surprisingly lively and varied.

A different question suggested by Woolf's is: What had happened to women's poetry by 1928, that made Virginia Woolf unable to perceive all that was truly there? Dale Spender states it well in *Man Made Language*:

> If every obstacle were overcome and a woman found the courage to write, the confidence to write, the chance of publication and the conquest of the literary and public world in her own age, her efforts could still be minimized with the passage of time and her writing fade till it disappeared entirely from public view. Many women writers have gone this way partly because male-controlled publishing institutions have "allowed them to go out of print," and partly because literary history . . . has been written by men with men's concerns in mind.

Spender ends this summation by saying, "One of the fundamental tasks facing contemporary women is the unearthing of the 'lost' writers and their work."[2] That task of reclamation is precisely what I have undertaken to begin for the women poets of nineteenth-century England.

Much more remains to be done. Many of the poets I read in preparing this book are at least as good as the numerous minor male poets now included in standard anthologies and studied at length in literary history and criticism. It is clear to me that the comparable women poets of the century have been unjustifiably consigned to oblivion. In particular, I recommend the reevaluation, reissue, and renewed study of Sara Coleridge, Jean Ingelow, Emily Pfeiffer, Augusta Webster, Mathilde Blind, Amy Levy, Mary Elizabeth Coleridge, "Michael Field," and Alice Meynell.[3] Until fine women writers such as these are restored to us, we will continue to be deprived of the literary legacy that is rightfully ours.

Appendix:
The Poets

General sources of biographical and bibliographical information on the lesser-known poets covered in this book are listed below. In addition, the Selected Bibliography includes both anthologies and critical or biographical studies of minor and/or female poets.

Allibone, S. Austin. *A Critical Dictionary of English Literature and British and American Authors, Living and Deceased.* Philadelphia: Lippincott, 1858. Supplement. Ed. J. F. Kirk. 1891.

Baugh, Albert C., ed. *Literary History of England.* New York: Meredith, 1967.

Black, Helen C. *Notable Women Authors of the Day.* Glasgow: David Bryce & Son, 1893.

Cambridge Bibliography of English Literature, vol. 3, 1800–1900. Ed. F. W. Bateson. Cambridge: Cambridge Univ. Press, 1940.

Cambridge History of English Literature. Ed. A. W. Wood and A. R. Waller. Cambridge: Cambridge Univ. Press, 1963.

Dictionary of National Biography. Ed. Leslie Stephen and Sidney Lee. London: Oxford Univ. Press, 1927. Supplements.

Kunitz, Stanley, and Howard Haycraft. *British Authors of the Nineteenth Century.* New York: Wilson, 1936.

New Cambridge Bibliography of English Literature, vol. 3, 1800–1900. Ed. George Watson. Cambridge: Cambridge Univ. Press, 1969.

AIKIN, LUCY ("MARY GODOLPHIN"), 1781–1864. Resources: "Introduction" to *Epistles on Women* (Boston: W. Wells, 1810). Like her aunt, Anna Barbauld, Lucy Aikin was an educational theorist. She believed that "no talent, no virtue, is masculine alone; no fault or folly exclusively feminine." For herself, she hoped that "the scholars, the sages, and the patriots" of coming days would "greet her as a sister and a friend." The four *Epistles* survey the history and geography of woman's unhappy lot and her progress within culture, in order to show "that it is impossible for man to degrade his companion without degrading himself, or to elevate her without receiving

a proportional accession of dignity and happiness." This "Great Truth" Aikin regarded as "the chief 'moral of my song.' "

BARBAULD, ANNA LETITIA AIKIN, 1743–1825. Resources: *Memoir of Mrs.
Barbauld* by her greatniece Anna Letitia Aikin Le Breton (London: G. Bell & Sons,
1874). The daughter of a schoolteacher, the young Anna Aikin was for awhile a part
of the Joseph Priestley circle. She married a teacher, bore several children and, relying
on her own broad classical education, helped him administer a boys' school and
wrote children's textbooks. Her husband, a Presbyterian minister, was liable to "fits
of insane fury"; in 1811 he went mad and died. During her fourteen-year widowhood, Barbauld established her literary reputation, publishing poems, hymns for children, essays on education, and editions of various literary works. In declining the
opportunity to administer the first college for women, she wrote to Elizabeth
Montagu wondering whether it appeared that she had "stepped out of the bounds of
female reserve in becoming an author."

BEVINGTON, LOUISA SARAH [GUGGENBERGER] ("ARBOR LEIGH"),
1845–? Resources: *Key Notes*, by Arbor Leigh (1876); republished three years later
under her own name (London: C. K. Paul, 1879). Bevington was an evolutionist. In
1881 she published an article in the *Fortnightly Review* defending evolutionary morality. *Key Notes* was verse based in evolutionary science; Charles Darwin expressed satisfaction with it, but literary critics were less impressed. Bevington also believed that
suffering was the source of art; she took an evolutionist approach to the amelioration
of such social ills as wife beating. In 1883, at the age of thirty-eight, she married a
Munich artist. I was unable to locate any further poetry by her after that date.

BLESSINGTON, LADY MARGUERITE [BORN MARGARET POWER],
1789–1849. Resources: Prudence Hannay, "Lady Blessington: A Literary Club for
Editors," *Affairs of the Mind*, ed. Peter Quennell (Washington, D.C.: New Republic
Books, 1980), pp. 23–33. Married at age fifteen to a sadistic and violent English
army officer, Margaret fled and lived under the protection of another man for ten
years. When her husband was killed in a brawl, she married the Irish peer Lord Blessington. The rest of her life was equally unconventional, including marrying off her
husband's young daughter to her own close friend Count Alfred D'Orsay and then
supporting the entire household as a journalist when Lord Blessington died. She
wrote and edited several annuals and in 1839 published a novel, *The Governess*. Her
best known publication is *Conversations with Lord Byron* (1832).

BLIND, MATHILDE ("CLAUDE LAKE"), 1841–1896. Resources: Cora Kaplan,
Salt and Bitter and Good: Three Centuries of English and American Woman Poets (New
York: Paddington, 1975), pp. 159–61. Mathilde Blind moved to England in 1848
when her stepfather, a political writer, was exiled from Germany for revolutionary
activities. At age thirty, still single, she moved out of her parents' home and established an independent life. In addition to poetry, she published criticism, biography

(including a life of George Eliot), and translations (among them the *Journal of Marie Bashkirtseff*). She was a strong advocate of higher education for women and left her inheritance to Newnham College. Vita Sackville-West believed that Blind's poetic gifts and her vision of nature were underestimated by contemporary critics of her work.

BROWNE, MARY ANN [GRAY], 1812–1844. Mary Ann Browne was considered to have left her considerable promise as a poet unfulfilled because of her early death. When her first volume of verses was published, she was only fifteen years old. The bulk of her poetry appeared in various annuals and periodicals and has evidently never been collected. She married James Gray, a Scot, when she was thirty; two years later she was dead.

COLERIDGE, MARY ELIZABETH, 1861–1907. Resources: Theresa Whistler's "Introduction" to *Collected Poems* (London: Rupert Hart-Davis, 1954). Mary Coleridge's great-grandfather was the elder brother of Samuel T. Coleridge; consequently, her home was frequently visited by literary men such as Tennyson and Browning. Robert Bridges encouraged her to publish her verses, calling them "original" and "imaginative." Much of her poetry is in the Gothic or fantastic vein of the Romantics. Although her mother tried to push her toward a conventional life-style, Mary chose to devote her time and energies to a small circle of close women friends and their activities—including teaching working women, both at the Working Women's College and in private homes. According to Whistler, "No one so feminine can ever have longed more to be a man. . . . In her novels it is always the portraits of young men which are attempted from within."

COLERIDGE, SARA, 1802–1852. Resources: E. L. Griggs, *Coleridge Fille* (London: Oxford Univ. Press, 1940). Although her parents' marriage was unhappy, Sara Coleridge was much loved by both her mother and her famous father, Samuel T. Coleridge, who wrote several beautiful poems about her. She received an excellent education and knew six or seven languages. In 1830 she married her cousin Henry Coleridge. Griggs compares the couple to the Brownings for their shared intellectual interests and mutual respect. Sara was pregnant seven times in her thirteen years of married life; only two of the children survived. After her husband's death, she made numerous literary friendships, followed the course of women's writing, and contributed to the scholarship on her father. She died of cancer at the age of fifty.

COOK, ELIZA, 1818–1889. Resources: Marcia Kutrieh, "Popular British Romantic Poets" (Ph.D. dissertation, Bowling Green State Univ., 1974), pp. 435–48. Entirely self-educated, Eliza Cook was the youngest of eleven children. Her mother encouraged her interest in literature; Eliza's first book of poems was published, to favorable reviews, when she was seventeen years old. From 1849 to 1854 she edited and published *Eliza Cook's Journal*, a lively and clear collection of essays, poems, and sketches written with a view to improving and entertaining middle-class women. She was, for a time, an intimate friend of the famous actress Charlotte Cushman. In 1863 Cook received a Civil List pension. She was an invalid for the last twenty-five years of her life.

CRAIK, DINAH MULOCK, 1826–1887. Resources: Sally Mitchell, *Dinah Mulock Craik* (Boston: Twayne Publishers, 1983); Elaine Showalter, "Dinah Mulock Craik and the Tactics of Sentiment: A Case Study in Victorian Female Authorship," *Feminist Studies*, 2(1975), 5–23. Dinah Mulock was the daughter of a dissenting preacher and a mother who died when Dinah was in her teens. Besides poetry, she published fiction, including *John Halifax, Gentleman* (1856–1857) and *The Little Lame Prince* (1875), and essays, including *A Woman's Thoughts about Women* (1858) and *Concerning Men* (1888). In 1864 she married George Craik, an editor for Macmillan, and they adopted a daughter. While disapproving of "strong-mindedness, down to the lowest depth of bloomerism, cigarette-smoking, and talking slang," as Craik wrote in *A Woman's Thoughts*, she nevertheless recognized the virtues of "Self-Dependence" and "Female Friendships."

DUFFERIN, LADY HELEN [BORN HELEN SELINA SHERIDAN], 1807–1867. Resources: Harold Nicolson, *Helen's Tower* (London: Constable, 1937), pp. 52–141. Helen Sheridan was the granddaughter of Richard Brinsley Sheridan, the dramatist, and the sister of Caroline Norton. She married Price Blackwell, later Lord Dufferin, in 1825. After her husband died in 1841, Lady Dufferin devoted herself to raising their son. In 1862, after a twenty-year friendship, she married Lord Gifford. She died of breast cancer in 1867. Lady Dufferin was best known for witty, light-hearted songs satirizing society and for some fine ballads on the miseries in Ireland, including her best-known piece "The Irish Emigrant." Nicolson ranked her work above Caroline Norton's.

"FANE, VIOLET" (MARY MONTGOMERIE LAMB, LADY CURRIE), 1843–1905. After the death of her first husband, Henry Singleton, in 1864, Mary Lamb married Sir Philip Currie, the British ambassador to Turkey, and moved to Constantinople. She published five volumes of verse under the name "Violet Fane" between 1872 and 1895. *Denzil Place* (1875) was a verse novel after the manner of Barrett Browning's *Aurora Leigh*. She also published several other novels and one drama.

"FIELD, MICHAEL" (KATHERINE HARRIS BRADLEY, 1846–1913, AND EDITH EMMA COOPER, 1862–1914). Resources: Mary Sturgeon, *Michael Field* (London: Harrap, 1922); Charles Ricketts, *Michael Field* (Edinburgh: Tragara Press, 1976). Bradley and Cooper were constant companions from 1865, when Bradley joined the household of her older sister, Cooper's mother. Among their friends were Robert Browning, George Meredith, and Oscar Wilde. In addition to poetry, "Michael Field" wrote tragic dramas which were, for a time, compared to Shakespeare's. Contemporary critics were disappointed to find that "Michael Field" was not an exciting new (male) poet but a spinster aunt and her spinster niece, who were passionately devoted to one another.

GREENWELL, DORA, 1821–1882. Greenwell was born into the rural aristocracy, but her family fell on hard times and in 1848 moved to London to live with relatives. An invalid much of her long life, Greenwell never married. She was interested and active in many social movements and philanthropic projects, including women's suffrage, prison visiting, and the treatment of "imbeciles." A friend of Christina Rossetti and an admirer of Elizabeth Barrett Browning, she published both poetry and essays. Much of her writing was spiritual or religious.

HAVERGAL, FRANCES RIDLEY, 1836–1879. Resources: T. H. Darlow, *Frances Ridley Havergal: A Saint of God* (London: Nisbet & Co., 1927). Havergal wrote many devotionals, Christmas poems, children's tales, and religious verses. She refused several offers of marriage, one when she was forty-three years old and had been an invalid for five years. Her middle name was after the English martyr Bishop Ridley; biographers credited her with a lifelong monastic impulse and a sense of consecration to God. However, many of her poems are secular in both subject and theme.

HEMANS, FELICIA DOROTHEA, 1793–1835. Resources: Vols. 64–70 of *Romantic Context*, ed. Donald H. Reiman (New York: Garland, 1978). Best remembered (somewhat disdainfully) for "Casabianca," Felicia Hemans was the most popular woman poet of her day. She was a friend of Sir Walter Scott, and from time to time she visited Wordsworth in the Lake Country. She married a militia captain, Alfred Hemans, who left her shortly before the birth of their fifth son; Lydia Sigourney, the American poet, suggested that Captain Hemans may have been jealous of his wife's literary career. Reiman concludes that Hemans' poetry suffered from "cultural lag," remaining closer to Pope and Cowper than to her own contemporaries, and that her present obscurity has resulted because "she spoke only from the past to her age, and not, as well, from her age to the next."

HOWITT, MARY, 1799–1888. Resources: Carl Woodring, *Victorian Samplers: William and Mary Howitt* (Lawrence: Univ. of Kansas Press, 1952). Mary Botham married William Howitt in 1821, and the two of them shared an active and complex life as authors, parents, social reformers, and political leaders. Among the causes they supported were anti-slavery, peace, national compulsory education, Irish relief, Catholic emancipation, women's economic rights, Poor Law reform, and the prevention of cruelty to animals. Besides poetry, Mary wrote social essays and edited or co-edited several periodicals. She also translated Frederika Bremer and Hans Christian Andersen and wrote poems and tales for children. Born into a strict Quaker family, Mary went through several religious conversions before ending her life as a Roman Catholic.

HUNTER, ANNE, 1742–1821. Hunter's poems and songs were widely known in her day; some of her verses were set to music by Franz Joseph Haydn. The dramatist Joanna Baillie took an active interest in her career. John Hunter, an eminent surgeon, was her husband; Everard Home was her brother.

INGELOW, JEAN, 1820–1897. Resources: Naomi Lewis, "A Lost Pre-Raphaelite: Jean Ingelow," *Times* (London) *Literary Supplement*, December 8, 1972, p. 1487; Maureen Peters, *Jean Ingelow: Victorian Poetess* (Ipswich, England: Boydell, 1972). Ingelow was educated at home by her mother, who was of a poetical turn of mind. Her books were composed at home on the dining room table, where she worked every morning for two or three hours. The best known of her poems was "The High Tide on the Coast of Lincolnshire, 1571." In later years, she wrote mostly fiction. A spinster aunt who was anti-marriage may have influenced Ingelow to remain single and helped form some of her more cynical views on the subject of marriage. Ingelow was a friend of Jane and Ann Taylor and on friendly terms also with Tennyson, Ruskin, and Christina Rossetti. In 1892 she was mentioned for the Poet Laureateship.

KEMBLE, FRANCES ANNE (FANNY), 1809–1893. Resources: Margaret Armstrong, *Fanny Kemble: A Passionate Victorian* (New York: Macmillan, 1938); Joseph C. Furnas, *Fanny Kemble: Leading Lady of the Nineteenth-Century Stage* (New York: Dial Press, 1982); *The Terrific Kemble: A Victorian Self-Portrait from the Writings of Fanny Kemble*, ed. Eleanor Ransome (London: Hamish Hamilton, 1978); Constance Wright, *Fanny Kemble and the Lovely Land* (New York: Dodd, Mead, 1972). The daughter of Charles Kemble and the niece of John Philip Kemble and Sarah Siddons, Fanny decided at an early age to become famous, either as a writer or as an actress; she accomplished both. She married an American, Pierce Butler, who took her to live on his Georgia plantation. To Fanny's dismay, he turned out to be a slaveholder. Their marriage broke up in a sensational manner over her ideas of female independence and her moral horror at the source of his wealth. They were divorced in 1849 and Fanny returned to the stage, giving one-woman shows and readings from Shakespeare. Among her friends were Anna Jameson, Frances Power Cobbe, Caroline Norton, and Lucretia Mott. The example of her opinions, choices, and independence made her a feminist symbol in both England and America.

LAMB, LADY CAROLINE, 1785–1828. Resources: Henry Blyth, *Caro: The Fatal Passion, The Life of Lady Caroline Lamb* (New York: Coward, McCann & Co., 1973); Lord David Cecil, *The Young Melbourne, and the Story of His Marriage with Caroline Lamb* (New York: Bobbs-Merrill, 1939). Born Caroline Ponsonby into a Regency aristocratic family, Caro always wanted to be a boy and chafed at the constraints upon female behavior. She was beautiful and flirtatious as an adolescent, and her marriage at the age of twenty to William Lamb (later Lord Melbourne) did not satisfy her needs. After one miscarriage and the subsequent birth of a child who became a hopeless invalid, she began to take lovers. Her highly indiscreet liaison with Lord Byron, which occurred in 1812, scandalized society, and her subsequent publication of a thinly veiled account of the affair in her novel *Glenarvon* ruined her permanently. She separated from her husband in 1825, and three years later she died of dropsy at the age of forty-two.

LANDON, LETITIA ELIZABETH ("L.E.L."), 1802–1838. Resources: Helen Ashton, *Letty Landon* (London: Collins, 1951); Laman Blanchard, ed., *The Life and Literary Remains of L.E.L.* (London: H. Colman, 1841); D. E. Enfield, *L.E.L.: A Mystery of the Thirties* (London: Hogarth Press, 1928); Lionel Stevenson, "Miss Landon, 'The Milk-and-Watery Moon of Our Darkness,' 1824–30," *Modern Language Quarterly*, 9 (September 1947), 355–63. Landon's career was launched by William Jerdan, who hailed her as a female Byron, an expectation that could never be met. When her father died, she had somehow to support herself, so she ingratiated herself with the editor William Maginn; but here she ran afoul of social mores, and her reputation for chastity came into question. In 1838, following a broken engagement to John Forster, a biographer, she secretly married George Maclean, the governor of Cape Coast Castle, and sailed with him for a three-year stint in Africa (despite rumors that he already had an African wife). Within a few months, she was found dead in her room with a bottle of prussic acid in her hand. Whether she died by accident, suicide, or murder has never been proved.

LEVY, AMY, 1861–1889. The daughter of an editor, Amy Levy was a consciously Jewish writer. Her novel *Reuben Sachs* (1888) begins, "Reuben Sachs was the pride of his family. . . . The fact that he was a Jew had proved no bar to his popularity." Those who knew her reported that she had a melancholy nature and a fear of insanity. Shortly after correcting the proofs for her last publication, *A London Plane Tree*, she suffocated herself by inhaling charcoal fumes.

MEYNELL, ALICE THOMPSON, 1847–1922. Resources: June Badeni, *The Slender Tree: A Life of Alice Meynell* (Padstow, Cornwall, England: Tabb House, 1981); Viola Meynell, *Alice Meynell: A Memoir* (London: Jonathan Cape, 1929, 1947), Vita Sackville-West, "Introduction," *Alice Meynell: Prose and Poetry—Centenary Volume*, ed. Frederick Page (London: Jonathan Cape, 1947); Anna K. Tuell, *Mrs. Meynell and Her Literary Generation* (New York: Dutton, 1925). Alice Thompson grew up in Italy, returning to England at the age of eighteen. Her first volume of poetry (1875) was praised by George Eliot, Dante Rossetti, and Robert Browning. In 1877 she married Wilfred Meynell. The couple had eight children, one of whom did not survive. Meynell devoted herself both to her family and to social causes such as women's suffrage, housing reform, and the prevention of cruelty to animals. She and her husband rescued the poet Francis Thompson from poverty and opium. Meynell and Coventry Patmore admired one another's talents and the Roman Catholic orientation in each other's work. Her busy life as a mother, editor, essayist, columnist, and humanitarian led Meynell to set poetry aside for awhile, but she returned to it in later years. Several small volumes appeared after her death.

NESBIT, EDITH [BLAND], 1858–1924. Resources: Doris L. Moore, *E. Nesbit: A Biography* (New York: Chilton Books, 1966). Edith Nesbit and her husband Hubert Bland, whom she married in 1879 when she was seven months pregnant, were both Socialists. Their son was named Fabian. Bland's mistress lived with them and bore him two children whom Nesbit raised along with her own. She herself had various lovers and was unconventional in her dress, recreation, child-rearing methods, etc. She started out writing poetry in the eighties and nineties but turned to children's books, for which she is best known, around 1900. After Bland's death, she remarried when she was nearly sixty years old. She died at the age of sixty-five.

NORTON, CAROLINE ELIZABETH, 1808–1877. Resources: Alice Acland, *Caroline Norton* (London: Constable, 1948); James O. Hoge and Clarke Olney, eds., *The Letters of Caroline Norton to Lord Melbourne* (Columbus: Ohio State Univ. Press, 1974); Joan Huddleston, ed., *Caroline Norton's Defense: English Laws for Women in the Nineteenth Century* (Chicago: Academy Chicago, 1982). Caroline Sheridan was married to George Norton, an abusive husband who accused her in 1836 of marital misconduct with Lord Melbourne (Queen Victoria's Prime Minister, and the widower of Lady Caroline Lamb). The case went to court, but the jury dismissed it without leaving the box. Caroline and her husband separated, but were unable to divorce. George Norton claimed both of Caroline's children and all of her earnings from her writing, as the law permitted him to do. The publicity surrounding this situation, along with Caroline Norton's published defense, secured changes in the marriage law, but not soon enough to restore to Caroline all that she had lost, including her son and her reputation in society. George Meredith's *Diana of the Crossways* (1885) was based in part upon Caroline Norton's life.

PFEIFFER, EMILY JANE DAVIS, 1827–1890. Emily Pfeiffer was a committed, active feminist. Denied a thorough and systematic education for reasons of class and gender, she campaigned all her life for better education for women. Her many political and social essays were collected and reprinted in 1888 as *Women and Work*. When her wealthy husband, a German merchant, died in 1889, she took her inheritance and used it to found an orphanage and a School of Dramatic Art for women. Though plagued by ill health and insomnia for much of her life, she published numerous stories, essays, and volumes of poetry.

PROCTER, ADELAIDE ANNE ("MARY BERWICK"), 1825–1864. Resources: Margaret M. Maison, "Queen Victoria's Favourite Poet," *The Listener*, 73 (April 29, 1965), 636–37. As the daughter of Bryan Procter ("Barry Cornwall"), Adelaide grew up in the company of Wordsworth, Lamb, Hazlitt, Patmore, and other Romantic authors. Dickens and Thackeray were her regular correspondents. Under the "Mary Berwick" pseudonym she contributed to Dickens' *Household Words* in 1853 and 1854. Her most famous poem, "A Lost Chord," appeared first in the *English Woman's Journal* which she helped to found and to which she contributed other poems and articles. She helped organize the Society for Promoting the Employment of Women and supported other activities of the Langham Place feminists. After her death at the age of thirty-nine from tuberculosis, her poetry went through more editions than any other English poet except for Tennyson.

RADFORD, DOLLIE MAITLAND, 1858–? Dollie Radford and her husband Ernest were members of the Hammersmith group that centered on William Morris. Dollie contributed to the *Savoy* and the *Yellow Book,* published chapbooks of her verse with John Lane, and wrote several books for children. She had at least one child, a son born in 1884. I found several hints that she and her husband may have separated; after her last publication in 1910 I was unable to find any further information about her except a tantalizing reference in a biographical sketch of her son to "the many burdens that fate laid upon her."

ROBINSON, AGNES MARY FRANCES [DARMESTETER DUCLAUX], 1857–1944. Mary Robinson was the daughter of an architect who served as a newspaper correspondent during the Franco-German war. She was educated in Belgium and in Italy and studied English and classical literature at University College, London. Her first collection of verses appeared in 1878; it was admired at Oxford and remarked upon by Tennyson and by Robert Browning. Robinson was learned in several languages; some of her most popular works were translated into French, German, and Italian and were quite well known on the Continent. Arthur Symons pronounced her poetry "very modern." Besides poems, she wrote criticism, prose fiction, and biography, including a monograph on Emily Brontë for the "Eminent Women" series. She married James Darmesteter and moved to Paris in 1888. He died in 1894, and she remarried a Frenchman named Duclaux.

SOUTHEY, CAROLINE BOWLES, 1786–1854. Caroline Bowles was the only child of an East India Company official. Early in life she was disfigured by smallpox, and she subsequently developed a shy, retiring manner. Her autobiographical poem *The Birthday* (1836) recounts a happy childhood, spent mostly in the company of women: her mother, grandmother, great-grandmother, aunt, and nurse. She received one proposal of marriage as a young woman but turned it down in deference to her parents' judgment. Her mother died in 1816. In 1818 Caroline initiated a twenty-year correspondence with Robert Southey which culminated in her marriage to the aging, invalid poet after his first wife died. Caroline married Southey in 1839 and cared for him until his death in 1843. She received a Civil List pension in 1852.

TAYLOR, JANE, 1783–1824. Resources: Doris M. Armitage, *The Taylors of Ongar* (Cambridge, England: Heffer, 1939). The entire Taylor family was literary; the father was a clergyman and engraver and the mother a writer of some reputation. Like her sister Ann, Jane Taylor wrote mostly for children. She lived at home and worked with her father as an engraver, writing poems and essays in the "room of her own" that he provided for her. Her poems were noted for both their sense of humor and their piety. Her chief period of literary activity was from 1812 to 1816; in 1822 she gave up writing altogether because of declining health.

VELEY, MARGARET, 1843–1887. Resources: "Preface" by Leslie Stephen in Veley's *A Marriage of Shadows* (Philadelphia: Lippincott, 1889). Margaret Veley lived quietly, writing poetry and caring for her sickly sisters. She published in various magazines, including *Century* and *Blackwood's*, mostly during the seventies and eighties. Often, as in "A Lutanist" or "Private Theatricals," she wrote from a masculine point of view. Her death came very suddenly in 1887.

WEBSTER, AUGUSTA, 1837–1894. Augusta Webster's *A Housewife's Opinions* (1879) was not a household manual, but a series of reflections upon important issues related to the lives of married women like herself. For example, she considered seriously the consequences of expecting housewives to do their own housework, anticipating that women's time for study, art, or music would be drastically curtailed, as would their time with their husbands. Cooperative housekeeping she ruled out, because of the English ideal of private home life. An ardent feminist, Webster believed that gaining women's suffrage was only a matter of time, despite the six Parliamentary defeats she had personally witnessed. Besides poetry and social essays, she also wrote long dramatic monologues on Christian saints, and on the glory (and the difficulty) of asceticism and submission to God. William Michael Rossetti praised one of her several dramas: *The Sentence* (1887) about Caligula.

WORTLEY, LADY EMMELINE STUART, 1806–1855. Resources: Janet Courtney, *The Adventurous Thirties: A Chapter in the Women's Movement* (1933; reprinted, Freeport, N.Y.: Books for Libraries Press, 1967). An aristocrat by birth and by marriage, Lady Emmeline Stuart Wortley was a world traveller. As a writer, she was best known and most respected for her travel journals. Her poetry, on the other hand, was mercilessly attacked by critics and reviewers. She married in 1831, and from 1833 on wrote enough each year to fill an entire volume of verse. She was widowed in 1844. In 1855 she and her only daughter Victoria (named after the Queen) were travelling in the wilds of northern Lebanon, when Lady Stuart Wortley suddenly died.

Notes

INTRODUCTION

1. Ellis, *The Women of England*, p. 155.

2. See Basch, Calder, Mews, and Thomson.

3. Mews includes two chapters with this phrase as the title in her study of women's roles in women's novels, *Frail Vessels* (cited above).

4. John Stuart Mill, p. 26.

5. One final exclusion should be mentioned. I did not evaluate poetry by most of the nineteenth-century women writers discussed by Agress in *The Feminine Irony*. (Most of them are chiefly prose writers anyway.) Agress found that these early writers "subscribed to and reinforced women's subordinate role in their writings—even though many did not themselves accept it" (Abstract, no page).

6. These references are then excluded from the Selected Bibliography. I did not include Elizabeth Barrett Browning, Emily Brontë, George Eliot, or Christina Rossetti in the Appendix; however, critical and biographical sources on these more famous writers are listed in the Selected Bibliography.

7. Tayler and Luria, p. 100.

8. Showalter, *A Literature of Their Own*, p. 82.

9. See Homans.

10. Diehl, p. 31.

11. Marcus, *Representations*, p. xiv.

12. Edwin Ardener, "Belief and the Problem of Women," *Perceiving Women*, ed. Shirley Ardener (London: Malaby, 1975).

13. Marcus, *Representations*, p. xiv.

14. Spender, *Man Made Language*, p. 225.

15. Gilbert and Gubar, *The Madwoman in the Attic*, p. 69.

16. Ibid., p. 73.

17. Rogers, *Feminism in Eighteenth-Century England*, p. 4.

18. Pratt, p. 10.

19. Elaine Showalter, "Towards a Feminist Poetic," in Jacobus, p. 35.

20. Cheryl Walker, p. 20.

21. Judith Newton, *Women, Power, and Subversion: Social Strategies in British Fiction, 1778-1860* (Athens: Univ. of Georgia Press, 1981), p. 9.

22. Showalter, *A Literature of Their Own*, pp. 15-16.

23. Ibid., p. 11.

24. Ibid.

25. Showalter, "Towards a Feminist Poetic," in Jacobus, p. 33.

26. Spender, *Man Made Language*, p. 200. On the double standard, see also Showalter, *A Literature of Their Own*, pp. 73-99.

27. A good discussion of "female poetry" appears in Watts, pp. 68-74.

28. Agress, p. 172.

29. Cheryl Walker, p. 32.

30. Quoted in Showalter, "Women Writers and the Double Standard," p. 332.

31. Showalter, *A Literature of Their Own*, pp. 85-86.

32. Vita Sackville-West, "Introduction," in Wellesley, pp. v, iii.

33. See Quinlan, p. 228.

34. Showalter, "Women Writers and the Double Standard," p. 343.

35. Patricia Stubbs, *Women and Fiction: Feminism and the Novel 1880-1920* (New York: Barnes and Noble, 1979), p. 25.

36. Wollstonecraft, *A Vindication of the Rights of Woman*, p. 143.

37. Spender, *Man Made Language*, p. 216.

38. Harriet Taylor Mill, "The Emancipation of Women," *Westminster Review*, 55 (July 1851): 310.

39. Jones, Abstract, no page.

40. Eliot, *Writings*, 22: 217-19.

41. Hill, p. 153.

42. Greer, "Flying Pigs and Double Standards," p. 785.

CHAPTER 1. REPRESENTATIONS OF WOMAN, 1792-1901

1. Barbara Welter, "The Cult of True Womanhood," *American Quarterly*, 18 (1966): 151-74.

2. See Delamont and Duffin; and Jill Conway, "Stereotypes of Femininity in a Theory of Sexual Evolution," *Victorian Studies*, 14 (September 1970): 47-62.

3. Rorabacher, no page.

4. Sandford, pp. 11, 114.

5. On contemporary understanding of sex roles, see also the many recent collections of nineteenth-century essays and other documents: e.g., Bauer and Ritt; Burstyn; Hellerstein et al.; and Murray.

6. Ruskin, *Works*, 18: 121-22.

7. "The Subjection of Women," *Edinburgh Review*, 130 (October 1869): 602.

8. Wollstonecraft, *A Vindication of the Rights of Woman*, pp. 81-82.

9. Hays, pp. 136-37.

10. Dryden, p. 183.

11. Wollstonecraft, *A Vindication of the Rights of Woman*, pp. 108-9.

12. Harriet Taylor Mill, "The Emancipation of Women," *Westminister Review*, 55 (July 1851): 301.

13. Patmore, "The Social Position of Women," p. 524.

14. Strachey, p. 15. The single most important document in the struggle for marriage law reform was a carefully researched pamphlet by Barbara Leigh Smith Bodichon: *A Brief Summary in Plain Language of the Most Important Laws Concerning Women* (1854); it is excerpted in Murray, pp. 118-20.

15. Quoted in Strachey, p. 15.

16. Killham, p. 87.

17. Quoted in Brittain, p. 29.

18. Brittain, p. 29.

19. Crow, pp. 250-51.

20. Brittain, p. 23.

21. Hill, pp. 90-91.

22. Landon, *Poetical Works*, p. 160. The poem is from *The Golden Violet*, first published in 1827.

23. Caroline Norton, "Woman's Love," in Hale, p. 147.

24. Frances Anne Kemble, *Poems* (1844), p. 78.

25. Craik, *Mulock's Poems, New and Old*, p. 48.

26. Landon, *Poetical Works*, p. 69.

27. Cook, *Poetical Works*, p. 255.

28. Caroline Lamb, "Woman's Love," in Wellesley, p. 136. This poem was first published in the 1830 *Keepsake*.

29. All three women were in unhappy marriages; eventually, each separated from her husband. Fanny Kemble was divorced in 1849. See Appendix.

30. Mary Ann Browne, "Man's Love," in Hale, p. 188.

31. Hemans, *Poetical Works*, p. 239.

32. See Margaret M. Maison, "Queen Victoria's Favourite Poet," *The Listener*, 73 (April 29, 1965): 636-37.

33. Procter, *Poems*, p. 219.

34. Ibid., pp. 158-59.

35. Aikin, *Epistles on Women*, pp. 32, v, 22.

36. Anna Barbauld, "The Rights of Women," in Bax and Stewart, pp. 37-38.

37. Mary Howitt, "Beatrice," in *Friendship's Offering* (London: Smith, Elder, 1835), pp. 58-61.

38. Caroline Norton, "The Visionary Portrait," in Bethune, p. 391.

39. Ingelow, *Poems*, p. 398.

40. Kemble, *Poems* (1883), p. 193.

41. Hemans, *Poetical Works*, p. 336.

42. Mary Howitt, "The Three Ages of Woman," *Ladies' Companion*, 2 (July 6, 1850; August 17, 1850; November 23, 1850): 24-25, 120-21, 344-45.

43. See Maureen Peters, *Jean Ingelow: Victorian Poetess* (Ipswich, England: Boydell, 1972), p. 34.

44. Ingelow, *Poems*, p. 108.

45. Havergal, *Poetical Works*, p. 253.

46. Greenwell, *Poems* (1889), pp. 117-18.

47. Emily Brontë, *The Poems of Emily Jane Brontë and Anne Brontë*, p. 13. From childhood through adulthood, the Brontë siblings created, acted out, and wrote poems depicting the imaginary kingdoms of Gondal and Angria. Passionate and heroic, the characters in the saga "loved with brute passion, committed adultery and incest, bore illegitimate children, moldered in dungeons, murdered, revenged, conquered, and died unrepentant" (Moers, p. 262). See *The Complete Poems of Emily Jane Brontë*, ed. C. W. Hatfield (New York: Columbia Univ. Press, 1941), pp. 17-19, for Fannie Ratchford's outline of the Gondal story.

48. For examples of this new approach, see " 'It Would Not Do': Emily Brontë as Poet," in Smith, pp. 33-67; Gilbert and Gubar, *The Madwoman in the Attic*, pp. 83-88; Gallant; and Patricia Meyer Spacks, "The Rebellions of Good Women," in Todd, *Be Good, Sweet Maid*, pp. 103-12. See also C. Day Lewis, "The Poetry of Emily Brontë: A Passion for Freedom," *Brontë Society Transactions*, 13 (1957): 83-99. Lewis remarks, somewhat daringly, "My own belief is that the source of Emily Brontë's proud recalcitrance, her preoccupation with themes of captivity, exile and freedom, was her sex; the limitation of not being a man." Lewis hastens to add, however, "There is no reason whatsoever to suppose that Emily Brontë *knew* what was the cause of her trouble, or consciously rebelled against being a woman" (p. 95).

49. A representative treatment of this kind is Irving H. Buchen, "Emily Brontë and the Metaphysics of Childhood and Love," *Nineteenth-Century Fiction*, 2 (June 1967): 63-70; rpt. in Petit, pp. 248-55. See also Richard Benvenuto, *Emily Brontë* (Boston, Twayne, 1982), pp. 58-60.

50. Brontë's relationship to Romanticism is a central issue in Lawrence Starzyk, "Emily Brontë: Poetry in a Mingled Tone," *Criticism*, 14 (1972): 119-36; and, more recently, and from a feminist perspective, in Nina Auerbach, "This Changeful Life: Emily Brontë's Anti-Romance," in Gilbert and Gubar, *Shakespeare's Sisters*, pp. 49-64; and Homans, pp. 104-61.

51. Charles Morgan, "Emily Brontë," in Petit, p. 91.

52. Smith, "Introduction: Towards a New Assessment," pp. 7-8.

53. Gilbert and Gubar, *The Madwoman in the Attic*, p. 85.

54. See Moers, pp. 245-51, on bird imagery in women's poetry.

55. Greenwell, *Poems* (1861), pp. 116-17.

56. She was also a friend of Christina Rossetti and an ardent admirer of Elizabeth Barrett Browning.

57. E.g., Kaplan, *Salt and Bitter and Good*; and Stanford. The title of the former comes, of course, from "A Curse for a Nation" by Elizabeth Barrett Browning.

58. Kaplan, *Salt and Bitter and Good*, p. 21.

59. Ibid., pp. 21-22.

60. Pfeiffer, *Under the Aspens*, p. 106.

61. Mary Elizabeth Coleridge, *Collected Poems*, p. 189. This poem is also available in Auden, p. 349.

62. Mary Elizabeth Coleridge, *Collected Poems*, p. 161.

63. In *Woman and the Demon*, Nina Auerbach expands upon this juncture of the angelic and demonic in the contemporary idealization of Victorian womanhood.

CHAPTER 2. DAUGHTERS

1. Gregory, pp. 5, 41, 26-27. A new edition appeared as late as 1877.

2. John Keats, *The Poetical Works*, ed. H. W. Garrod, 2d ed. (Oxford: Clarendon Press, 1958), p. 27.

3. Trevelyan, p. 501.

4. Patricia Branca, "Image and Reality," in Hartman and Banner, pp. 184-85. See also Gorham, pp. 20-24, on the variability of women's education in nineteenth-century England.

5. Spender, *Women of Ideas*, pp. 46-47.

6. Blease, p. 77.

7. Quoted in Blease, pp. 76-77.

8. Anna Barbauld, "To a Lady, with Some Painted Flowers," in Squire, p. 313.

9. Wollstonecraft, *Thoughts on the Education of Daughters*, pp. 25-26, 56.

10. See Doris M. Armitage, *The Taylors of Ongar* (Cambridge, England: Heffer, 1939).

11. Jane Taylor, *Writings*, 2, 2: 92-93.

12. Jane Taylor, "Accomplishment," in Hale, p. 111.

13. Jane Taylor, *Writings*, 1, 3: 95.

14. Frances Power Cobbe, *Life of Frances Power Cobbe, by Herself*, vol. 2 (Boston: Houghton, Mifflin, 1894), pp. 55, 56.

15. Crow, p. 60.

16. Southey, *Select Literary Works*, 1: 17.

17. Muzzey, pp. 57-58, 73.

18. Reid, p. 6; excerpted in Murray, pp. 212-13.

19. Lady Emmeline Stuart Wortley, "To Woman," in *Keepsake* (London: Longmans, 1840), p. 147.

20. Reid, p. 121.

21. See Ann Colley, "The Conflict between Tradition and Modern Values in Tennyson's *The Princess*," in *Women, Literature, Criticism [Bucknell Review]*, ed. Harry R. Garvin (Lewisburg, Pa.: Bucknell Univ. Press, 1978), pp. 37-48.

22. Killham, p. 3.

23. Tennyson, *The Princess*, in *The Poems of Tennyson*, Prologue, lines 124-26. Further citations from Tennyson's poems will be identified internally by part and/or line number.

24. Burstyn, p. 26.

25. See Gorham on the psychology of the idealized child-woman, pp. 6-7.

26. Mary Howitt, "Childhood, or the Triad," in Wellesley, pp. 258-60. This poem was first published in *Friendship's Offering* (London: Smith, Elder, 1835).

27. Southey, *Select Literary Works*, pp. 12-13.

28. Ingelow, *Poems*, p. 188.

29. See Burstyn, pp. 20-22, and Gorham, p. 11, on the economic contradictions of middle-class girls' lives.

30. Hemans, *Poetical Works*, pp. 349-50. Korner was a German poet and soldier, killed in battle in 1813. His sister survived him just long enough to complete his portrait and a drawing of his burial place and then died of grief.

31. Eliot, *Writings*, 19: 186-87. For a thorough analysis of the autobiographical element in "Brother and Sister," see Redinger, pp. 44-65.

32. See Gorham, p. 44, on the significance of brothers to sisters.

33. See Smith-Rosenberg; Faderman; and Gorham, pp. 112-15.

34. Kemble traveled extensively in the United States. See Constance Wright, *Fanny Kemble and the Lovely Land* (New York: Dodd, Mead, 1972).

35. See Houghton, pp. 348-53, for a thorough discussion of this phenomenon. For provocative analyses of woman as angel in Victorian literature and iconography, see Alexander Welsh, "The Bride from Heaven," in *The City of Dickens* (Oxford: Clarendon Press, 1971), pp. 141-228; and Auerbach, *Woman and the Demon*, pp. 64-88.

36. Patmore, "The Social Position of Women," pp. 525-28.

37. Linton, *The Girl of the Period*, 1: 1-2, 8-9. This controversial series of essays was first published in the *Saturday Review*, 25 (March 14, 1868): 339-40, and subsequent numbers. A contemporary response is Penelope Holland, "Our Offence, Our Defence, and Our Petition," *Macmillan's Magazine*, 19 (February 1869): 323-31; excerpted in Murray, pp. 45-47.

38. Mary Howitt, "The Morning Walk," in *Friendship's Offering* (London: Smith, Elder, 1833), pp. 109-13.

39. Caroline Norton, "Twilight," *The Dream*, pp. 7, 13, 70, 71.

40. "Violet Fane," "Time," in Miles, 7: 598.

41. See Utter and Needham, pp. 43-95.

42. Norton, *Poems* (1854), pp. 183-85.

43. Nesbit, *Songs of Love and Empire*, p. 152.

44. See Doris L. Moore, *E. Nesbit: A Biography* (Philadelphia: Chilton Books, 1966).

45. Letitia Landon, "The Adieu," in *Keepsake* (London: Longmans, 1833), p. 104.

46. Vita Sackville-West, "The Women Poets of the Seventies," in Granville-Barker, p. 124.

47. Webster, *Portraits*, pp. 23-24.

48. Mary Elizabeth Coleridge, "The Making of Heroines," *Gathered Leaves*, p. 179. This essay was first published in the *Reflector* for March 1888.

49. Mary Elizabeth Coleridge, *Collected Poems*, p. 215.

CHAPTER 3. WIVES

1. *Woman As She Is, and As She Should Be* (London: J. Cochrane, 1835), p. 272.

2. Sarah Ann Sewell, *Woman and the Times We Live In* (Manchester, England: n.p., 1869), pp. 28-29.

3. Dunbar, p. 20.

4. Banks and Banks, p. 59.

5. James Baldwin Brown, *Young Men and Maidens* (London: Hodder and Stoughton, 1871), pp. 38-39. Quoted in Houghton, p. 345. See Houghton's discussion of the Victorian concept of "home," pp. 341-48.

6. Linton, p. 59.

7. Patricia Branca, "Image and Reality," in Hartman and Banner, p. 185; this essay is condensed from Branca's monograph, *The Silent Sisterhood*.

8. See, e.g., Houghton; Marcus, *The Other Victorians*; Pearsall; and Trudgill.

9. Acton, *Functions and Disorders of the Reproductive Organs*, pp. 115-16. Acton's book, written for physicians, proved quite popular with the general public, reaching its sixth London edition in 1875. Not all of Acton's contemporaries agreed with him, of course. [See Branca, *The Silent Sisterhood*, p. 125; and Patricia Robertson, *An Experience of Women: Pattern and Change in Nineteenth-Century Europe* (Philadelphia: Temple Univ. Press, 1982), p. 176.] Yet it still seems significant that a respected practicing physician could assert that women were essentially nonsexual and sell so many copies of his book.

10. Branca believes that Victorian women's continuing enthusiasm for their personal appearance, even after marriage, was an invitation to sexual activity from their husbands and that "most middle-class adult women made the transition relatively easily" from the sexual sublimation of girlhood to the sexual fulfillment of marriage (*The Silent Sisterhood*, p. 127).

11. Trudgill, pp. 58-59. Trudgill's book contains a succinct but admirably researched discussion of Victorian sexual beliefs, wedding-night trauma, etc.

12. See Nancy Cott, "Passionlessness," in Cott and Pleck, p. 173.

13. Kitchener, pp. 152-53.

14. Havelock Ellis, *Studies in the Psychology of Sex*, vol. 3 (Philadelphia: F. A. Davis, 1901-1928), Appendix B, pp. 303-6.

15. Quoted in Pearsall, p. 40.

16. See also Robertson, pp. 109-13.

17. Not until 1891 was the husband's right to impose conjugal relations on his unconsenting wife legally disallowed. Murray, p. 118.

18. Mews, p. 9.

19. Murray, p. 121. See Frances Power Cobbe, "Wife Torture in England," *Contemporary Review*, 32 (April 1878): 55-87; excerpted in Murray, pp. 121-23. See also Cobbe, "Criminals, Idiots, Women, and Minors."

20. John Stuart Mill, p. 35. A brief account of legal reforms related to wife-beating may be found in William L. Burn, *The Age of Equipoise* (London: Unwin University Books, 1964), pp. 155-56.

21. William Scott, "Queen Bees or Working Bees?" *Saturday Review*, 8 (November 12, 1859): 575-76.

22. Jameson, pp. 216-18.

23. Strachey, p. 47.

24. Hill, p. 97.

25. Houghton, pp. 348-49.

26. Mews points out the difficulty inherent in unmarried women's attempts to portray marriage: they tended to analyze the more public aspects of the wife's relationship with her husband. Generally their concern was "not so much with the psychological adjustments involved in the relationship, and certainly not with any more than hints about the physical side of marriage" (p. 126). The Brontë sisters, Mews finds, were exceptional in this regard.

27. See Johnson for the marriage theme in Tennyson and Browning and a survey of sex and marriage in English poetry from 1830 to 1880.

28. Dante Gabriel Rossetti, *The House of Life*, ed. P. F. Baum (Cambridge: Harvard Univ. Press, 1928), p. 73.

29. Quoted by Baum, p. 31.

30. Meredith, *Modern Love*, Sonnet 43, in *Poems*, p. 141.

31. McGhee, p. 167.

32. Certain earlier works by Robert Browning, notably "My Last Duchess" (*Dramatic Lyrics*, 1842) and "Andrea del Sarto," "A Woman's Last Word," and "Another Way of Love" (*Men and Women*, 1855), may be exceptions to this generalization, in respect to Browning's intent, if not to the poems' reception. On *The Ring and the Book*, McGhee remarks, "The mockery that men have made of marriage . . . [is] fully revealed [through] Pompilia's sad and strange life" (p. 90).

33. Reed, p. 77. For a discussion of the "commercial marriage" theme in nineteenth-century fiction and poetry, see pp. 105-15.

34. Stone, p. 422.

35. Letitia Landon, "The Choice," in *Forget Me Not* (London: Ackermann, 1826), p. 18.

36. J.M.S. Tompkins, *The Popular Novel in England 1770-1800* (Lincoln: Univ. of Nebraska Press, 1961; rpt. Westport, Conn.: Greenwood Press, 1976), p. 147. Mary Wollstonecraft's unfinished novel *Maria, or the Wrongs of Woman* (1798) paints a horrifying picture of a repugnant marriage—and the potentially disastrous consequences of even passive resistance to it—as does Robert Browning in *The Ring and the Book* some seventy years later. In 1869, one Frances Kelley related to an English court a tale of marital abuse that in reality rivalled Mary Wollstonecraft's fiction. See Hellerstein et al., pp. 260-64, for Kelley's testimony.

37. Norton, *Poems* (1857), pp. 249, 254; rpt. *Selected Writings*, 1: 117, 123.

38. Webster, *A Woman Sold*, pp. 109-10.

39. "Violet Fane," *Constance's Fate; or Denzil Place*, in *Poems*, 9-256.

40. Letitia Landon, "Remembrance," in *Keepsake* (London: Longmans, 1837), pp. 29, 30. See also "The Bridal Day" by Caroline Norton, *Poems* (1854), pp. 214-25.

41. Cook, *Poetical Works*, p. 74.

42. Webster, *A Woman Sold*, pp. 94, 95.

43. Havergal, *Poetical Works*, p. 153.

44. Craik, *Mulock's Poems, New and Old*, pp. 49-50.

45. See Craik, *A Woman's Thoughts about Women*.

46. Elaine Showalter, "Dinah Mulock Craik and the Tactics of Sentiment: A Case Study in Victorian Female Authorship," *Feminist Studies*, 2 (1975): 6.

47. Craik, *Mulock's Poems, New and Old*, p. 57.

48. "Michael Field," *A Selection from the Poems*, pp. 86, 87.

49. "Michael Field," *Works and Days*.

50. Foster, pp. 141-45. Bradley was about fifteen years older than Cooper.

51. Ingelow, *Poems*, p. 224.

52. "Violet Fane," *Autumn Songs*, p. 76.

53. Ingelow, *Poems*, p. 329.

54. Caroline Norton, "True Love," in Hale, p. 153.

55. For a full discussion of Caroline Norton's marriage, see Alice Acland, *Caroline Norton* (London: Constable, 1948).

56. See also *Caroline Norton's Defense: English Laws for Women in the Nineteenth Century*, ed. Joan Huddleston (Chicago: Academy Chicago, 1982).

57. Greenwell, *Poems* (1889), p. 541.

58. "Preface," *Poetical Works* of Felicia Hemans, p. 9.

59. Kaplan, *Salt and Bitter and Good*, p. 95.

60. Stubbs goes so far as to say that Victorian feminists and reformers supported the factory acts which restricted women's employment in industry not primarily because they objected to factory conditions as such, but because the reality of working women's lives was an affront to the ideal of home and family. Patricia Stubbs, *Women and Fiction: Feminism and the Novel 1880-1920* (New York: Barnes and Noble, 1979), p. 5.

61. Norton, *A Voice from the Factories*, p. 159.

62. Ingelow, *Poems*, p. 129.

63. Louisa Bevington [Guggenberger], "Bees in Clover," in Miles, 8: 270.

64. Bevington, *Poems, Lyrics, and Sonnets*, p. 148.

65. Helen Selina Sheridan, Lady Dufferin, "The Charming Woman," in Stanford, pp. 118-19.

66. Southey, *Select Literary Works*, pp. 151-52.

67. Amy Levy, "Xantippe," *A Minor Poet*, pp. 24, 25, 28, 32, 33, 34.

68. Bax and Stewart, p. 96.

69. E. Nesbit, "A Tragedy," in Miles, 8: 589, 590.

70. Caroline Norton, "The Two Pictures," *Court Magazine*, 4 (January 1834): 26, 27.

71. Fanny Kemble, "Paolo and Francesca," in Bax and Stewart, p. 75.

72. "Violet Fane," "Divided," in Miles, 7: 601, 602.

73. Ingelow, *Poems*, p. 404.

74. Hemans, *Poetical Works*, p. 171.

75. Agnes Mary Frances Robinson, *Collected Poems*, p. 194.

CHAPTER 4. MOTHERS

1. Trudgill, p. 63.

2. Several prominent medical authorities, notably Thomas Nichols (1853) and George Drysdale (1854), confusing menstruation with the period of estrus in lower

mammals, considered the rest of the month to be generally "safe." See Elaine and English Showalter, "Victorian Women and Menstruation," in Vicinus, *Suffer and Be Still*, pp. 38-44. At least one handbook, *Notes on the Population Question* (1831), advised vaginal use of corrosive sublimate, which was sometimes fatal. A Dr. Soule (*The Science of Reproduction and Reproductive Control*) recommended strychnine and iodine, taken internally. The latter two books are cited in Pearsall, p. 217.

3. Calder, p. 161.

4. Trall, p. 203.

5. Basch, p. 34.

6. Sara Coleridge, *Phantasmion*, p. 79.

7. According to Banks and Banks, pp. 53-57, the trend beginning in the late 1860s toward smaller families among the English middle class was *not* the result of the feminist movement, though certain contemporary writers, notably William Acton and Eliza Lynn Linton, did attempt to make this connection. Angus McLaren disagrees, postulating a type of "domestic feminism" in women's readiness to adopt birth control devices and noting that "all the leading birth control advocates were sympathetic" to the cause of women's rights. *Birth Control in Nineteenth-Century England* (New York: Holmes & Meier, 1978), pp. 94-101.

8. Webster, *Mother and Daughter*, p. 39.

9. Ibid., p. 38.

10. Meynell, *Collected Poems*, p. 86.

11. Rich, pp. 151-55. Actually, puerperal fever was not a contagious disease at all, but a type of blood poisoning caused by contamination at the hands of doctors. It was most prevalent among women whose confinement took place in lying-in hospitals. Mary Wollstonecraft was among its victims.

12. Ellis, *The Mothers of England*, p. 13.

13. Riley, pp. 130-31.

14. Letter from Queen Victoria to the Princess Royal, June 15, 1858, in *Dearest Child: Letters between Queen Victoria and the Princess Royal (1858-1861)*, ed. Roger Fulford (London: Evans Bros., 1864), p. 115. Quoted by John Hawkins Miller, in " 'Temple and Sewer': Childbirth, Prudery and Victoria Regina," in Wohl, pp. 23-43. Queen Victoria, who lived to be eighty-two years old, was a notable exception to the way in which multiple pregnancies often doomed a woman to an early death. She gave birth to nine children, the first seven of them before the introduction of chloroform as a childbirth anesthetic. But although "by her own admission she suffered less than the average woman . . . she hated the condition that reduced her to a heavy suffering body." In January 1841, after bearing only one child, she wrote to her uncle, "you cannot really wish me to be a *'Mamma d'une nombreuse famille,'* . . . men never think . . . what a hard task it is for us women to go through this very often." Basch, pp. 35-36.

15. Blind, *The Ascent of Man*, p. 76.

16. Kaplan, *Salt and Bitter and Good*, p. 160. For more information on Blind's youthful attempts to reconcile science and religion, see pp. 159-61.

17. Trall, pp. 203-4.

18. Caroline Bowles, "The Dying Mother to Her Infant," in *The Literary Souvenir* (London: Longmans, 1830), pp. 33, 34, 37.

19. Mary Elizabeth Coleridge, *Collected Poems*, p. 205.

20. Caroline Norton, "Crippled Jane," in *Home Thoughts and Home Scenes*, p. 35. I am indebted to Courtney, pp. 79-80, for calling this poem and its Wordsworthian overtones to my attention.

21. Sara Coleridge, *Phantasmion*, p. 33.

22. Branca, *The Silent Sisterhood*, pp. 98-99.

23. Ibid., p. 96.

24. Mary Anne Browne, "The Departed," in *Forget Me Not* (London: Ackermann, 1838), pp. 349-50.

25. Kemble, *Poems* (1844), pp. 164-65.

26. Ingelow, *Poems*, pp. 485, 589, 493.

27. Ibid., p. 494.

28. Maureen Peters, *Jean Ingelow: Victorian Poetess* (Ipswich, England: Boydell, 1972), p. 44. For more examples of infant death poetry, see also Emily Brontë, "Geraldine," *Poems of Emily Jane Brontë and Anne Brontë*, pp. 121-22; Sara Coleridge, "The Mother," in Bax and Stewart, pp. 64-65, and "O Sleep My Babe," *Phantasmion*, p. 126; Jane Taylor, "On the Death of an Infant," *Writings*, 1, 2: 340; Caroline Norton, "The Widow and Her Son," in Hale, pp. 145-56; and Caroline Bowles Southey, "To a Dying Infant," in Bethune, pp. 328-30.

29. *Home Thoughts and Home Scenes* was originally published in London by the Camden Press.

30. Caroline Norton, "Affection," in *Friendship's Offering* (London: Smith, Elder, 1833), pp. 61-63.

31. Caroline Norton, "To My Child," in *Friendship's Offering* (London: Smith, Elder, 1834), pp. 179-80.

32. For full details, see Alice Acland, *Caroline Norton* (London: Constable, 1948), pp. 97-139.

33. Alexander H. Japp, "E. Nesbit," in Miles, 8: 580.

34. E. Nesbit, "Song," in Miles, 8: 581.

35. Miles, 8: 580.

36. William Michael Rossetti, "Introduction," *Mother and Daughter* by Augusta Webster, p. 11.

37. Quoted in Basch, p. 33.

38. Basch, p. 33.

39. Alexander Walker, p. 43.

40. Ellis, *The Mothers of England*, pp. 90, 23.

41. Patmore, "The Social Position of Women," p. 531.

42. "Rights and Conditions of Women," pp. 207-8.

43. See Ann Roberts, "Mothers and Babies: The Wetnurse and Her Employer in Mid-Nineteenth-Century England," *Women's Studies*, 3 (1976): 279-93.

44. Gisborne, pp. 378, 379.

45. For contemporary accounts of baby farming, abortion, and infanticide, see Hellerstein et al., pp. 238-40, 199, and 204-5.

46. See, e.g., "The Wife of Asdrubal," p. 50, and "The Suliote Mother," p. 266, in Hemans, *Poetical Works*.

47. Hemans, *Poetical Works*, p. 261.

48. Frances Power Cobbe, *The Duties of Women*, p. 81.

49. Ellis, *The Mothers of England*, pp. 50-51.

50. Ingelow, *Poems*, p. 467. This is the same Katie Harston who was to die two years later.

51. Landon, *Poetical Works*, pp. 303-5.

52. Procter, *Poems*, p. 138.

53. Webster, *Mother and Daughter*, Sonnet 11, p. 25.

54. Ibid., Sonnet 8, p. 22.

55. Ellis, *The Mothers of England*, p. 27.

56. Brontë, *Poems of Emily Jane Brontë and Anne Brontë*, p. 179.

57. Hemans, *Poetical Works*, p. 357.

58. Trudgill, p. 257.

59. Pfeiffer, *Under the Aspens*, pp. 84-85.

60. See, for example, *A Woman's View of Woman's Rights* (London: n.p., 1867), pp. 11-12; cited in Banks and Banks, p. 45.

61. Banks and Banks, p. 48.

62. D. B. Wyndham Lewis and Charles Lee, *The Stuffed Owl* (London: Dent, 1930), p. 192. Also Cook, *Poetical Works*, p. 31.

63. Cook, *Poetical Works*, pp. 107, 96, 131, 87.

64. Ibid., p. 132.

CHAPTER 5. THE FALLEN WOMAN

1. Engelman, pp. 314-15. See, e.g., Ellis, *The Wives of England*, pp. 196-205. See also Keith Thomas, "The Double Standard."

2. Elizabeth Janeway, "Who Is Sylvia? On the Loss of Sexual Paradigms," *Signs*, 5 (Summer 1980): 573-89.

3. Acton, *Prostitution*, p. 118. In Acton's pioneering study of 1857, he sought to bring the issue of prostitution squarely before the public. With that goal accomplished, he greatly expanded his book for the second edition in 1870. My quotations are from Peter Fryer's abridgement of Acton's expanded second edition.

4. Elizabeth R. Chapman, "The New Godiva," in *The New Godiva* (London: T. Fisher Unwin, 1885), p. 44. This essay previously appeared as a pamphlet published by Isbister, reaching "but a limited circle of readers," according to Chapman in her introduction (p. xii). She does not give the dates for first publication of any of the five essays in the collection, but says that all were "written before the attention of the country . . . was drawn to the subjects with which they deal" (p. vii).

5. Greg, "Prostitution," p. 503.

6. W.E.H. Lecky, *History of European Morals*, vol. 2 (London: Longmans, 1869), p. 299.

7. For a full account of Josephine Butler and the Contagious Diseases Acts, see Walkowitz.

8. Quoted by her husband, George W. Johnson, *The Evolution of Woman* (London: Holden, 1926), pp. 211-12.

9. E. M. Sigsworth and T. J. Wyke, "A Study of Victorian Prostitution and Venereal Disease," in Vicinus, *Suffer and Be Still*, p. 78, n.10.

10. Wollstonecraft, *A Vindication of the Rights of Woman*, p. 228.

11. Kitchener, p. 52.

12. E.g., Michael Ryan, *Prostitution in London* (London: Bailliere, 1839), p. 89.

13. Ryan; Greg, "Prostitution"; Acton, *Prostitution*; James B. Talbot, *The Miseries of Prostitution* (London: James Madden, 1844); and William Tait, *Magdalenism* (London: P. Rickard, 1840) are a few of the better-known such studies.

14. Radcliffe, pp. 403, 439.

15. See Acton, *Prostitution*, pp. 118-20.

16. Mayhew, p. 116.

17. See Greg, "Prostitution," pp. 468-70. For more on incest, see Anthony S. Wohl, "Sex and the Single Room: Incest among the Victorian Working Classes," in Wohl, pp. 197-216.

18. Acton, *Prostitution*, p. 25.

19. For a recent, feminist perspective on this controversy, see Deborah Gorham, "The 'Maiden Tribute of Modern Babylon' Re-examined: Child Prostitution and the Idea of Childhood in Late-Victorian England," *Victorian Studies*, 21 (Spring 1978): 353-79; and Walkowitz, pp. 246-47. While the accuracy of Stead's reporting has been questioned, it is clear that he catalyzed the reform movement.

20. See Sigsworth and Wyke, in Vicinus, *Suffer and Be Still*, pp. 77-99.

21. Acton, *Prostitution*, pp. 72, 26.

22. Logan, pp. 96-97.

23. Recent reevaluations can be found in Walkowitz, pp. 13-47, and Finnegan, pp. 1-33 and 212-15.

24. See Basch, pp. 266-67, and Mitchell, *The Fallen Angel*.

25. Distasteful as the term "illegitimate child" may be, it accurately reflects the nineteenth-century attitude toward children born outside of marriage and conveys a distinction essential to my discussion.

26. John Clare, *Poems*, vol. 2, ed. J. W. Tibble (London: Dent, 1935), pp. 178-79. The date of composition of "A Maid's Tragedy" is uncertain. It was written at Helpstone between 1824 and 1832.

27. "Violet Fane," *Poems*, pp. 254-56.

28. Caroline Norton, "The Sorrows of Rosalie," *The Undying One*, 127ff; rpt. *Selected Writings*, 1: 3-77.

29. Sara Coleridge, *Phantasmion*, pp. 158, 159.

30. Dora Greenwell, "Christina," *Poems* (1861), p. 3.

31. Anne Hunter, "A Simile," in Bax and Stewart, p. 56.

32. Bax and Stewart, p. 56.

33. Procter, *Poems*, p. 412. This poem was included in *A Chaplet of Verses*, which Procter published in 1862 in order to donate the profits to a Protestant night refuge for the homeless poor.

34. Agnes Mary Frances Robinson, *The New Arcadia*, pp. 31-32. *The New Arcadia* was an anti-pastoral poem which, according to Arthur Symons, strained too hard in the attempt to pull heavy tragedy out of peasant life. Miles, 8: 523.

35. Landon, *Poetical Works*, pp. 328, 329. The date of first publication of this poem cannot be precisely assigned; however, it was, obviously, written before 1838, the year of Landon's death.

36. Mary Howitt, "Judgment," in Bethune, p. 355.

37. Mary Howitt, "The Heart of the Outcast," in Bethune, p. 356.

38. Mary Howitt, *Ballads*, p. 194.

39. Caroline Norton, "The Prison Chaplain," in Bethune, p. 411.

40. Ingelow, *Poems*, p. 134.

41. Caroline Norton, *The Child of the Islands*, p. 39. The title refers to the Prince of Wales, born in 1841. The point of the poem was to acquaint him with the distressed circumstances of the English poor in the year of his first birthday. Publication was delayed for several years by the Nortons' domestic problems; rpt. *Selected Writings*, 5: 39.

42. Hood, p. 317. Subsequent references to the poems of Hood will be identified internally by line number.

43. Pfeiffer, *Under the Aspens*, Preface, no page.

44. Ibid., pp. 15, 23.

45. Kemble, *Poems* (1844), pp. 113-14.

46. Auerbach, *Woman and the Demon*, p. 168.

47. Hemans, *Poetical Works*, p. 344.

48. Ibid., p. 314.

49. Caroline Norton, "The New-Born Child," in Bethune, p. 405.

50. Norton, *The Dream*, p. 94.

51. See also Caroline Norton's novel *Lost and Saved* (1863); excerpted in *Selected Writings*, 8.

52. E. Nesbit, *Leaves of Life*, pp. 82, 87.

53. Levy, *A Minor Poet*, pp. 65, 67-68.

54. Procter, *Poems*, pp. 210, 212, 213.

55. Thomas Hardy, *The Collected Poems*, 2d ed. (London: Macmillan, 1920), p. 145. "The Ruined Maid" was written in 1866 at Westbourne Park Villas and published for the first time in *Poems of the Past and Present* (1901).

56. Dante Gabriel Rossetti, *The Complete Poetical Works*, ed. William Michael Rossetti (Boston: Little, Brown, 1903), p. 110, lines 252-254. "Jenny" was rewritten for the 1870 *Poems* from earlier versions in 1847 and 1858-1859.

57. Webster, *Portraits*, p. 52. Further quotations from this poem will be documented internally by page number.

58. Mackenzie Bell, in Miles, 7: 503.

59. Sackville-West, "The Women Poets of the Seventies," p. 125.

60. Evans, p. 374.

61. Meynell, *Poems*, p. 63. Further quotations from this poem will be documented internally by page number.

62. Evans suggests that Meynell later rejected "A Study" and certain other pieces from *Preludes* because she (rightly, in his opinion) detected in them "the sadness of adolescent *malaise*"; yet, as he also points out, "this first volume had a larger and more generous movement than the narrower perfection of her later verse" (p. 158).

CHAPTER 6. THE SPINSTER

1. Susan Gorsky chronicles this transition in the popular novel in "Old Maids and New Women."

2. Banks and Banks, p. 27.

3. Greg, "Why Are Women Redundant?" in *Literary and Social Judgments*, pp. 282-83, 276.

4. Tabitha Bramble appears in *Humphry Clinker* (1771). On the stereotype of the ridiculous old maid in eighteenth-century life and literature, see Utter and Needham, pp. 214-58, and Rogers, *The Troublesome Helpmate*, pp. 201-3.

5. Hayley, 1: xvi, 9, 18.

6. Gisborne, p. 428.

7. Patmore, "The Social Position of Women," p. 535.

8. Greenwell, "Our Single Women," p. 69.

9. Frances Power Cobbe, "What Shall We Do with Our Old Maids?" *Fraser's Magazine*, 66 (November 1862); rpt. in *Essays on the Pursuits of Women*, ed. Frances Power Cobbe, p. 60.

10. Banks and Banks, pp. 28-32, and Hammerton, pp. 129-31.

11. Greg, "Why Are Women Redundant?" pp. 289-91.

12. Cook, "Old Maids," p. 404.

13. Gorsky, p. 72.

14. Greenwell, "Our Single Women," p. 64.

15. Frances Power Cobbe, "Celibacy vs. Marriage," *Fraser's Magazine*, 65 (February 1862); rpt. in *Essays on the Pursuits of Women*, p. 53.

16. *Harriet Martineau's Autobiography*, vol. 1, ed. Maria Weston Chapman (London: Smith Elder, 1877), pp. 131-33. For a detailed discussion of Martineau's celibacy—its sources and implications—see Margaret Walters, "The Rights and Wrongs of Woman: Mary Wollstonecraft, Harriet Martineau and Simone de Beauvoir," in *The Rights and Wrongs of Women*, ed. Juliet Mitchell and Ann Oakley (Hammondsworth, England, 1976), pp. 329-51.

17. See Lee Chambers-Schiller, "The Single Woman Reformer: Conflicts between Family and Vocation, 1830-1860," *Frontiers*, 3 (Fall 1978): 41-48; and Harriet Warm Schupf, "Single Women and Social Reform in Mid-Nineteenth-Century England: The Case of Mary Carpenter," *Victorian Studies*, 17 (March 1974): 301-17.

18. Showalter, *A Literature of Their Own*, p. 47. Only about 65 percent of married women writers had children, and they tended to have fewer than the nineteenth-century average of five or six, according to Showalter (p. 65).

19. Cobbe, "What Shall We Do with Our Old Maids?" p. 69.

20. Cobbe, "Celibacy vs. Marriage," p. 52.

21. Cook, "Old Maids," p. 404.

22. Cobbe, "Celibacy vs. Marriage," p. 51.

23. Cook, "Old Maids," p. 403.

24. Cook, "A Brief Chapter on Old Maids," p. 222.

25. Cobbe, "Celibacy vs. Marriage," p. 50.

26. Greenwell, "Our Single Women," p. 62.

27. Symons, *Collected Works*, 2: 49.

28. Lady Emmeline Stuart Wortley, "I Am Come But Your Spirits to Raise," in *Keepsake* (London: Longmans, 1837), pp. 30-31, 32.

29. Letitia Landon, "The Secret Discovered," in *Friendship's Offering* (London: Smith, Elder, 1837), p. 324.

30. Procter, *Poems*, p. 300. Further quotations from this poem will be identified internally by page number.

31. Ibid., p. 269. Further quotations from this poem will be identified internally by page number.

32. Cook, *Poetical Works*, p. 303. Further quotations from this poem will be identified internally by page number.

33. Carl Woodring, *Victorian Samplers: William and Mary Howitt* (Lawrence: Univ. of Kansas Press, 1952), p. 104.

34. Webster, *Dramatic Studies*, p. 150. Further quotations from this poem will be identified internally by page number.

35. Eliot, *Writings*, 25: 163.

36. Ibid., 19: 51. Further quotations from this poem will be identified internally by line number.

37. "The old maid is frequently associated in popular culture with the witch, the two stereotypes springing from a common gynophobic fear of self-determined women" (Pratt, p. 123). See also Auerbach, *Woman and the Demon*, pp. 107-15, on the Victorian old maid as "an authentic female hero, with angelic and demonic capacities shaping the proud uniqueness of her life" (p. 111).

38. Robinson, *The New Arcadia*, pp. 80-81, 85.

39. Ibid., p. 57. Further quotations from this poem will be identified internally by page number.

CHAPTER 7. REPRESENTATIONS OF WOMEN AT WORK

1. See Hewitt; Holcombe; Neff; Pinchbeck; and Rowbotham.

2. "It has been roughly calculated that the middle ranks are about three times as numerous as the aristocratic, and that the working classes are about three times as numerous as the middle ranks; or in other words, of thirteen units, *one* would

represent the aristocracy, *three* the middle ranks, and the remaining *nine* stand for the 'masses.' " Parkes, pp. 73-74.

3. Quoted in Josephine Butler, *Memoir of John Grey of Dilston* (1894); excerpted in Murray, pp. 266-67.

4. Kaye, pp. 293, 295.

5. Davidoff, *The Best Circles*, p. 39.

6. Patricia Branca, "Image and Reality," in Hartman and Banner, p. 189.

7. Davidoff, *The Best Circles*, p. 39.

8. Margaret, Countess of Blessington, "Soliloquy of a Modern Fine Lady," in *Keepsake* (London: Longmans, 1845), pp. 185-86.

9. Quoted in Courtney, p. 249.

10. Adburgham, p. 250.

11. Patmore, "The Social Position of Women," p. 537; Frances Power Cobbe, "Female Charity: Lay vs. Monastic," in *Essays on the Pursuits of Women*, ed. Frances Power Cobbe, pp. 109-10.

12. Norton, *The Lady of La Garaye*, pp. 27, 102.

13. M. Jeanne Peterson, "The Victorian Governess: Status Incongruence in Family and Society," in Vicinus, *Suffer and Be Still*, p. 6.

14. See Showalter, "Women Writers and the Double Standard," pp. 323-43. By the end of the century, the use of a male pseudonym had all but lost its original purpose of gaining an unbiased critical appraisal for a new book.

15. Edward Carpenter, *My Days and Dreams* (London: Allen & Unwin, 1916), pp. 30-32.

16. Barbara Bodichon, *Women and Work* (1856); excerpted in Murray, p. 269.

17. Webster, *Portraits*, p. 87.

18. On nineteenth-century women artists, see Ellen C. Clayton, *English Female Artists*, vol. 2 (London: Tinsley Brothers, 1876); Karen Petersen and J. J. Wilson, *Women Artists* (New York: Harper Colophon Books, 1976), pp. 64ff.; and Ann Sutherland Harris and Linda Nochlin, *Women Artists 1550-1950* (New York: Knopf, 1976), pp. 50-58.

19. "Rights and Conditions of Women," pp. 197-98.

20. See, e.g., Germaine Greer, *The Obstacle Race: The Fortunes of Women Painters and Their Work* (London: Secker & Warburg, 1979).

21. Greenwell, *Poems*, (1889), p. 213.

22. For a discussion of this theme in nineteenth-century women's fiction, see Showalter, *A Literature of Their Own*, pp. 65-72. Critical interest in *Armgart* has revived in the past few years; two treatments which complement mine may be found in the essays by Blake and Midler.

23. "We are reading 'Aurora Leigh' for the third time with more enjoyment than ever," she wrote to Sara Hennell on June 8, 1857. "I know no book that gives me a deeper sense of communion with a large as well as beautiful mind" (Eliot, *Writings*, 24: 55).

24. Eliot, *Writings*, 19: 86-89. Further quotations from the play will be

documented internally by page number. *Armgart* was written in 1870 and published in July 1871 simultaneously in *Macmillan's Magazine* and in the *Atlantic Monthly*.

25. Spacks, p. 160.

26. See Moers, pp. 189-92, on the plausibility and the appeal of the opera singer heroine in women's literature.

27. Mews, pp. 190-91.

28. Cook, "Lines," *Poetical Works*, p. 493.

29. Havergal, "The Children's Triumph," *Poetical Works*, p. 253.

30. Moers, p. 198.

31. Greer, "Flying Pigs and Double Standards," p. 134.

32. Lionel Stevenson, "Miss Landon, 'The Milk-and-Watery Moon of Our Darkness,' 1824-30," *Modern Language Quarterly*, 9 (September 1947): 358.

33. Landon, *Poetical Works*, p. 103.

34. Quoted in Williams, p. 517.

35. Margaret, Countess of Blessington, "Stock in Trade of Modern Poetesses," in *Keepsake* (London: Longmans, 1833), pp. 208-9.

36. Letitia Landon, in *The Life and Literary Remains of L.E.L.*, vol. 2, ed. Laman Blanchard (London: H. Colman, 1841), p. 277.

37. Havergal, "Making Poetry," *Poetical Works*, p. 59.

38. Havergal, "Autobiography," *Poetical Works*, p. 193.

39. Havergal, *Poetical Works*, p. 59.

40. Mary Elizabeth Coleridge, *Collected Poems*, p. 92. This untitled poem was composed in 1882.

41. "Michael Field," *A Selection from the Poems*, p. 18.

42. Ibid., p. 44.

43. "Michael Field," *Works and Days*, p. 16.

44. See Charlotte Brontë's many letters to her school friend Ellen Nussey in 1836. *The Letters of the Brontës: A Selection*, ed. Muriel Spark (Norman: Univ. of Oklahoma Press, 1954), pp. 53-61.

45. Ellis, *The Wives of England*, p. 107.

46. Quoted in Dunbar, p. 132.

47. Jane Taylor, *Writings*, 1, 1: 296.

48. Hemans, *Poetical Works*, p. 243.

49. Norton, *The Dream*, pp. 153-56; rpt. *Selected Writings*, 4: 153-56.

50. Courtney, p. 22. The definitive explanation for the Hemans' separation has never been given.

51. Hemans, *Poetical Works*, p. 160.

52. Letitia Landon, "Felicia Hemans," *Poetical Works*, p. 545.

53. Pinchbeck, p. 316.

54. Hammerton believes this particular image was so pervasive that "it obscured the real resourcefulness of many Victorian women"; furthermore, "even in literature, the downtrodden victimised woman was not the only type to appear as a governess . . . " (pp. 20, 27).

55. Branca, "Image and Reality," in Hartman and Banner, p. 185.

56. See Peterson, in Vicinus, *Suffer and Be Still*, on the "status incongruence" issue.

57. "A governess would work for perhaps twenty-five years at the most, at a salary which would perhaps start at £25 a year and seldom rise beyond £80" (Crow, p. 68). For comparison, £20 per annum would be "about five times as much as the cost of laundering a governess' not very extensive wardrobe" (Moers, p. 119).

58. In 1849, Eliza Cook was horrified to have to report that the largest class of inmates in England's lunatic asylums were former governesses. "Governesses," p. 306.

59. Southey, "The Birthday," in *Select Literary Works*, pp. 55-56.

60. Ingelow, *Poems*, p. 315. Further quotations from this poem will be documented internally by page number.

61. Hellerstein et al., pp. 323-29. Excerpts from Great Britain, *Parliamentary Papers*: Children's Employment Commission, 1843 and 1865, and Select Commission of the House of Lords on the Sweating System, 1888.

62. Cook, "The Wrongs of Englishwomen," p. 355. See also Eliza Cook's "A Song for Workers," *Poetical Works*, pp. 440-42.

63. Norton, *The Child of the Islands*, pp. 20, 29; rpt. *Selected Writings*, 5: 20, 29.

64. Nesbit, *Leaves of Life*, pp. 137, 138, 139.

65. Edelstein, p. 210.

66. Inspired by Anna Jameson, these women included Barbara Leigh Smith (later Madame Bodichon), Bessie Rayner Parkes (later Mrs. Belloc), Jessie Boucherett, Adelaide Anne Procter, and Maria Rye. They were joined in their efforts by Josephine Butler, Frances Power Cobbe, John Stuart Mill, Elizabeth Westenholme, and Harriet Martineau. See Clara Thomas, *Love and Work Enough: The Life of Anna Jameson* (Toronto: Univ. of Toronto Press, 1967).

67. Thomson, p. 85.

68. Meynell, "The Lady Poverty," *Collected Poems*, p. 71.

69. Pinchbeck, p. 100.

70. Mary Howitt, "Tibbie Inglis," in Bethune, p. 343.

71. Ingelow, *Poems*, pp. 66, 68.

72. Mathilde Blind, "Reapers," in Stanford, p. 140.

73. Norton, *A Voice from the Factories*, pp. 163, 162.

74. Mary Howitt, "The Rich and the Poor," *Forget Me Not* (London: Ackermann, 1838), pp. 203, 205.

75. Norton, *The Child of the Islands*, p. 110; rpt. *Selected Writings*, 5: 110.

76. Crow, p. 71.

77. Pike, p. 156.

78. Theresa McBride, *The Domestic Revolution: The Modernisation of Household Service in England and France* (London: Croom Helm, 1976), p. 14.

79. Jane Taylor, *Writings*, 2, 2: 279-82.

80. Marion Glastonbury, "The Best-Kept Secret—How Working-Class Women Live and What They Know," *Women's Studies International Quarterly*, 2 (1979): 171.

81. Deborah Gorham, "The 'Maiden Tribute of Modern Babylon' Re-examined:

Child Prostitution and the Idea of Childhood in Late-Victorian England," *Victorian Studies*, 21 (Spring 1978): 378.

82. See Leonore Davidoff, "Mastered for Life: Servant and Wife in Victorian and Edwardian England," *Journal of Social History*, 7 (Summer 1974): 406-28.

CHAPTER 8. THE NEW WOMAN

1. Mona Caird, "The Morality of Marriage," *Fortnightly Review*, 53 (March 1890): 310-30; Margaret Oliphant, "The Anti-Marriage League," *Blackwood's*, 159 (January 1896): 135-49.

2. Showalter, *A Literature of Their Own*, pp. 28-29. See also Elaine Showalter, "Family Secrets and Domestic Subversion: Rebellion in the Novels of the 1860s," in Wohl, pp. 101-16; and Winifred Hughes, *The Maniac in the Cellar: Sensation Novels of the 1860s* (Princeton, N.J.: Princeton Univ. Press, 1980).

3. Calder, p. 168. See also the symposium, "Does Marriage Hinder a Woman's Self-Development?" *Lady's Realm*, 5 (March 1899): 576-86.

4. See Rover, "The New Woman and Bachelor Motherhood," in *Love, Morals and the Feminists*, pp. 132-39.

5. Cobbe, *The Duties of Women*, p. 112.

6. Strachey, pp. 387-88.

7. Amelia Bloomer was editor and publisher of *The Lily*, a paper devoted to the rights of women. For details on bloomers, see Crow, pp. 127-30.

8. Crow, pp. 127-30. See also Cunnington; and Helene Roberts, "The Exquisite Slave: The Role of Clothes in the Making of the Victorian Woman," *Signs*, 2 (Spring 1977): 554-69.

9. Eliza Lynn Linton, "The Epicene Sex," *The Girl of the Period*, 2: 241.

10. "The Future of Single Women," *Westminster Review*, 65 (January 1884): 158.

11. In her chapter on misogyny in the nineteenth century, Rogers demonstrates how "the *Saturday Review* plainly revealed its misogyny by disapproving of women whatever they did" (*The Troublesome Helpmate*, p. 217).

12. See Cunningham. A contemporary example of critics' reactions to the literature of the nineties is Hugh E. M. Stutfield, "Tommyrotics," *Blackwood's*, 158 (June 1895): 833-45.

13. Dowling, p. 436.

14. Colby, pp. 61-62.

15. Scanlon, p. 153.

16. Cruse, p. 337.

17. Scanlon, p. 141.

18. Cruse, p. 338.

19. Showalter, *A Literature of Their Own*, p. 185, n.5. The offending novels included Grant Allen's *The Woman Who Did* (1895), George Gissing's *The Odd Women* (1893), and Thomas Hardy's *Jude the Obscure* (1896).

20. See, e.g., George Meredith, *Diana of the Crossways* (1885); George Egerton

(Mary Chavelita Dunne), *Keynotes* (1893) and *Discords* (1894). A host of lesser writers also treated the New Woman: Sarah Grand, "John Oliver Hobbes" (Pearl Craigie), Mona Caird, and others. See Jackson, p. 224, and Cunningham, pp. 178-85.

21. Davidson, *Poems*, 1: 71, lines 7-11, 16-18, and 25-26. Dowling finds affinities as well as antagonisms between the ideology of the Decadents—including Davidson—and the ideology of the New Woman.

22. Showalter, *A Literature of Their Own*, pp. 184-85, 216, 192-93.

23. Veley, *A Marriage of Shadows*, pp. 73-74.

24. Dyhouse, p. 160.

25. Evans, p. 372.

26. Dyhouse, p. 160.

27. Mary Elizabeth Coleridge, *Collected Poems*, p. 94.

28. See also "Regina" and "The Other Side of the Mirror." The former is discussed in Carol Pearson and Katherine Pope, *The Female Hero* (New York: R. R. Bowker, 1981), p. 250, and the latter in Gilbert and Gubar, *The Madwoman in the Attic*, pp. 15-17.

29. Showalter, *A Literature of Their Own*, p. 217.

30. Pfeiffer, *Under the Aspens*, p. 107.

31. Nesbit, *Leaves of Life*, pp. 46-48.

32. Radford, *Songs and Other Verses*, pp. 78, 81.

33. Ibid., pp. 87, 90-91, 93.

34. Dowling, p. 451.

35. Quoted in Showalter, *A Literature of Their Own*, p. 182. No author or bibliographical data are provided.

36. Showalter, *A Literature of Their Own*, pp. 191-92.

37. Ibid., p. 29.

38. Ibid., p. 192.

39. Mary Elizabeth Coleridge, *Collected Poems*, pp. 212-13.

40. Gilbert and Gubar devote Chapter 3 of *The Madwoman in the Attic* to uncovering the subtext of a visionary mother-land in women's literature (pp. 93-104).

41. Gorsky, p. 77.

CHAPTER 9. ELIZABETH BARRETT BROWNING

1. Barrett Browning, *Letters*, ed. Frederic G. Kenyon, 2: 228 (February 28, 1856). All citations of Barrett Browning's letters will be from this edition—identified by volume number, page number, and date—unless otherwise specified.

2. Barrett Browning, *The Complete Works*, ed. Charlotte Porter and Helen A. Clarke, 4: 80-81, book 3, lines 68-79. Further citations from the poems of Barrett Browning will be from this edition and will be documented internally by line number. Citations from *Aurora Leigh* will include a reference to book number as well.

3. Published in the same year in *The Seraphim and Other Poems*.

4. Landon, *Poetical Works*, pp. 529-30.

5. *Athenaeum*, no. 521 (October 21, 1837): 783, and *Literary Gazette*, no. 1083 (October 21, 1837): 668.

6. *Athenaeum*, no. 573 (October 20, 1838): 758.

7. "Preface," *The Seraphim and Other Poems*, in *Complete Works*, 1: 168.

8. Ibid.

9. See Barrett Browning, "Felicia Hemans, to L.E.L., Referring to Her Monody on the Poetess" (1838), *Complete Works*, 2: 81-83; and "L.E.L.'s Last Question" (1839), *Complete Works*, 3: 117-19. Christina Rossetti wrote a poem in response to Barrett Browning's. See "L.E.L.," *Victoria Magazine*, 1 (May 1863): 40-41.

10. Besides *Findens' Tableaux*, Barrett Browning published in *Keepsake*, the *Amaranth*, and the *English Bijou Almanack*.

11. Taplin, pp. 95, 21.

12. *Letters*, 1: 232 (January 7, 1845).

13. Helen Cooper, "Working into Light: Elizabeth Barrett Browning," in Gilbert and Gubar, *Shakespeare's Sisters*, p. 66.

14. Harriet Waters Preston, ed., *The Complete Poetical Works of Elizabeth Barrett Browning*, p. 140.

15. Mark A. Weinstein, *William Edmondstoune Aytoun and the Spasmodic Controversy* (New Haven, Conn.: Yale Univ. Press, 1968), p. 26. On Barrett Browning and the Spasmodics, see also Buckley, *The Victorian Temper*, pp. 61-63; and Hayter, pp. 197-200.

16. See Taplin, pp. 128, 237, 411.

17. Taplin, p. 129.

18. See Donaldson.

19. See "Christopher in His Cave," *Blackwood's*, 44 (August 1838): 279-84.

20. As amatory verse, *Sonnets from the Portuguese* falls outside the limits of the present study, notwithstanding the recent controversy over whether the sequence may be read as an epithalamion. See Susan Zimmerman, "*Sonnets from the Portuguese*: A Negative and a Positive Context," in Todd, *Be Good, Sweet Maid*, pp. 69-81; and McGhee, p. 248.

21. In fact, just the reverse: McGhee feels, "It was a nice accident of history that Victoria could become queen of England and so by her marriage typify, if not symbolize, the great hope of her subjects (including many poets) that domestic order is political order because both derive from the divine order made possible by the sacramental power of marriage" (p. 243). For other nineteenth-century poems on Queen Victoria, see Barrett Browning, "The Young Queen," and "Victoria's Tears," *Complete Works*, 2: 106-8, 108-10; Eliza Cook, "Lines to the Queen of England," *Eliza Cook's Journal*, 6 (November 22, 1851): 57; "Victoria," *Victoria Magazine*, 1 (May 1863): 1-2; and Christina Rossetti, "Our Widowed Queen," *New Poems*, pp. 133-34.

22. Taplin, p. 194.

23. Letter to Mary Russell Mitford (July 22, 1842), available in *Elizabeth Barrett to Miss Mitford: The Unpublished Letters of Elizabeth Barrett Browning to Mary Russell Mitford*, ed. Betty Miller (London: John Murray, 1954), pp. 125-26.

24. "My Kate," in *Keepsake* (London: Smith, Elder, 1855), pp. 16-17; rpt. in *Last Poems* (1862), in *Complete Works*, 6: 20-21.

25. Algernon C. Swinburne, "Aurora Leigh," *Complete Works of Algernon Charles Swinburne*, vol. 16, ed. Edmund Gosse and Thomas J. Wise (London: Heinemann, 1926), p. 4.

26. *Letters*, 2: 252-53 (February 2, 1857).

27. For a Marxist-feminist analysis of *Aurora Leigh*, see "Women's Writings: 'Jane Eyre,' 'Shirley,' 'Villette,' 'Aurora Leigh,' " in *1848: The Sociology of Literature*, Proceedings of the Essex Conference on the Sociology of Literature, July 1977, ed. Francis Barker, John Coombs et al., pp. 185-206. Cora Kaplan sees *Aurora Leigh* as "missing . . . any adequate attempt at analysis of the intersecting oppressions of capitalism and patriarchy." She pronounces the work "elitist." "Introduction," *Aurora Leigh* (London: Women's Press, 1978), p. 12.

28. The psychological coherence of Aurora's response to her mother's portrait is explicated in Gilbert and Gubar, *The Madwoman in the Attic*, pp. 18-19, and in Gelpi, pp. 36-40.

29. Barrett Browning had recognized and, to some extent, applauded this aspect of the character of George Sand. See the 1844 sonnets "To George Sand: A Desire" and "To George Sand: A Recognition." The former opens, "Thou large-brained woman and large-hearted man, / Self-called George Sand!" (*Complete Works*, 2: 239). George Sand and her novels are generally acknowledged as sources for *Aurora Leigh*. For more on the relationship between Barrett Browning and Sand, see Patricia Thomson, "Elizabeth Barrett Browning and George Sand," *Durham University Journal*, NS 33 (June 1972): 205-19. Steinmetz notes numerous passages in *Aurora Leigh* which show that although Barrett Browning "never used the term 'androgyny' . . . she would have understood the concept in the psychological sense of the androgynous mind" (p. 18, n.1).

30. Showalter asserts that although women "presented the permanently handicapped man as feminine in the pejorative sense, they believed that a limited experience of dependency, frustration, and powerlessness—in short, of womanhood—was a healthy and instructive one for a hero" (*A Literature of Their Own*, p. 150). For further implications of the poem's ending, see also Gilbert and Gubar, *The Madwoman in the Attic*, pp. 578-80; and Kaplan, "Introduction," *Aurora Leigh*, p. 24.

31. *The Letters of Robert Browning and Elizabeth Barrett Browning, 1845-1846*, vol. 2, ed. Elvan Kintner (Cambridge: Harvard Univ. Press, 1969), p. 957 (August 12, 1846). Kaplan notes several similarities between *Aurora Leigh* and *The Princess*. "Introduction," *Aurora Leigh*, pp. 26-28.

32. Gardner Taplin, "*Aurora Leigh*: A Rehearing," *Studies in Browning and His Circle*, 7 (Spring 1979): 22-23.

33. Moers, p. 40. Moers locates *Aurora Leigh* squarely in the "female tradition" by imagery, subject matter, sources, etc.

34. Swinburne, *Complete Works*, 16: 5.

35. Tompkins, "*Aurora Leigh*," The Fawcett Lecture.

36. Taplin, *Life*, p. 320, and Hayter, p. 171, respectively.

37. This character is perhaps named for the suicidal fallen woman in William Bell Scott's "Rosabell" (1837).

38. On July 16, 1853, Barrett Browning wrote Elizabeth Gaskell about *Ruth*, inquiring, "Was it quite impossible but that your Ruth should *die?*" Quoted in Aina Rubenius, *The Woman Question in Mrs. Gaskell's Life and Works* (Cambridge: Harvard Univ. Press, 1950), p. 211.

39. See Taplin, *Life*, p. 341.

40. *Letters*, 2: 254 (February 1857).

41. Taplin, *Life*, p. 348.

42. Hewlett, p. 42. So he said, anyhow. Hayter wonders if Thackeray wasn't perhaps "annoyed" because the poem "showed a clever woman convicting a man of hypocrisy and putting him [and by implication Thackeray himself] in his place." See Alethea Hayter, " 'These Men Over-Nice': Elizabeth Barrett Browning's 'Lord Walter's Wife,' " *Browning Society Notes*, 8 (August 1978): 5-7.

43. Taplin, *Life*, pp. 355-56.

44. *Dearest Isa: Robert Browning's Letters to Isabella Blagden*, ed. Edward C. McAleer (Austin: Univ. of Texas Press, 1951), p. 295 (March 19, 1868[?]).

45. Taplin, *Life*, pp. 382-84.

46. *Dearest Isa*, p. 295 (March 19, 1868[?]).

47. The term is Faderman's. She devotes an entire chapter to the nineteenth century, pp. 145-294.

48. *Dearest Isa*, pp. 294-95 (March 19, 1868[?]).

49. Hayter, *Mrs. Browning*, p. 224.

50. *Letters*, 2: 242 (November 1856).

CHAPTER 10. CHRISTINA ROSSETTI

1. *The Family Letters*, ed. William Michael Rossetti, p. 31. The approximate date of the letter is given as April 1870.

2. "Rossetti" will mean Christina; her brothers will be referred to as "Dante Gabriel" and "William Michael."

3. De la Mare, pp. x-xi. This essay was first delivered as a lecture before the Royal Society of Literature and printed in a collection of the Society's transactions in 1926.

4. Where possible, dates are dates of composition as reported by Crump in *The Complete Poems*, vol. 1. Volumes 2 and 3 have not yet appeared. Otherwise, they are the dates fixed by William Michael in *The Poetical Works*. Quotations from William Michael's annotations will be cited as "W. M. Rossetti," with the appropriate page number.

5. Crump, p. 149, lines 10-15. Further citations from the poems of Christina Rossetti will be from the Crump edition where possible, or otherwise from William Michael's edition, and will be documented internally by line number if from Crump and by page number if from William Michael. (There are no line numbers in William Michael's edition.)

6. Quoted in Sandars, p. 177.

7. Crump, p. 284.

8. Bell, p. 219.

9. Quoted in Bell, pp. 111-12.

10. Cora Kaplan, "The Indefinite Disclosed," in Jacobus, pp. 65, 77.

11. McGann, p. 254.

12. Quoted in W. M. Rossetti, p. 460.

13. W. M. Rossetti, p. 460.

14. Ibid., p. 486.

15. "A Helpmeet for Him," in W. M. Rossetti, p. 415.

16. William Michael revealed in the "Memoir" appended to the *Poetical Works* of 1904, which he edited, that two affairs of the heart had been foiled by Christina's religious scruples: the first with the Pre-Raphaelite painter James Collinson, between 1848 and 1850, and the second with the scholar Charles Bagot Cayley, beginning around 1860. Most subsequent biographers followed his lead. Recently, however, her reluctance to marry has been attributed to a misguided asceticism, by C. M. Bowra, *The Romantic Imagination* (Cambridge: Harvard Univ. Press, 1949), pp. 254-55; to an aversion to sexuality, by Germaine Greer, "Introduction," *Goblin Market*, pp. xxx-xxxi; or to a hopeless affair with the married poet William Bell Scott, by Lona Packer. Lionel Stevenson remarks, "one can only infer that she preferred spinsterhood to matrimony" (p. 114). Walsh agrees: "Christina Rossetti was not a selfless martyr but rather a self-centered, strong-willed person who sought to maintain her independence through the only means available to a respectable Victorian woman: by avoiding the servitude and total commitment of a lifetime as a governess, wife, or nun" (p. 27).

17. Sandars, p. 128.

18. Rossetti, *New Poems*, p. 383, note.

19. For an astute analysis of Rossetti's use of the sisterhood motif, see Weathers.

20. Packer, pp. 153-54.

21. Bell, p. 220.

22. W. M. Rossetti, p. 480.

23. Another Rossetti poem with a symbolic representation of loss of virginity is "On the Wing" (1862), in W. M. Rossetti, pp. 352-53; see Kaplan, "The Indefinite Disclosed," in Jacobus, pp. 74-75.

24. Packer, p. 154.

25. The referenced poems are "A Death of a First-Born" and "Michael F. M. Rossetti," in W. M. Rossetti, pp. 282, 412.

26. See Sandars, p. 149.

27. W. M. Rossetti, p. 487.

28. Dombrowski, p. 74.

29. As in "The Dead Bride" (1846), in W. M. Rossetti, p. 93; "After Death" (1849), in Crump, pp. 37-38; and "A Bird's Eye View" (1863), in Crump, pp. 134-36.

30. As in "The Hour and the Ghost" (1856), in Crump, pp. 40-42; and "The Poor Ghost" (1863), in Crump, pp. 120-21.

31. See, e.g., "Repining" (1847), in W. M. Rossetti, pp. 9-12; "Echo" (1854), in

Crump, p. 46; "L.E.L." (1859), in Crump, pp. 153-55; "Margery" (1863), in W. M. Rossetti, pp. 360-62; and "Somewhere or Other" (1863), in Crump, p. 161.

32. For more on the pining maiden figure in Christina Rossetti's poetry, see the Fass essay, which traces the influence of Keats' and Tennyson's poems about the legend of St. Agnes' Eve upon Rossetti's representations of passive, pining women.

33. Packer, p. 158.

34. Sandars, pp. 132-33.

35. W. M. Rossetti, p. 480.

AFTERWORD

1. Woolf, *Orlando*, pp. 214-15.

2. Spender, *Man Made Language*, p. 204.

3. Interest in Meynell seems to be reviving; see Beverly Ann Schlack, "The 'Poetess of Poets': Alice Meynell Rediscovered," *Women's Studies*, 7 (1980): 111-26. Also, in 1979 Hyperion Press in Westport, Conn., reissued the 1940 complete edition of Meynell's *Poems*.

Selected Bibliography

Acton, William. *Functions and Disorders of the Reproductive Organs*. 5th ed. London: Churchill, 1871.

———. *Prostitution*. Ed. Peter Fryer. New York: Praeger, 1969.

Adburgham, Alison. *Women in Print*. London: Allen & Unwin, 1972.

Agress, Lynne. *The Feminine Irony: Women on Women in Early Nineteenth-Century English Literature*. Teaneck, N.J.: Fairleigh Dickinson Univ. Press, 1978.

Aikin, Lucy. *Epistles on Women*. Boston: W. Wells and T. B. Wait, 1810.

Astell, Mary. *A Serious Proposal to the Ladies*. London: R. Wilkins, 1694.

———. *Some Reflections Upon Marriage*. London: William Parker, 1730.

Auden, W. H., ed. *Nineteenth-Century Minor Poets*. London: Faber, 1966.

Auerbach, Nina. *Woman and the Demon: The Life of a Victorian Myth*. Cambridge: Harvard Univ. Press, 1982.

Austen, Zelda. "Why Feminist Critics Are Angry with George Eliot." *College English*, 37 (February 1976): 549-61.

Banks, Joseph A., and Olive Banks. *Feminism and Family Planning in Victorian England*. New York: Schocken Books, 1964.

Barrett Browning, Elizabeth. *The Complete Works*. Ed. Charlotte Porter and Helen A. Clarke. New York: Thomas Y. Crowell, 1900.

———. *The Letters of Elizabeth Barrett Browning*. Ed. Frederic G. Kenyon. New York: Macmillan, 1897.

Basch, Françoise. *Relative Creatures: Victorian Women in Society and the Novel*. New York: Schocken Books, 1974.

Bauer, Carol, and Lawrence Ritt. *Free and Ennobled: Source Readings in the Development of Victorian Feminism*. New York: Pergamon Press, 1979.

Bax, Clifford, and Meum Stewart, eds. *The Distaff Muse: An Anthology of Poetry Written by Women*. London: Hollis & Carter, 1949.

Bell, Mackenzie. *Christina Rossetti: A Bibliographical and Critical Study*. 1898. Reprint. New York: Haskell House, 1971.

Bernikow, Louise, ed. *The World Split Open: Four Centuries of Women Poets in England and America, 1552-1950*. New York: Random House, 1974.

Bethune, George W. *The British Female Poets*. 1st ed. 1848. Reprint. Freeport, N.Y.: Books for Libraries Press, 1972.

Bevington, Louisa. *Poems, Lyrics, and Sonnets*. London: Elliot Stock, 1882.

Blake, Kathleen. "*Armgart*: George Eliot on the Woman Artist." *Victorian Poetry*, 18 (Spring 1980): 75-80.

Blease, W. Lyon. *The Emancipation of English Women*. London: David Nutt, 1913.

Blind, Mathilde. *The Ascent of Man*. London: T. Fisher Unwin, 1889.

Branca, Patricia. "Image and Reality: The Myth of the Idle Victorian Woman." *Clio's Consciousness Raised: New Perspectives on the History of Women*. Ed. Mary S. Hartman and Lois Banner. New York: Harper & Row, 1974, pp. 179-91.

_____. *The Silent Sisterhood: Middle-Class Women in the Victorian Home*. London: Croom Helm, 1975.

Brittain, Vera. *Lady into Woman*. New York: Macmillan, 1953.

Brontë, Emily. *The Poems of Emily Jane Brontë and Anne Brontë*. Oxford: Shakespeare Head, 1934.

Buckley, Jerome H. *The Victorian Temper: A Study in Literary Culture*. Cambridge: Harvard Univ. Press, 1951.

Buckley, Jerome H., and George B. Woods, eds. *Poetry of the Victorian Period*. 3d ed. Chicago: Scott, Foresman, 1965.

Burstyn, Joan N. *Victorian Education and the Ideal of Womanhood*. Totowa, N.J.: Barnes and Noble, 1980.

Burton, Elizabeth. *The Pageant of Early Victorian England*. New York: Scribner's, 1972.

Calder, Jenni. *Women and Marriage in Victorian Fiction*. New York: Oxford Univ. Press, 1976.

Clough, Arthur Hugh. *Poems*. Ed. A.L.P. Norrington. London: Oxford Univ. Press, 1968.

Cobbe, Frances Power. " 'Criminals, Idiots, Women, and Minors.' " *Fraser's Magazine*, 78 (December 1868): 777-94.

_____. *The Duties of Women*. London: Williams & Norgate, 1881.

_____. *Essays on the Pursuits of Women*. London: Emily Faithfull, 1863.

Colby, Vineta. *The Singular Anomaly: Women Novelists of the Nineteenth Century*. New York: New York Univ. Press, 1970.

Coleridge, Mary Elizabeth. *Collected Poems*. Ed. Theresa Whistler. London: Rupert Hart-Davis, 1954.

_____. *Gathered Leaves from the Prose of Mary Elizabeth Coleridge*. Ed. Edith Sichel. 1910. Reprint. Freeport, N.Y.: Books for Libraries Press, 1971.

Coleridge, Sara. *Phantasmion*. Boston: Roberts Brothers, 1874.

Cominos, Peter T. "Late Victorian Sexual Respectability and the Social System." *International Review of Social History*, 8 (1963): 18-48, 216-50.

Cook, Eliza. "A Brief Chapter on Old Maids." *Eliza Cook's Journal*, 1 (September 22, 1849): 333.

_____. "Governesses." *Eliza Cook's Journal*, 1 (September 15, 1849): 305-7.

_____. "Old Maids." *Eliza Cook's Journal*, 3 (October 26, 1850): 403-4.

_____. *Poetical Works*. London: Frederick Warne, 1870.

_____. "The Wrongs of Englishwomen." *Eliza Cook's Journal*, 3 (October 5, 1850): 353-56.

Cooper, Helen. "Working into Light: Elizabeth Barrett Browning." *Shakespeare's Sisters: Feminist Essays on Women Poets*. Ed. Sandra M. Gilbert and Susan Gubar. Bloomington: Indiana Univ. Press, 1979, pp. 65-81.

Cott, Nancy. "Passionlessness: An Interpretation of Victorian Sexual Ideology, 1790-1850." *A Heritage of Her Own*. Ed. Nancy Cott and Elizabeth Pleck. New York: Simon and Schuster, 1979, pp. 162-81.

Courtney, Janet. *The Adventurous Thirties: A Chapter in the Women's Movement*. 1933. Reprint. Freeport, N.Y.: Books for Libraries Press, 1967.

Craik, Dinah Mulock. *Mulock's Poems, New and Old*. New York: Hurst, 1883.

_____. *Poems*. London: Hurst & Blackett, 1859.

_____. *A Woman's Thought about Women*. Columbus, Ohio: Follet Foster, 1858.

Crow, Duncan. *The Victorian Woman*. London: Allen & Unwin, 1971.

Cruse, Amy. *The Victorians and Their Reading*. Boston: Houghton, Mifflin, 1935.

Cunningham, A. R. "The 'New Woman' Fiction of the 1890's." *Victorian Studies*, 17 (December 1973): 177-86.

Cunnington, C. Willett. *Feminine Attitudes in the Nineteenth Century*. London: Heinemann, 1935.

Davidoff, Leonore. *The Best Circles: Women and Society in Victorian England*. Totowa, N.J.: Rowman and Littlefield, 1973.

Davidson, John. *Poems*. Ed. Andrew Turnbull. London: Scottish Academic Press, 1973.

De la Mare, Walter. "Introduction." *Christina Rossetti: Poems Chosen by Walter de la Mare*. London: Gregynog Press, 1930.

Delamont, Sara, and Lorna Duffin. *The Nineteenth-Century Woman: Her Cultural and Physical World*. London: Croom Helm, 1978.

De Vitis, A. A. " 'Goblin Market': Fairy Tale and Reality." *Journal of Popular Culture*, 1 (Spring 1968): 418-26.

Diehl, Joanne Feit. " 'Come Slowly—Eden': The Woman Poet and Her Muse." *Dickinson and the Romantic Imagination*. Princeton, N.J.: Princeton Univ. Press, 1981, pp. 13-33.

Dombrowski, Theo. "Dualism in the Poetry of Christina Rossetti." *Victorian Poetry*, (Spring 1976): 70-76.

Donaldson, Sandra. " 'Motherhood's Advent in Power': Elizabeth Barrett Browning's Poems about Motherhood." *Victorian Poetry*, 18 (Spring 1980): 51-60.

Dowling, Linda. "The Decadent and the New Woman in the 1890's." *Nineteenth-Century Fiction*, 33 (March 1979): 434-53.

Dryden, Anne Richelieu Lamb. *Can Woman Regenerate Society?* London: J. W. Parker, 1844.

Dunbar, Janet. *The Early Victorian Woman: Some Aspects of Her Life*. London: G. Harrap, 1953.

Dyhouse, Carol. *Girls Growing Up in Late Victorian and Edwardian England.* Boston: Routledge & Kegan Paul, 1981.

Edelstein, T. J. "They Sang 'The Song of the Shirt': The Visual Iconology of the Seamstress." *Victorian Studies,* 23 (Winter 1980): 183-210.

Eliot, George. *The Writings of George Eliot.* Ed. J. W. Cross. 1907-1908. Reprint. New York: AMS Press, 1970.

Ellis, Sarah Stickney. *The Daughters of England.* London: Fisher, 1843.

_____. *The Mothers of England.* London: Fisher, 1844.

_____. *The Wives of England.* London: Fisher, 1843.

_____. *The Women of England.* London: Fisher, 1839.

Ellman, Mary. *Thinking about Women.* New York: Harcourt, Brace, 1968.

Elwin, Malcolm. *Victorian Wallflowers.* London: Jonathan Cape, 1934.

Engleman, Herta. "The Ideal English Gentlewoman in the Nineteenth Century." Ph.D. diss., Northwestern Univ., 1956.

Engels, Friedrich. *The Condition of the Working Class in England in 1844.* Trans. F. K. Wischnewetzky. London: Allen & Unwin, 1892.

An Essay in Defence of the Female Sex. London: M. A. Roper, 1697.

Evans, B. Ifor. *English Poetry in the Later Nineteenth Century.* London: Methuen, 1933.

Ewbank, Inga-Stina. *Their Proper Sphere: A Study of the Brontë Sisters as Early Victorian Novelists.* Cambridge: Harvard Univ. Press, 1966.

Faderman, Lillian. *Surpassing the Love of Men: Romantic Friendship and Love between Women from the Renaissance to the Present.* New York: Morrow, 1981.

"Fane, Violet." *Autumn Songs.* London: Chapman & Hall, 1889.

_____. *Poems.* New York: Dillingham, 1887.

Fass, Barbara. "Christina Rossetti and St. Agnes' Eve." *Victorian Poetry,* 14 (Spring 1976): 33-46.

"Field, Michael." *Long Ago.* Portland, Oreg.: Thomas B. Mosher, 1907.

_____. *A Selection from the Poems of Michael Field.* Ed. T. Sturge Moore. London: Poetry Bookshop, 1923.

_____. *Works and Days, from the Journal of Michael Field.* Ed. T. and D. C. Sturge Moore. London: John Murray, 1933.

Finnegan, Frances. *Poverty and Prostitution: A Study of Victorian Prostitutes in York.* Cambridge: Cambridge Univ. Press, 1979.

Foster, Jeanette. *Sex Variant Women in Literature.* New York: Vantage, 1956.

Gallant, Christine. "The Archetypal Feminine in Emily Brontë's Poetry." *Women's Studies,* 7 (1980): 79-94.

Gelpi, Barbara C. "*Aurora Leigh:* The Vocation of the Woman Poet." *Victorian Poetry,* 19 (Spring 1981): 35-48.

Gérin, Winifred. *Emily Brontë: A Biography.* Oxford: Clarendon Press, 1971.

Gilbert, Sandra M., and Susan Gubar. *The Madwoman in the Attic: The Woman Writer and the Nineteenth-Century Literary Imagination.* New Haven, Conn.: Yale Univ. Press, 1979.

————, eds. *Shakespeare's Sisters: Feminist Essays on Women Poets*. Bloomington: Indiana Univ. Press, 1979.

Gisborne, Thomas. *An Enquiry into the Duties of the Female Sex*. 5th ed. 1801. Reprint. New York: Garland Press, 1974.

Gorham, Deborah. *The Victorian Girl and the Feminine Ideal*. Bloomington: Indiana Univ. Press, 1982.

Gorsky, Susan. "Old Maids and New Women: Alternatives to Marriage in English-women's Novels, 1847-1915." *Journal of Popular Culture*, 7 (Summer 1973): 68-85.

Granville-Barker, Harley, ed. *The Eighteen Seventies*. New York: Macmillan, 1929.

Greenwell, Dora. "Our Single Women." *North British Review*, 36 (February 1862): 62-87.

————. *Poems*. Edinburgh: Alexander Strahan, 1861.

————. *Poems*. Ed. William Dorling. London: Walter Scott, 1889.

Greer, Germaine. "Flying Pigs and Double Standards." *Times* (London) *Literary Supplement*, July 25, 1974, pp. 784-85.

————. "Introduction." *Goblin Market* by Christina Rossetti. New York: Stonehill, 1975.

Greg, W. R. "Prostitution." *Westminster Review*, 57 (April-July 1850): 448-506.

————. "Why Are Women Redundant?" *National Review*, 57 (April 1862). Reprint. W. R. Greg. *Literary and Social Judgments*. Boston: Osgood, 1873.

Gregory, John. *A Father's Legacy to His Daughters*. London: John Sharpe, 1828.

Hale, Sarah Josepha, ed. *The Ladies' Wreath*. Boston: Marsh, Capen & Lyon, 1837.

Hammerton, A. James. *Emigrant Gentlewomen: Genteel Poverty and Female Emigration, 1830-1914*. London: Croom Helm, 1979.

Harris, Katharine. "The New Woman in the Literature of the 1890's: Four Critical Approaches." Ph.D. diss., Columbia Univ., 1963.

Harrison, Brian. "Victorian Philanthropy." *Victorian Studies*, 9 (June 1966): 353-74.

Hartman, Mary S., and Lois Banner. *Clio's Consciousness Raised: New Perspectives on the History of Women*. New York: Harper & Row, 1974.

Havergal, Frances Ridley. *Poetical Works*. Ed. Maria Havergal. New York: Dutton, 1885.

Haworth, Helen E. " 'A Milk-White Lamb That Bleats'? Some Stereotypes of Women in Romantic Literature." *Humanities Association Review* (Canada), 24 (1973): 277-93.

Hayley, William. *A Philosophical, Historical, and Moral Essay on Old Maids*. London: T. Cadell, 1785.

Hays, Mary. *Appeal to the Men of Great Britain in Behalf of Women*. Ed. Gina Luria. New York: Garland Press, 1974.

Hayter, Alethea. *Mrs. Browning: A Poet's Work and Its Setting*. New York: Barnes and Noble, 1963.

Hellerstein, Erna O., Leslie P. Hume, and Karen M. Offen. *Victorian Women: A Documentary Account of Women's Lives in Nineteenth-Century England, France, and the United States*. Stanford, Calif.: Stanford Univ. Press, 1981.

Hemans, Felicia. *Poetical Works*. New York: American Book Exchange, 1880.

Hewitt, Margaret. *Wives and Mothers in Victorian Industry*. London: Rockliff, 1958.

Hewlett, Dorothy. *Elizabeth Barrett Browning: A Life*. New York: Knopf, 1952.

Hill, Georgiana. *Women in English Life*. London: Bentley, 1896.

Holcombe, Lee. *Victorian Ladies at Work: Middle-Class Working Women in England and Wales, 1850-1914*. Devon, England: David and Charles, 1973.

Homans, Margaret. *Women Writers and Poetic Identity: Dorothy Wordsworth, Emily Brontë, and Emily Dickinson*. Princeton, N.J.: Princeton Univ. Press, 1980.

Hood, Thomas. *Selected Poems*. Ed. John Clubbe. Cambridge: Harvard Univ. Press, 1970.

Houghton, Walter E. *The Victorian Frame of Mind, 1830-1870*. New Haven, Conn.: Yale Univ. Press, 1957.

Howitt, Mary. *Ballads*. New York: Kiggins & Kellogg, 1854.

Ingelow, Jean. *Poems*. London: Oxford Univ. Press, 1921.

Jackson, Holbrook. *The Eighteen Nineties*. London: Jonathan Cape, 1931.

Jacobus, Mary, ed. *Women Writing and Writing about Women*. New York: Barnes and Noble, 1979.

Jaeger, Muriel. *Before Victoria*. London: Chatto & Windus, 1956.

Jameson, Anna. *Woman's Mission and Woman's Position*. London: R. Bentley, 1846.

Johnson, Wendell Stacy. *Sex and Marriage in Victorian Poetry*. Ithaca, N.Y.: Cornell Univ. Press, 1975.

Jones, Nellie Fern. "Survey of Critical Attitudes toward Women Writers." Master's thesis, Univ. of Colorado, 1944.

Kaplan, Cora. "The Indefinite Disclosed: Christina Rossetti and Emily Dickinson." *Women Writing and Writing about Women*. Ed. Mary Jacobus. New York: Barnes and Noble, 1979.

_____, ed. *Salt and Bitter and Good: Three Centuries of English and American Women Poets*. New York: Paddington, 1975.

Kaye, J. W. "The Employment of Women." *North British Review*, 26 (February 1857): 291-338.

Kemble, Frances Anne. *Poems*. Philadelphia: John Penington, 1844.

_____. *Poems*. London: Richard Bentley, 1883.

Killham, John. *Tennyson and "The Princess": Reflections of an Age*. London: Athlone Press, 1958.

Kinglake, A. W. "The Rights of Women." *Quarterly Review*, 85 (December 1844-March 1845): 94-125.

Kitchener, Henry T. *Letters on Marriage, on the Causes of Matrimonial Infidelity, and on the Reciprocal Relations of the Sexes*. London: C. Chapple, 1812.

Kutrieh, Marcia G. "Popular British Romantic Poets." Ph.D. diss., Bowling Green State Univ., 1974.

Landon, Letitia Elizabeth. *Poetical Works*. Ed. William Bell Scott. London: Routledge, 1850.

Leder, Sharon. "The Image of Woman in Christina Rossetti's Poetry." Ph.D. diss., New York Univ., 1979.

Levy, Amy. *A Minor Poet, and Other Verse*. London: T. Fisher Unwin, 1884.

Libertin, Mary. "Female Friendship in Women's Verse: Toward a New Theory of Female Poetics." *Women's Studies*, 9 (1982): 291-308.

Linton, Eliza Lynn. *The Girl of the Period: Essays Upon Social Subjects*. London: R. Bentley, 1883. First published in the *Saturday Review*, 25 (March 14, 1868): 339-40, and subsequent essays in subsequent numbers.

Lockhart, John G. "Modern English Poetesses." *Quarterly Review*, 66 (September 1840): 374-418.

Logan, William. *The Great Social Evil*. London: Hodder & Stoughton, 1871.

McGann, Jerome J. "Christina Rossetti's Poems: A New Edition and a Revaluation." *Victorian Studies*, 23 (Winter 1980): 237-54.

McGhee, Richard D. *Marriage, Duty, and Desire in Victorian Poetry and Drama*. Lawrence: Regents Press of Kansas, 1980.

Marcus, Steven. *The Other Victorians: A Study of Sexuality and Pornography in Mid-Nineteenth-Century England*. New York: Basic Books, 1964.

———. *Representations: Essays on Literature and Society*. New York: Random House, 1975.

Martineau, Harriet. "Modern Domestic Service." *Edinburgh Review*, 115 (April 1862): 409-39.

Mayhew, Henry. *London Labour and the London Poor*. Vol. 4. 1862. Reprinted as *London's Underworld*. Ed. Peter Quennell. London: Spring Books, 1957.

Meredith, George. *The Poems of George Meredith*. Ed. Phyllis B. Bartlett. New Haven, Conn.: Yale Univ. Press, 1978.

Mews, Hazel. *Frail Vessels: Woman's Role in Women's Novels from Fanny Burney to George Eliot*. London: Athlone Press, 1969.

Meynell, Alice. *Collected Poems*. London: Burnes & Oates, 1913.

———. *Poems*. London: Oxford Univ. Press, 1940.

———. *Preludes*. London: Henry S. King, 1875.

Midler, Marcia S. "George Eliot's Rebels: Portraits of the Artist as a Woman." *Women's Studies*, 7 (1980): 97-108

Miles, Alfred H., ed. *The Poets and the Poetry of the Century*. London: Hutchinson, 1892.

Milford, H. S., ed. *The Oxford Book of English Verse of the Romantic Period*. Oxford: Clarendon Press, 1928.

Mill, John Stuart. *The Subjection of Women*. Ed. Wendell Robert Carr. Cambridge, Mass.: M.I.T. Press, 1970.

Millett, Kate. *Sexual Politics*. New York: Doubleday, 1969.

Mintz, Steven: *A Prison House of Expectations: The Family in Victorian Culture*. New York: New York Univ. Press, 1983.

Mitchell, Sally. *The Fallen Angel: Chastity, Class and Women's Reading 1835-1880*. Bowling Green, Ohio: Bowling Green Univ. Popular Press, 1981.

Moers, Ellen. *Literary Women*. New York: Doubleday, 1976.

Moore, Katharine. *Cordial Relations: The Maiden Aunt in Fact and Fiction*. London: Heinemann, 1966.

_____. *Victorian Wives*. London: Allison and Busby, 1974.

More, Hannah. *Strictures on the Modern System of Female Education, with a View of the Principles and Conduct Prevalent Among Women of Rank and Fortune*. 6th ed. London: Cadell & Davies, 1799.

Murray, Janet H. *Strong-Minded Women and Other Lost Voices from Nineteenth-Century England*. New York: Pantheon Books, 1982.

Muzzey, Artemas Bowers. *The Young Maiden*. Boston: Crosby and Nichols, 1847.

Neff, Wanda. *Victorian Working Women: An Historical and Literary Study of Women in British Industries and Professions, 1832-1850*. New York: Columbia Univ. Press, 1929.

Nesbit, E. *Leaves of Life*. London: Longmans, 1888.

_____. *Songs of Love and Empire*. Westminster, England: Archibald Constable, 1898.

Norton, Caroline. *The Child of the Islands*. London: Chapman & Hall, 1846.

_____. *The Dream*. London: Colburn, 1840.

_____. *The Lady of La Garaye*. New York: John Bradburn, 1864.

_____. *Poems*. New York: C. S. Francis, 1854.

_____. *Poems*. New York: Leavitt & Allen, 1857.

_____. *Selected Writings of Caroline Norton*. Ed. James O. Hoge and Jane Marcus. Delman, N.Y.: Scholars' Facsimiles & Reprints, 1978.

_____. *The Undying One and Other Poems*. New York: C. S. Francis, 1854.

_____. *A Voice from the Factories*. Boston: John Putnam, 1847.

_____, ed. *Home Thoughts and Home Scenes*. Boston: J. E. Tilton, 1865.

Olsen, Tillie. *Silences*. New York: Delacorte Press, 1978.

O'Malley, Ida Beatrice. *Women in Subjection: A Study of the Lives of Englishwomen before 1832*. London: Duckworth, 1933.

Owenson, Sydney, Lady Morgan. *Woman and Her Master*. London: Colburn, 1840.

Packer, Lona M. *Christina Rossetti*. Los Angeles: Univ. of California Press, 1963.

Parkes, Bessie Rayner. *Essays on Woman's Work*. London: Alexander Strahan, 1865.

Patmore, Coventry. *Poems*. Ed. Frederick Page. London: Oxford Univ. Press, 1949.

_____. "The Social Position of Women." *North British Review*, 14 (February 1851): 515-40.

Pearsall, Ronald. *The Worm in the Bud: The World of Victorian Sexuality*. London: Macmillan, 1969.

Penny, Anne Judith (Brown). *The Afternoon of Unmarried Life*. London: Longmans, 1858.

Petit, Jean Pierre, ed. *Emily Brontë: A Critical Anthology*. Baltimore: Penguin Books, 1973.

Pfeiffer, Emily. *The Rhyme of the Lady of the Rock*. London: Kegan Paul, 1884.

_____. *Under the Aspens, Lyrical and Dramatic*. 2d ed. London: Kegan Paul, 1882.

Pike, E. Royston. *Human Documents of the Victorian Golden Age, 1850-1875*. London: Allen & Unwin, 1974.

Pinchbeck, Ivy. *Women Workers and the Industrial Revolution, 1750-1850*. London: Routledge, 1930.

Pratt, Annis. *Archetypal Patterns in Women's Fiction.* Bloomington: Indiana Univ. Press, 1981.

Preston, Harriet Waters, ed. *The Complete Poetical Works of Elizabeth Barrett Browning.* Boston: Houghton, Mifflin, 1900.

Procter, Adelaide Anne. *Poems: Complete Edition, with an Introduction by Charles Dickens.* 1866. Reprint. New York: Worthington, 1889.

Quinlan, Maurice J. *Victorian Prelude.* London: Frank Cass, 1965.

Radcliffe, Mary Ann. *The Female Advocate.* Edinburgh: Manners & Miller, 1810. Reprint. New York: Garland Press, 1974.

Radford, Dollie. *Songs and Other Verses.* London: John Lane, 1895.

Redinger, Ruby. *George Eliot: The Emergent Self.* New York: Knopf, 1975.

Reed, John. *Victorian Conventions.* Athens: Ohio Univ. Press, 1975.

Reid, Marion. *A Plea for Woman.* New York: Farmer and Daggers, 1845.

Rich, Adrienne. *Of Woman Born: Motherhood as Experience and Institution.* New York: Norton, 1976.

"Rights and Conditions of Women." *Edinburgh Review,* 73 (April 1841): 189-209.

Riley, Madeline. *Brought to Bed.* New York: A. S. Barnes, 1968.

Robinson, Agnes Mary Frances. *Collected Poems.* London: T. Fisher Unwin, 1902.

_____. *Emily Brontë.* Boston: Roberts Brothers, 1883.

_____. *The New Arcadia and Other Poems.* Boston: Roberts Brothers, 1884.

Rogers, Katharine. *Feminism in Eighteenth-Century England.* Urbana: Univ. of Illinois Press, 1982.

_____. *The Troublesome Helpmate: A History of Misogyny in Literature.* Seattle: Univ. of Washington Press, 1966.

Rorabacher, Louise E. *Victorian Women in Life and in Fiction.* Urbana: Univ. of Illinois Press, 1942.

Rosenblum, Dolores. "Christina Rossetti: The Inward Pose." *Shakespeare's Sisters: Feminist Essays on Women Poets.* Ed. Sandra M. Gilbert and Susan Gubar. Bloomington: Indiana Univ. Press, 1979, pp. 82-98.

Rossetti, Christina. *Complete Poems of Christina Rossetti.* Vol. 1. Ed. (with textual notes and introduction) R. W. Crump. Baton Rouge: Louisiana State Univ. Press, 1978.

_____. *New Poems, Hitherto Unpublished or Uncollected.* Ed. William Michael Rossetti. New York: Macmillan, 1896.

_____. *The Poetical Works.* Ed. William Michael Rossetti. London: Macmillan, 1904.

Rossetti, William Michael, ed. *The Family Letters of Christina Georgina Rossetti.* London: Brown, Langhams, 1908.

Rover, Constance. *Love, Morals and the Feminists.* London: Routledge and Kegan Paul, 1970.

Rowbotham, Sheila. *Hidden from History.* London: Pluto Press, 1973.

Rowton, Frederic. *The Female Poets of Great Britain.* London: Longmans, 1850.

Ruskin, John. *Works.* Ed. E. T. Cook and Alexander Wedderburn. London: George Allen, 1905.

Sackville-West, Vita. "Introduction." *The Annual: Being a Selection from the Forget-Me-Nots, Keepsakes, and Other Annuals of the Nineteenth Century*. Ed. Dorothy Wellesley. London: Cobden-Sanderson, 1930.

———. "The Women Poets of the Seventies." *The Eighteen Seventies*. Ed. Harley Granville-Barker. London: Macmillan, 1929, pp. 112-34.

Sandars, Mary F. *The Life of Christina Rossetti*. London: Hutchinson, 1930.

Sandford, Elizabeth Poole. *Woman in Her Social and Domestic Character*. London: Longmans, 1839.

Scanlon, Leone. "The New Woman in the Literature of 1883-1909." *University of Michigan Papers in Women's Studies*, 2 (1976): 133-58.

Schreiner, Olive. *The Story of an African Farm*. London: Chapman & Hall, 1883.

Sheridan, Helen Selina, Lady Dufferin. *Songs, Poems and Verses, with a Memoir by Her Son*. London: John Murray, 1884.

Showalter, Elaine. "Desperate Remedies: Sensation Novels of the 1860's." *Victorian Newsletter*, no. 49 (Spring 1976): 1-5.

———. *A Literature of Their Own: British Women Novelists from Brontë to Lessing*. Princeton, N.J.: Princeton Univ. Press, 1977.

———. "Women Writers and the Double Standard." *Woman in Sexist Society*. Ed. Vivian Gornick and Barbara Moran. New York: Basic Books, 1971, pp. 323-43.

———. "Women Writers and the Female Experience." *Notes from the Third Year: Women's Liberation*. Ed. Anne Koedt. New York: Notes from the Second Year, Inc., 1971, pp. 134-41.

Smith, Anne, ed. *The Art of Emily Brontë*. New York: Barnes and Noble, 1976.

Smith-Rosenberg, Carroll. "The Female World of Love and Ritual: Relations between Women in Nineteenth-Century America." *Signs*, 1 (Autumn 1975): 1-29.

Southey, Caroline Bowles. *Select Literary Works*. Hartford: Silas Andrus, 1851.

Spacks, Patricia Meyer. *The Female Imagination*. New York: Knopf, 1975.

Spender, Dale. *Man Made Language*. Boston: Routledge & Kegan Paul, 1980.

———. *Women of Ideas and What Men Have Done to Them, from Aphra Behn to Adrienne Rich*. Boston: Routledge & Kegan Paul, 1982.

Squire, J. C., ed. *The Cambridge Book of Lesser Poets*. Cambridge, England: Cambridge Univ. Press, 1927.

Stanford, Ann, ed. *The Women Poets in English: An Anthology*. New York: Herder, 1972.

Stedman, Edmund C., ed. *A Victorian Anthology*. Cambridge, Mass.: Riverside Press, 1895.

Steinmetz, Virginia. "Beyond the Sun: Patriarchal Images in *Aurora Leigh*." *Studies in Browning and His Circle*, 9 (Fall 1981): 18-41.

Stenton, Doris Mary. *The English Woman in History*. New York: Macmillan, 1957.

Stevenson, Lionel. "Christina Rossetti." *The Pre-Raphaelite Poets*. Chapel Hill: Univ. of North Carolina Press, 1972, pp. 78-122.

Stone, Lawrence. *The Family, Sex and Marriage in England 1500-1800*. Abridged edition. New York: Harper & Row, 1977, 1979.

Strachey, Rachel C. (Ray). *The Cause: A Short History of the Women's Movement in Great Britain*. London: G. Bell, 1928.

Stuart, Dorothy M. *Christina Rossetti*. London: Macmillan, 1930.

Symons, Arthur. *Collected Works*. London: Martin Secker, 1924.

Taplin, Gardner B. *The Life of Elizabeth Barrett Browning*. New Haven, Conn.: Yale Univ. Press, 1957.

Tayler, Irene, and Gina Luria. "Gender and Genre: Women in British Romantic Literature." *What Manner of Woman: Essays on English and American Life and Literature*. Ed. Marlene Springer. New York: New York Univ. Press, 1977.

Taylor, Harriet. "The Enfranchisement of Women." *Westminster Review*, 55 (October 29, 1850): 289-311.

Taylor, Jane. *Writings*. New York: Saxton & Miles, 1835.

Tennyson, Alfred, Lord. *The Poems of Tennyson*. Ed. Christopher Ricks. London: Longmans, 1969.

Thomas, Eleanor. *Christina Georgina Rossetti*. New York: Columbia Univ. Press, 1931.

Thomas, Keith. "The Double Standard." *Journal of the History of Ideas*, 20 (April 1959): 195-216.

Thompson, William. *Appeal of One Half the Human Race, Women, Against the Pretensions of the Other Half, Men, to Retain Them in Political, and Thence in Civil and Domestic Slavery*. London: Longmans, 1825.

Thomson, Patricia. *The Victorian Heroine: A Changing Ideal, 1837-1873*. New York: Oxford Univ. Press, 1965.

Todd, Janet, ed. *Be Good, Sweet Maid: An Anthology of Women and Literature*. New York: Holmes & Meier, 1981.

_____. *Gender and Literary Voice*. New York: Holmes & Meier, 1980.

Tompkins, J.M.S. "*Aurora Leigh*." The Fawcett Lecture, 1961-1962. London: Bedford College, 1961.

Trall, R. T. *Sexual Physiology*. London: M. A. Orr, 1881.

Trevelyan, G. M. *English Social History*. London: Longmans, 1942.

Trudgill, Eric. *Madonnas and Magdalens: The Origins and Development of Victorian Sexual Attitudes*. New York: Holmes & Meier, 1976.

Utter, Robert P., and Gwendolyn B. Needham. *Pamela's Daughters*. London: Macmillan, 1936.

Veley, Margaret. *A Marriage of Shadows*. Philadelphia: Lippincott, 1889.

Vicinus, Martha, ed. *Suffer and Be Still: Women in the Victorian Age*. Bloomington: Indiana Univ. Press, 1972.

_____. *A Widening Sphere: Changing Roles of Victorian Women*. Bloomington: Indiana Univ. Press, 1977.

Walker, Alexander. *Women Physiologically Considered as to Mind, Morals, Marriage, Matrimonial Slavery, Infidelity and Divorce*. London: A. H. Baily, 1840.

Walker, Cheryl. *The Nightingale's Burden: Women Poets and American Culture before 1900*. Bloomington: Indiana Univ. Press, 1982.

Walkowitz, Judith R. *Prostitution and Victorian Society: Women, Class, and the State.* Cambridge, England: Cambridge Univ. Press, 1980.

Walsh, Eve. "A Reading of Christina Rossetti's 'Three Stages.' " *Pre-Raphaelite Review*, 2 (November 1978): 27-35.

Watts, Emily Stipes. *The Poetry of American Women from 1632 to 1943.* Austin: Univ. of Texas Press, 1977.

Weathers, Winston. "Christina Rossetti: The Sisterhood of Self." *Victorian Poetry*, 3 (Spring 1965): 81-89.

Webster, Augusta. *Dramatic Studies.* London: Macmillan, 1866.

_____. *Mother and Daughter.* Ed. William Michael Rossetti. London: Macmillan, 1895.

_____. *Portraits.* London: Macmillan, 1870.

_____. *A Woman Sold, and Other Poems.* London: Macmillan, 1867.

Wellesley, Dorothy, ed. *The Annual: Being a Selection from the Forget-Me-Nots, Keepsakes, and Other Annuals of the Nineteenth Century.* London: Cobden-Sanderson, 1930.

White, Cynthia. *Women's Magazines, 1693-1968.* London: Michael Joseph, 1971.

Williams, Jane. *Literary Women of England.* London: Saunders, Otley, 1861.

Wohl, Anthony S. *The Victorian Family: Structure and Stresses.* London: Croom Helm, 1978.

Wolff, Cynthia G. "A Mirror for Men: Stereotypes of Women in Literature." *Massachusetts Review*, 13 (Winter-Spring 1972): 205-18.

Wollstonecraft, Mary. *Thoughts on the Education of Daughters.* London: Joseph Johnson, 1787.

_____. *A Vindication of the Rights of Woman.* Ed. Miriam Kramnick. Baltimore: Penguin Books, 1975.

Woolf, Virginia. "*Aurora Leigh.*" *Yale Review*, 20 (1931): 677-90. Reprint. Virginia Woolf. *The Common Reader.* Vol. 2. 2d series. New York: Harcourt, Brace, 1925, pp. 218-31.

_____. *Orlando.* London: Hogarth Press, 1928.

_____. *A Room of One's Own.* New York: Harcourt, Brace, 1929.

Yonge, Charlotte M. *Womankind.* London: Mozley & Smith, 1877.

Zaturenska, Marya. *Christina Rossetti: A Portrait with Background.* New York: Macmillan, 1949.

Index

About the Author

KATHLEEN HICKOK is Associate Professor of English and Chair of Women's Studies at Iowa State University. Her other works include articles in the *International Journal of Women's Studies* and the *Journal of Popular Culture*, and contributions to *The Dichotomy of Domestic Space*, a work in progress, and a multivolume anthology of short stories by American women writers.